MW00804353

Russia, the Near Abroad, and the West

Russia, the Near Abroad, and the West

Lessons from the Moldova-Transdniestria Conflict

William H. Hill

Woodrow Wilson Center Press
Washington, D.C.

The Johns Hopkins University Press
Baltimore

EDITORIAL OFFICES

Woodrow Wilson Center Press
One Woodrow Wilson Plaza
1300 Pennsylvania Avenue, N.W.
Washington, D.C. 20004-3027
Telephone: 202-691-4029
www.wilsoncenter.org

ORDER FROM

The Johns Hopkins University Press
Hampden Station
P.O. Box 50370
Baltimore, Maryland 21211
Telephone: 1-800-537-5487
www.press.jhu.edu/books/

© 2012 by William H. Hill
Printed in the United States of America
2 4 6 8 9 7 5 3 1

Library of Congress Cataloging-in-Publication Data

Hill, William H. (William Holway), 1945–
    Russia, the near abroad, and the West : lessons from the Moldova-Transdniestria conflict / William H. Hill.
        pages : maps ; cm
    Includes bibliographical references and index.
    ISBN 978-1-4214-0565-0 (hardcover : alkaline paper)
    1. Russia (Federation)—Foreign relations—Moldova.   2. Moldova—Foreign relations—Russia (Federation)   3. Dniester Moldovan Republic—International status.   4. Dniester Moldovan Republic—History—Autonomy and independence movements.   5. Russia (Federation)—Foreign relations—Western countries.
    6. Western countries—Foreign relations—Russia (Federation)   I. Title.
DK67.5.M58H55   2012
947.6086—dc23

Wilson Center

The Woodrow Wilson International Center for Scholars is the national, living U.S. memorial honoring President Woodrow Wilson. In providing an essential link between the worlds of ideas and public policy, the Center addresses current and emerging challenges confronting the United States and the world. The Center promotes policy-relevant research and dialogue to increase understanding and enhance the capabilities and knowledge of leaders, citizens, and institutions worldwide. Created by an act of Congress in 1968, the Center is a nonpartisan institution headquartered in Washington, D.C., and supported by both public and private funds.

Conclusions or opinions expressed in Center publications and programs are those of the authors and speakers and do not necessarily reflect the views of the Center staff, fellows, trustees, advisory groups, or any individuals or organizations that provide financial support to the Center.

The Center is the publisher of *The Wilson Quarterly* and home of Woodrow Wilson Center Press and *dialogue* television and radio. For more information about the Center's activities and publications please visit us on the Web at www .wilsoncenter.org.

Jane Harman, Director, President, and CEO

Board of Trustees
Joseph B. Gildenhorn, Chairman of the Board
Sander R. Gerber, Vice Chairman

Public Members: James H. Billington, Librarian of Congress; Hillary R. Clinton, Secretary, U.S. Department of State; G. Wayne Clough, Secretary, Smithsonian Institution; Arne Duncan, Secretary, U.S. Department of Education; David Ferriero, Archivist of the United States; James Leach, Chairman, National Endowment for the Humanities; Kathleen Sebelius, Secretary, U.S. Department of Health and Human Services; Fred P. Hochberg, designated appointee of the President from within the federal government

Private Members: Timothy Broas, John T. Casteen III, Charles E. Cobb Jr., Thelma Duggin, Carlos M. Gutierrez, Susan Hutchison, Barry S. Jackson

National Cabinet
Eddie & Sylvia Brown, Melva Bucksbaum & Raymond Learsy, Ambassadors Sue & Chuck Cobb, Lester Crown, Thelma Dugin, Judi Flom, Sander R. Gerber, Ambassador Joseph B. Gildenhorn & Alma Gildenhorn, Harman Family Foundation, Susan Hutchison, Frank F. Islam, Willem Kooyker, Linda B. & Tobia G. Mercuro, Dr. Alexander V. Mirtchev, Wayne Rogers, Leo Zickler

Contents

Preface

Many Western listeners were stunned, offended, and puzzled at Russian president Vladimir Putin's vituperative diatribe against the United States at the February 2007 annual Munich Security Conference. Russian protests against alleged American unilateralism melded in 2008 into denunciations from Moscow of NATO's plans to expand into Ukraine and Georgia. The August 2008 war against Georgia brought Russia's relations with Western Europe and the United States to their lowest point since the later days of the Cold War. Western political leaders and analysts were left asking themselves what had happened to make the once-hopeful process of Russia's democratization and integration into the West go so wrong. Some argued that with its strength restored by an economy bolstered by high oil prices, Moscow was attempting through neo-imperial policies to restore its exclusive sphere of influence in the former Soviet space. Others argued that Russia's anger had been fueled by its failure to achieve true integration into Euro-Atlantic institutions. According to this line, Moscow felt threatened by its loss of influence even in neighboring states to the encroaching NATO and European Union, of which it was not a member, and over which it had little influence and no control.

Many disciplines in the social sciences frequently employ the study of individual cases to draw or illustrate broader theoretical conclusions. This book attempts to identify some of the reasons for Russia's failure to achieve full integration into the European and Euro-Atlantic institutions and for Moscow's increasing insecurity and resentment over the involvement of other parties—states and international organizations—in its so-called near abroad, where it asserted a right to "privileged interests." The most detailed portion of this volume offers a study of the case of Moldova, examining the search during the past two decades for an agreement that would reunite this small post-Soviet country divided by civil war. The study focuses especially on the events of 2003, a crucial year in the pursuit of a political settlement between the recognized government in Chisinau and the separatist authorities in Transdniestria (or Transnistria), a narrow sliver of land on the east, or left, bank of the Dniestr (or Nistru) River, which beginning in 1990 fought to secede from Moldova as the latter sought independence from Moscow. The conflict was one of a number of small wars that broke out on the periphery of the USSR over the distribution of territory and political authority during the process of the dissolution of the multinational Soviet empire. Along with Georgia, Armenia, Azerbaijan, and Tajikistan, Moldova was an exception to the peaceful unraveling of the Soviet Union. The summer 2008 war in Georgia demonstrates that even after twenty years, the process of violent confrontation over ethnic divisions and national borders in some parts of the former USSR has not yet reached its conclusion.

From the moment the Soviet Union dissolved, Russia asserted a primary if not exclusive right to peacemaking and conflict resolution in the various small wars that broke out on the former Soviet periphery. Russian military intervention and mediation almost solely produced a settlement of the civil war in Tajikistan by 1997. Russian forces intervened in Georgia in both South Ossetia and Abkhazia from 1992 to 1994, and were mandated as the chief peacekeepers by the Conference on Security and Cooperation in Europe (CSCE, which in 1995 became the Organization for Security and Cooperation in Europe, OSCE) and the United Nations, respectively, for these conflicts. In the conflict between Armenia and Azerbaijan over Nagorno-Karabakh, Russia played (and still plays) a leading role in the settlement process, along with the United States and France, the other cochairs of the OSCE Minsk Group. Finally, in Moldova's conflict with its breakaway region of Transdniestria, Russian troops unilaterally intervened to halt the fighting and remain as the sole foreign peacekeepers (except for a few military observers from Ukraine). For much of the 1990s, Russia's involvement and mediation efforts in each of these conflicts were generally not opposed and even drew support from some Western European states and the United States.

Moldova and its Transdniestrian region fought a small, brief, but bitter war in the spring and summer of 1992. The open military hostilities of June and July 1992 followed two years of rising tensions in the republic, marked by Tiraspol's resistance to Chisinau's attempts to assert its political authority and physical control over the left bank. With the involvement of local Russian military forces, remnants of a large Soviet Red Army force stationed in the Moldavian Soviet Socialist Republic, the separatists in Transdniestria won de facto independence in July 1992. During the conflict, the Moldovan authorities in Chisinau appealed for support and assistance to the United Nations, the OSCE, and a variety of European and North American states. The only response came from Russia, and Moscow became the first mediator between Chisinau and Tiraspol.

Negotiations for a political settlement between the Moldovan government and the separatist Transdniestrian region have gone on since late 1992. In April 1993, Western nations joined the process through the establishment of an OSCE Mission in Moldova, which has been led by British, Canadian, and, since 1995, American diplomats. Neighboring Ukraine formally joined the settlement process as a mediator in 1995. The negotiations have come close to a deal twice. The first time was in May 1997, when Moldova and Transdniestria signed the so-called *Moscow Memorandum,* which had been negotiated largely under the auspices of Russian foreign minister, Yevgeniy Primakov. The *Moscow Memorandum,* which was also signed by the three mediators from Russia, Ukraine, and the OSCE, called for the two parties to "construct their relations within the framework of a common state." Alas, Chisinau and Tiraspol (the seat of the Transdniestrian authorities) could not agree on what was meant by "common state," and no further steps were taken.

The other near settlement occurred in 2003, when Moldovan president Vladimir Voronin proposed writing a new Constitution for Moldova as a federal state, with Transdniestria having the status of a highly autonomous federal unit. Voronin asked for President Putin's assistance in this effort, and Putin sent the deputy head of his Presidential Administration, Dmitri Kozak, to facilitate negotiations between the Moldovans and Transdniestrians. Working alongside of but not as a part of the formal negotiating process, Kozak's effort produced a *Memorandum* that both President Voronin and Transdniestrian leader Igor Smirnov accepted in November 2003. However, just hours before Putin was to travel to Chisinau to preside over the *Memorandum*'s signing, Voronin called him—ostensibly influenced by pressure from the United States, EU, and OSCE—to call off the deal.

Putin was furious; even years later, he still reportedly remains angry at this last-minute embarrassment. But his personal offense at Voronin's last-minute rejection was not the only significant fallout of the Kozak incident. The Western sabotage of a Russian-brokered settlement in Moldova came two years after Putin had accepted a U.S. military presence in Central Asia in the wake of the September 11, 2001, terrorist attacks on the United States. After the 2003 debacle in Moldova, some four months later, the OSCE's Office for Democratic Institutions and Human Rights sharply criticized the democratic bona fides of Putin's reelection. This was followed by the offering of strong Western support for Ukraine's Orange Revolution, which successfully called into question the initial victory of Putin's favored candidate, Viktor Yanukovych, and led to the election of the Western-leaning Viktor Yushchenko. Western responses to the so-called Tulip Revolution in Kyrgyzstan in early 2005 and Uzbekistan's violent repression of protesters in Andijon offered further evidence to Russian leaders so inclined to believe that the West was out to supplant Russian influence throughout the former Soviet Union and perhaps even advocate regime change in Russia itself.

The events in Moldova in 2003 did not of themselves convince Moscow that Washington, Brussels, and other Western actors were out to get it. However, relations between Russia and the Western mediators in Moldova were never the same after the Kozak history. Whereas Russian diplomats and military officers and Westerners in Moldova had worked cooperatively and at times effectively together before, their working relations deteriorated badly from that time. In addition, what was for most Western capitals a relatively minor incident for the Russians was a personal affront to their president and a denial of Russia's right to play an independent political and diplomatic role in a part of the world that had once been theirs exclusively. Thus, for many Russian politicians and analysts, these events in Moldova remain an early and important part of a pattern they claim to discern in Western behavior, which they find to be evidence of an intentional campaign to weaken Russia and displace its influence even in Russia's neighbors, former imperial possessions, and traditional friends.

I believe that the history of the political settlement negotiations in Moldova and in particular the involvement of Dmitri Kozak also makes a fascinating story in and of itself. I am clearly prejudiced in this respect. I served as head of the OSCE Mission in Moldova twice, from June 1999 to November 2001, and from January 2003 through July 2006. When I finished my second tour in Moldova, I contemplated writing a history of the Transdniestrian conflict. Once embarked on this process, as I followed the political disputes ongoing within Moldova/Transdniestria, among the states of the former Soviet Union, and between Russia and the United States and EU over the Russian near abroad, I became increasingly convinced of the logic and necessity of paying particular attention to these events of 2003—the reasons for Kozak's involvement, the way it played out, why it failed, and what were the consequences of this failure. I believe this study tells us much, not just about Moldova but also about Russia and its relations with its neighbors, the EU, and the United States.

Although many of the principal actors in this story have moved on to other activities, the Transdniestrian question remains an existential political issue in Moldova. Therefore, some of the conclusions I draw in this narrative are still bound to be politically controversial. In addition to published sources, for this narrative I have drawn extensively on my own notes, papers, and recollections. Although I may refer in some instances to conversations with or information provided by other individuals, I alone remain responsible for any lapses of memory or errors of fact. Also, all the judgments offered or conclusions drawn are entirely my own and do not reflect the position of the National War College, the Department of Defense, or the U.S. government.

In addition, some notes on language, terminology, and transliteration are in order. Early in the Soviet period, Stalin and his associates "discovered" the Moldovan language as a means of furthering the Soviet claim to Bessarabia, which from 1812 on was a province of Russia, and from 1918 to 1940 was a part of Romania. During Soviet times, Moscow insisted that the majority population of the Moldavian Soviet Socialist Republic spoke Moldovan, a different language from Romanian and written in Cyrillic script. After Moldova gained independence in 1991, the country's new leaders referred to the state language as Moldovan. Citizens of the Republic of Moldova may be Moldovans, but in my personal experience and observation (which are shared by many linguists in and citizens of Moldova), the majority speak Romanian, with minorities having Russian, Ukrainian, Gagauz (a Turkic tongue), and Bulgarian as their native language. I therefore refer throughout this work to Romanian speakers in Moldova. This signifies no political affiliation or prediction of the political orientation or fate of the Moldovan state; in my opinion, it is merely a recognition of linguistic fact.

One illustration of the extent and depth of the political dispute in Moldova and the role played by language is the name of its separatist region itself. This narrow sliver of land lies along the east, or left, bank of the Dniestr (in Russian), or Nistru (in Romanian), River. I tend to use "Dniestr" when quoting Russian speakers or materials, and "Nistru" when quoting from the Romanian. It is of course the same river. Romanian speakers in the country call this territory Transnistria (the land across the Nistru). Russian speakers call the territory Pridnestrov'e, or the land along the Dniestr. For reasons that remain obscure (at least to me), some English-language studies of the country combined the two to form the hybrid "Transdniestria." This variant was in use in the OSCE when I arrived at the Mission to Moldova in June 1999, and I have used it ever since (as does the OSCE). From time to time, I have been criticized by both parties to the conflict for this usage, because it ostensibly shows I favor one side or the other. Whether out of neutrality, consistency, or stubbornness, I have maintained this usage throughout this volume.

The transliteration of foreign terms, place names, and personal names is also always an issue in works of this nature. For Romanian, I have used the terms and names as written in that language, complete with dia-critical marks, except in cases where there is a broadly accepted English version (e.g., Bucharest, as opposed to Bucureşti, or Chisinau, as opposed to Chişinău). For Russian terms and names, I have used the Library of Congress system of transliteration, again with a few exceptions where there is a broadly accepted English variant.

Finally, I am grateful to a number of people who helped me, not only in the compilation and composition of this volume, but also during the more than seven years of my work and life in Moldova. I wish to thank the many representatives at all levels of the OSCE Chairs that appointed me, worked with me, and supported me during my time in Moldova— Norway, Austria, Romania, Portugal, the Netherlands, Bulgaria, Slo-venia, and Belgium. I owe a special debt of gratitude to Ambassador Adriaan Jacobovits de Szeged, with whom I worked especially closely and harmoniously during his tenure both as special representative of the Dutch OSCE Chair and later as special representative for Moldova of the European Union. U.S. negotiators Carey Cavanaugh, David Kramer, and Rudolf Perina are close and valued colleagues, whose wis-dom, advice, and support aided me immeasurably. My immediate suc-cessor in Moldova, Ambassador Louis O'Neill, was kind enough to per-mit me to check my recollections against records in the archive of the OSCE Mission. U.S. ambassadors to Moldova Pamela Smith and Heather Hodges were valued colleagues during much of the period of this narrative. Many present and former colleagues were kind enough to read and comment on the manuscript at various stages of its development, including Lyndon Allin, Neil Brennan, Rebecca Chamberlain-Creanga, Jeff Goldstein, Ryan Grist, Gottfried Hanne, Jelle Marseille, Wayne Merry, Ambassador Kalman Mizsei, and Claus Neukirch. To these and other friends and colleagues, my thanks for your patience, support, and good advice. I alone remain responsible for any errors or omissions of fact or opinion in the text or elsewhere.

Considerable portions of the research on European security and security institutions reflected in this work were accomplished while I was a Public Policy Scholar at the Woodrow Wilson International Center for Scholars in 2001 and 2002, supported by a grant from the U.S. Institute of Peace. Georgetown University's Institute for the Study of Diplomacy provided a superb setting and support during my initial compilation and checking of sources and drafting for this work during 2006 and 2007, after my departure from Moldova.

I am especially grateful to my many friends and colleagues in Moldova, in society, government, and the OSCE Mission on both sides of the Nistru/Dniestr, who are too numerous to name individually. You made Moldova a wonderful place for me to live and work, a land that I sorely miss since my departure and that I continue to visit regularly.

Last but most important, I owe more than I can express to Greg, Natalie, and Joyce for their love and support throughout the events chronicled in this volume, and during the time after while I tried to make sense of them.

William H. Hill
McLean, Virginia
July 2011

Map 1. Moldova and Its Neighborhood.

Map 2. Moldova and Transdniestria.

Russia, the Near Abroad, and the West

Chapter 1

Introduction:
How Things All Went Bad

Relations between the newly independent Russian Federation and the United States, the European Union, and the major Western European powers were launched in 1992 in an atmosphere of great hope and cooperation, but gradually deteriorated to near confrontation and bitter recriminations following Russia's 2008 war with Georgia. The most commonly accepted Western narrative for this process describes an open, democratizing government led by Russian president Boris Yeltsin gradually being replaced after 2000 by an increasingly closed, authoritarian, suspicious regime installed by his successor, KGB veteran Vladimir Putin.

The most common Russian narratives explain this deterioration in relations with the accusation that the West, led by the United States, sought to exclude Russia from post–Cold War Europe's key political and security structures. In the Russian perception, Washington and its Allies took geopolitical advantage of the dissolution of the Warsaw Pact and the Soviet Union, and the relative Russian weakness to turn Europe into a giant security and politico-economic bloc arrayed against and hostile to Russia. This view found its clearest expression in Putin's diatribe to the annual Munich Security Conference in February 2007.[1]

There were two major points of contention between Russia and the West during the 1990s. The first was the extension of NATO to the east, as three Central European states that had been Soviet Warsaw Pact satellites—Poland, Hungary, and the Czech Republic—became members of the North Atlantic Alliance by April 1999. Russian objections to the extension of NATO membership to three of the Visegrad four were ameliorated somewhat by launching a special relationship between NATO and Russia through the NATO-Russia Founding Act (signed in

May 1997) and the establishment of the NATO-Russia Permanent Joint Council. The second sore point was the increasing involvement of NATO's military forces in combat and peacekeeping operations in the former Yugoslavia. At first, Russia cooperated with NATO—directly or indirectly—such as in the February 1994 introduction of the Sarajevo exclusion zone and then the post–Dayton Accords peacekeeping operations with the NATO International Force in Bosnia-Herzegovina.

However, by the end of the 1990s and throughout the 2000s, Moscow was increasingly vexed by NATO's wholesale expansion into Eastern Europe and more muscular out-of-area military operations undertaken without the United Nations' blessing. The Russians were particularly indignant at NATO's war with Serbia in the spring of 1999 in response to the slaughter and refugee crisis provoked in Kosovo by the regime of Slobodan Miloševic. Moscow was largely excluded from the political process seeking to obtain concessions from Belgrade without war; the decision to go to war was made in the North Atlantic Council, without referral to or approval from the United Nations, a fact that heightened Russia's fury. Although Moscow (through the good offices of former prime minister Viktor Chernomyrdin) eventually collaborated with NATO in bringing Miloševic to the table and adopting a UN resolution ending the hostilities, the depth of Moscow's resentment was evident in the apparently unauthorized dash of Russian military units from NATO's Stabilization Force in Bosnia to seize the Pristina Airport in Kosovo, an action that nearly led to armed conflict with NATO forces also deploying in Kosovo.

Moscow was also uncomfortable with the second wave of NATO expansion to seven Eastern European countries—including the three Baltic states, which had once been unwilling republics of the Soviet Union—that was decided at the 2002 Prague Summit and ratified by all Allies by mid-2004. The deepening of NATO-Russia relations at the Prague Summit and the replacement of the Permanent Joint Council by the NATO-Russia Council arguably took some of the sting out of the second tranche of NATO enlargement. However, by mid-decade the establishment of U.S. and NATO facilities in Poland, Romania, and Bulgaria, which were seen by Moscow as a violation of commitments made in 1997 to then–foreign minister Yevgeny Primakov not to introduce permanent NATO military facilities to the territory of new members, did much to sour relations between Moscow on the one hand, and Washington and Brussels on the other.

Western actions during the years 2007–8 in determining the status of Kosovo, separated de facto from Serbia-Montenegro with the June 1999 cease-fire but formally recognized by United Nations Security Council Resolution 1214 still to be de jure a part of Serbia, were the next significant steps in souring Russia's relations with the major Western powers. In Moscow's view, when agreement proved difficult to reach in negotiations between Belgrade and Pristina brokered by the contact group of which Russia was a member, the United States and its Allies simply implemented over Russian and Serbian objections former Finnish president Martti Ahtisaari's plan to grant Kosovo independence and to recognize the new state.

During these two decades, it is not clear whether Moscow has been more frustrated by the substance of NATO's policy of enlargement and out-of-area military operations in the Balkans or by the fact that Russia was effectively prevented from meaningfully participating in or influencing the process. In the view of Putin and his colleagues, Russia's exclusion from NATO and the Alliance's actions without seeking UN debate and authorization meant that Russia was unable to participate in deliberations or influence decisions on the most important political and security questions in Europe.

During these two decades, in particular after 2000, Russian political leaders were increasingly disturbed by a third major development on the European security landscape: the growing interest and involvement of major Western actors—the United States, the European Union, and NATO—in key political and security questions in a number of countries in the former Soviet Union, an area that Moscow had long considered (and to this day would like to consider) its exclusive turf—its "near abroad." Russia's sensitivity and hostility to Western penetration of its near abroad was starkly demonstrated by the reaction of Putin and his colleagues to the announcement at the April 2008 NATO Bucharest Summit that Ukraine and Georgia would one day be members of NATO. However, Moscow's unhappiness with Western involvement and actions in a number of former Soviet republics considerably predated Bucharest, which was merely one of the more recent and visible in a long series of events and actions that had persuaded the Kremlin that the West was out to diminish and eventually supplant Russia's influence in the former Soviet space.

Russia's claim to preponderant influence in most of the former Soviet states could be seen with particular clarity in its activities as primary mediator and peacekeeper in a number of intrastate and interstate conflicts that broke out on the periphery of the USSR as the Soviet empire fell apart. In some cases, such as the Minsk Group formed to mediate the conflict between Azerbaijan and Armenia over Nagorno-Karabakh, Moscow worked cooperatively with major Western partners in pursuit of common interests in preventing the escalation of violence and reducing the influence of other regional actors. In other cases, such as the conflicts in Abkhazia and South Ossetia in Georgia, Russia intervened and became the sole provider of peacekeeping forces, albeit with the initial support or approval of the United States and the major European powers. In like fashion, in Moldova Russia was the sole external power prepared to intervene and broker a cease-fire, while other Euro-Atlantic states joined the process of conflict resolution—via the Organization for Security and Cooperation in Europe (OSCE)—only some six months after the cessation of hostilities.

During much of the 1990s, Moscow was able to nurture the notion that it had the lead, if not the exclusive right, in international efforts to resolve these conflicts that broke out in the aftermath of the Soviet dissolution. Russia was the equal partner to other states in the Minsk process, and after 1997 cochair with the United States and France. Most of the conflict resolution efforts on Nagorno-Karabakh were channeled through the OSCE, as were similar international initiatives on the South Ossetian and Transdniestrian conflicts. Abkhazia was the exception, for there Russian peacekeepers operated under a UN mandate, and the international negotiations on the conflict were conducted in the "Friends of Georgia" group in the UN. Most important in each case, however, was that Russia was a full participant in the conflict resolution process, with a veto over any unwanted OSCE or UN initiatives. Thus Moscow could consider its regional interests fully protected.

The NATO bombing of Serbia in the spring of 1999, over Russia's vehement objections and without the imprimatur of the United Nations, was an especially rude shock for Moscow. In light of NATO's actions in the Balkans, the continued expansion to the east after 2000 of both NATO and the EU took on a particularly ominous appearance, as the United States, the EU, and leading European states also became much more interested and active in the former Soviet republics on Russia's periphery, often on a bilateral basis, independent of the established OSCE and UN conflict resolution mechanisms. At the November 1999 OSCE Summit in Istanbul, the United States and its Allies pressed for

Russian commitments to complete the withdrawal of its military forces from Moldova and Georgia as a condition for signing the Adapted Treaty on Conventional Armed Forces in Europe (CFE). Russia's Western partners then refused to begin ratification of the adapted treaty until Russia completed this withdrawal, a position that caused the Russian military considerably greater discomfiture. After Estonia, Latvia, and Lithuania became NATO members in 2004, they were unable to accede to the adapted CFE regime and Moscow was left without any treaty-based limitations on possible NATO military deployments on Russia's northwestern border.

By mid-2005, in Moscow's eyes, this series of political and military developments constituted a growing Western threat to Russia. Russia's chief CFE partners refused to ratify and accede to an arms control regime that they had negotiated with Russia only a few years before. Furthermore, the Western powers enthusiastically supported the sudden, extralegal replacement of Georgian president Shevardnadze with the militant, Western-oriented nationalist Mikheil Saakashvili, called President Putin's 2004 reelection significantly flawed, in effect unfree and unfair, and offered strong backing to Ukrainian opposition candidate Viktor Yushchenko and the crowds protesting election fraud in the initial victory of Viktor Yanukovych. Many observers in Moscow concluded that the West was out to replace Russian influence in the countries of the former Soviet Union and perhaps even to engage in regime change via a "color revolution" in Russia itself.

To a Western observer, such fears seem wildly exaggerated, perhaps even laughable. Nonetheless, it appears that by the mid-2000s a sizable portion of the Russian public, perhaps even a majority, had drawn such conclusions about Western intentions toward Russia. This process of disillusionment, suspicion, distrust, and fear led directly to Putin's angry outburst in Munich in February 2007 and the deep chill in Russia's relations with the West following the August 2008 war with Georgia. The damage done to relations between Russia and the United States and its Allies has only begun to be mended with the first years of the Barack Obama administration and its "reset" of the U.S. policy toward Russia.

There was another important incident early in this process of deterioration of Russia's working relations with its major Western partners and growing suspicion of Western involvement in Russia's near abroad. This incident involved Russia's collaboration with the United States and its

European partners via the OSCE in seeking a political settlement of the Transdniestrian conflict in Moldova. Between 1993 and 2003, Russia, the United States, and major OSCE participating states worked together, often with relative harmony, to negotiate a special status for Moldova's breakaway Transdniestrian region and for the reunification of the country and to facilitate the withdrawal of the Russian military units, arms, and equipment that were still left in Moldova from Soviet times. This cooperation between Russia and its Western partners went spectacularly bad in late 2003, when the United States, EU, and OSCE Chair effectively blocked a settlement agreement that had been negotiated unilaterally by Putin's close adviser and friend Dmitri Kozak only hours before Putin was to arrive in Moldova to preside over the signing of the agreement—titled the *Memorandum on Basic Principles of State Structure of the Unified State,* and called here the Kozak *Memorandum.*

This incident was little reported in major Western press outlets and little remarked upon outside narrow circles in the major Western capitals, in part because it occurred at the same time as the Rose Revolution in Georgia. However, the failure of the Kozak settlement plan was taken as a major disaster and major insult by Moscow. President Putin and his colleagues complained loudly and bitterly that the West, in particular the United States, had operated according to a double standard—unilateral intervention, even military action, was permitted to NATO in the Balkans; but unilateral Russian initiatives, even to settle a long-standing conflict in a country Russia long considered its exclusive turf, would be thwarted by the United States and its Allies. The events in Moldova in 2003 form an essential part of the Russian narrative of how the West has sought over the past decade to displace and weaken Russia. In fact, with the U.S. invasion of Iraq, the rejection of the Kozak plan, and the Rose Revolution in Georgia, one might plausibly argue that 2003 was when Russia's relations with the West, and in particular the United States, really started to go bad. As such, these events in Moldova deserve more attention than they have received almost everywhere in the world but Russia.

The failure of the Kozak *Memorandum* offers at least four key lessons. First, the events of 2003 in Moldova illustrate vividly many of the difficulties in finding solutions to the unresolved territorial, ethnic, linguistic, and national issues in a number of the states on the periphery of the former Soviet Union, such as Georgia, Armenia, Azerbaijan, and perhaps Ukraine and Russia's North Caucasus. Second, Moscow's policies and behavior in Moldova and Transdniestria during the negotiation process in 2003 provide a striking example of Russia's self-perception of its proper role, position, and relationship to the states of the near abroad, that is, the former USSR. Third, a detailed examination of Russia's activity vis-à-vis the Transdniestrian settlement process, in particular the near attainment of a settlement in 2003, lends considerable insight into the sources of Russia's increasingly deep resentment of and difficult relations with the United States and the European Union since the turn of this century. Fourth and finally, the details of the Transdniestrian political settlement negotiations during the fateful year of 2003 offer a number of lessons for prospective mediators, especially of the "how not to" variety.

Since gaining independence in 1991, Moldova has generally been too small, too quiet, and too obscure to attract the attention of Western policymakers. Nonetheless Moldova, in particular its Transdniestrian region, remains for Moscow an area of important Russian interest, but even more a country where Moscow considers Russian influence ought to be unchallenged. It is not my purpose to review the centuries-long history of Russia's competition for influence and political control in Bessarabia and the northwestern part of the Black Sea region, although it is certainly imperative to keep that history in mind when attempting to recount and interpret contemporary political events and aspirations.[2] My point is rather that what Western leaders in 2003 saw as a minor matter of blocking a unworkable political settlement in a small, remote post-Soviet divided state, Kremlin leaders saw as a direct geopolitical challenge and defeat on turf that had been theirs, relatively unchallenged, for centuries. Russian perceptions of what occurred in Moldova in November 2003 then colored Russian interpretations of the Western presence and actions in Georgia after the Rose Revolution, Ukraine in 2004–5, Kyrgyzstan, Uzbekistan, and elsewhere throughout the former Soviet empire. As such, Moldova may have been one of the first places in the former USSR where Russia–United States and Russia–European Union relations moved from an uneasy, peripatetic cooperation to a more clearly adversarial posture.

Thus a study of the events in Moldova during 2003 leading up to the failure of the Kozak *Memorandum* is arguably of interest beyond local Bessarabian and Transdniestrian history and politics. In particular, an examination of the Transdniestrian political settlement process, set in the context of regional and European politics, can contribute insights into Russia's understanding of its interests in its near abroad, its perception of Western attitudes toward Moscow's interests in the region, and the means whereby the Kremlin thought best to manage its interaction with external actors in the post-Soviet space in order to defend and promote Russian interests. In addition, a review of the events of 2003 in Moldova may provide insights (lessons may not be too strong a word) for external—particularly Western—interlocutors who continue to be involved with Russia and its neighbors in attempting to settle those unresolved territorial and political questions remaining from the Soviet breakup. Finally, the chain of circumstances and events that produced the Kozak *Memorandum* is (at least for me) a fascinating vignette of negotiation and mediation, replete with close calls, seemingly inexplicable blunders, and caveats for aspiring diplomats and do-gooders.

As of this writing, the Transdniestrian conflict seems farther than ever from resolution. Since early 2009, Moldova on the right bank of the Dniestr has been in a deep political crisis, from which there is now only a faint promise of emergence. The global economic crisis hit the Transdniestrian entity especially hard, demonstrating clearly the non-viability of the entity as an independent state, but not swaying the determination of Tiraspol's leaders to remain separate from Chisinau. The external mediators and observers—Russia, Ukraine, the OSCE, EU, and United States—remain involved in the "five-plus-two" political settlement negotiation process, which did not meet formally for more than five years. Meanwhile, political stability and economic prosperity continue to elude all the region's residents. The narrative that follows— irrespective of any other merits or lessons—tells a sad tale of how ambition, self-righteousness, and stubbornness can frustrate determined efforts to reach agreement that might provide security and stability—and thus a victory—for all.

Chapter 2

Russia and the Post–Cold War Euro-Atlantic Security Architecture

The Transdniestrian conflict in Moldova, like the other wars on the periphery of the USSR, arose against a common background of internal reform and loosening of central control within the Soviet Union and the sudden disappearance of the external tensions with the major powers of Western Europe and North America. With the end of the Cold War, beginning with the demise of the Warsaw Pact system of satellites in 1989 through the collapse of the Soviet Union, the USSR's confrontational stance toward the United States changed with stunning swiftness into a cooperative relationship characterized by a seemingly total embrace by Moscow of Washington's major norms with respect to global political, economic, and security affairs. Soviet president Mikhail Gorbachev did nothing to rescue the pro-Soviet governments of the Central and Eastern European Warsaw Pact states from the popular movements that swept them away in the autumn of 1989. During the forty years of the Cold War, the East/West standoff divided Europe into two hostile armed camps and paralyzed international organizations such as the United Nations. Scarcely a year after the fall of the Berlin Wall, Gorbachev and Soviet foreign minister Eduard Shevardnadze worked in tandem with the United States in the UN Security Council to craft and authorize a forceful, united international response to Saddam Hussein's invasion of Kuwait.[1]

Gorbachev and Shevardnadze during this same period worked with U.S. president George H. W. Bush and other Western leaders to completely refashion the European security system. At meetings of the Conference on Security and Cooperation in Europe (CSCE, which on January 3, 1995, became the Organization for Security and Cooperation in Europe, OSCE) on human rights in Copenhagen in June 1990 and of the heads of state in Paris in November 1990, Soviet leaders joined with their Western counterparts in adopting landmark documents on democracy, political freedoms, and human rights about which U.S. and Western leaders had only dreamed during the forty-five years since the end of World War II.[2] As one reads the sweeping, unqualified commitments to fundamental freedoms and basic political rights in the *Copenhagen Document* and *Charter of Paris,* it is easy to see how otherwise sober, responsible leaders of Western liberal democratic states might have actually believed they had reached the "end of history."[3] At the same time, Gorbachev cooperated readily in the reunification of the two German states, and he acquiesced to the insistent U.S. proposal that all of reunited Germany should remain within NATO.[4] At its summer 1990 summit in London, NATO itself announced that it would be fundamentally transformed to take into account emerging post–Cold War realities in Europe and to reach out to its former adversaries in the Warsaw Pact.[5] By the final months of 1990, the Soviet Union had also accepted the basic terms of the Treaty on Conventional Armed Forces in Europe (CFE), an agreement that effectively ended the military confrontation in Europe between NATO and the Soviet camp. Though formal entry into force of the CFE Treaty took almost another two years, by the end of 1990 the prospect of a major NATO-Soviet military conflict in Europe had vanished.

The Collapse of Yugoslavia and the USSR—and the West's Responses

Unfortunately, the end of the Cold War and the turn to democracy and market economics, which brought peace and eventual prosperity to much of the European continent, also carried the seeds of destruction for Eastern Europe's two multiethnic, multinational socialist states—Yugoslavia and the USSR. The Socialist Federative Republic of Yugoslavia—or Tito's Yugoslavia—was the first to disintegrate, with the delicate ethnic balance among republics and provinces upset by Serbian leader Slobodan Miloševic's bid for dominance. The warning signs of the impending Yugoslav train wreck were visible long before the country descended into war in June 1991, with Miloševic's brazen attempts in 1988 and 1989 to assert Serbian dominance within the country's federal presidency and other federal bodies.[6]

In contrast to Yugoslavia, the Soviet Union fell apart relatively suddenly, peacefully, and unexpectedly.[7] To be sure, there was real turmoil in Russia and the other Soviet republics over Gorbachev's proposed political and economic reforms. The political liberalization in Gorbachev's perestroika was also used by several republics—notably the three Baltic states and Moldova—to seek a reversal of the Molotov-Ribbentrop Pact and independence from Soviet rule. Democratization under Gorbachev's rule also afforded disgruntled national and ethnic minorities in a number of Soviet republics an opening to protest or appeal their status, including the Armenian population in the Nagorno-Karabakh region in Azerbaijan; the Ossetian and Abkhaz minorities in Georgia; ethnic Russians and Tatars on Ukraine's Crimean Peninsula; and Kyrgyz, Tajik, and Uzbek enclaves in several Central Asian republics. However, the struggle between advocates of democratic reform and hard-line Soviet conservatives in the Russian Republic, in particular in the capital, generally tended to overshadow the debates and conflicts in the Soviet hinterlands.[8]

Then came the August 19 coup against Gorbachev, the resistance in Moscow led by Russian president Boris Yeltsin, and the stunning collapse within days of the authority of both the reactionary plotters and Gorbachev himself. Within three weeks, at a CSCE human dimension meeting in Moscow, the participating states—including the USSR—recognized the independence of Estonia, Latvia, and Lithuania. Within four months of the coup, Yeltsin, Ukrainian president Leonid Kravchuk, and Belarusan president Stanislav Shushkevich had dismantled the USSR. The leaders of the other Soviet republics went along, without significant resistance.[9] On December 25, 1991, Boris Yeltsin moved into Kremlin offices just vacated by Gorbachev, president of a country that no longer existed, and the Russian tricolor replaced the Soviet hammer and sickle over the Kremlin.

In retrospect, the signs of impending Soviet collapse seem more evident than they did to external observers at the time. Although indications of possible disintegration were clear enough by early 1991 for the U.S. Embassy in Moscow to warn Washington of the possibility, the response from President George H. W. Bush was to try to defend Gorbachev and his democratic reforms against his nationalist critics, allegedly one of the major motives behind the president's July 31 "Chicken Kiev" speech (so called by critics in the West and the Ukrainian diaspora who saw Bush's reservations about a Soviet breakup as a lack of courage).[10] U.S. secretary of state James Baker also worried about possible harmful consequences of the disintegration of the Soviet Union, famously warning of the danger of a possible "Yugoslavia with nukes."[11] After the failure of the August coup, the U.S. and European powers were forced to perform a rapid transfer of support from Gorbachev to Yeltsin, for it appeared that the shift in domestic political allegiance within Russia was irreversible and the movement of the western and Transcaucasus Soviet republics toward total independence was irresistible.

The stunningly rapid, largely unexpected demise of the Soviet Union put incredible stress on the process of reforming the European security institutions, which were already under unprecedented strain from the tectonic political realignment and fundamental normative changes brought by the end of the Cold War. During the 1980s, American political leaders and diplomats denounced the USSR's authoritarianism and domination of Eastern Europe and called for the creation of a "Europe whole and free." As events during 1990 moved with stunning speed, Western Cold Warriors saw a new, free Europe forming almost instantaneously as they watched. With the desertion of most of its members, the Warsaw Treaty Organization disappeared and along with it the four-decade confrontation of military blocs in Europe. The *Charter of Paris* adopted at the CSCE's November Summit established for the first time standing political structures in this hitherto episodic, serial process of political-security negotiations among all the nations of the Euro-Atlantic space. Many participants, in particular the Soviets, conjectured that the end of the bloc-to-bloc military confrontation in Europe would also lead to the disappearance of NATO and its replacement by the CSCE, as a universal Euro-Atlantic security organization. Indeed, within both NATO and the U.S. government, senior officials seriously debated whether NATO still had a purpose and a role in European security.[12]

From 1991 on, the CSCE began to develop institutions and take on many of the attributes of a full-fledged international security organization, beyond its previous identity as a continuing negotiating forum. In accordance with the terms of the *Charter of Paris,* the CSCE launched political consultation mechanisms at the senior and working levels. In June 1991 in Berlin, the foreign ministers of the participating states held the first meeting of the CSCE Ministerial Council. At this meeting, Secretary of State Baker urged the establishment of a uninterrupted zone of peace and security "from Vancouver to Vladivostok," reinforcing notions held by many participants that the CSCE's broad geographic scope and universality of membership would make it the leading post–Cold

War European security body.[13] At the working level, the CSCE introduced the Committee of Senior Officials (CSO), which was composed of ambassadors representing the participating states, and which was to meet regularly to discuss topics of interest ("current issues") to any CSCE member state and make recommendations to the Ministerial Council.[14] In addition, the CSCE established its first permanent offices—a Secretariat in Prague and a Conflict Prevention Center in Vienna—and began preparations for opening an Office for Free Elections in Warsaw (which soon became the current Office for Democratic Institutions and Human Rights).[15] CSCE political consultations were largely carried out by staff members provided from delegations in Vienna who were engaged in the ongoing negotiations on confidence- and security-building measures (CSBMs), which eventually produced the 1992 Vienna Document on CSBMs.[16]

Yet at the same time that political leaders were building new pan-European institutions in the CSCE, the security situation in Southeastern Europe was descending into turmoil and war. Tensions had been gradually growing in Yugoslavia during the winter of 1990–91, and a number of violent incidents in the spring of 1991 in disputed areas of Croatia involving Serbian-supported bands made it clear that war was on the horizon. Secretary of State Baker visited Belgrade immediately after the CSCE Berlin Ministerial Council in June 1991 and met with representatives of all the Yugoslav republics, but he did not succeed in convincing the Serb, Croat, and Slovene leaders to avoid secession and violence.[17] War broke out when Slovenia and Croatia seceded from the Yugoslav Federation on June 25, 1991. Essentially reporting to the Serbian leader Slobodan Milosevic, the Yugoslav National Army (Jugoslovenska Narodna Armija, JNA) attacked both breakaway republics. After a brief, two-week war, Slovenia broke away cleanly. Croatia was not so lucky, because Serb-supported local forces controlled most of the Krajina, a mountainous crescent along much of the border with Bosnia, while JNA armor and infantry forces mounted attacks against major Croatian population centers near Serbia in eastern Slavonia.

As war erupted and spread in Yugoslavia, CSCE representatives were assembled at a meeting on national minorities in Geneva. Through consultations of senior delegation representatives in Geneva and emergency sessions of the CSO (in Prague and Vienna), the CSCE debated how to deal with the Yugoslav conflict, the first real security crisis in Europe since the upbeat gathering of the CSCE heads of state in Paris the previous November. U.S. leaders, still weary from the nine-month effort at coalition building to oust Saddam Hussein from Kuwait, were reluctant to get involved. Secretary Baker's alleged comment that "we don't have a dog in that fight," epitomized the American attitude. However, the soon-to-be European Union stepped up to the plate. With the Maastricht Treaty still some months away on the horizon, member states of the European Community were nonetheless ambitious to use the Yugoslav crisis as an opportunity to demonstrate the development of a separate European security and defense capability. The European Community's Troika—consisting of the past, current, and future presidency countries—intervened, conducted negotiations, inserted observers (along with UN peacekeepers), and ultimately failed utterly to curtail current and head off future violence.[18]

The insecurity in Europe from the growing war in Yugoslavia was augmented by a spate of local conflicts that broke out or escalated as the Soviet Union fell apart. All these conflicts demanded attention from a system of Euro-Atlantic security structures that was still very much in transition and could be easily overwhelmed by the sudden, unexpectedly broad demand. Hostilities between Armenia and Azerbaijan posed the greatest immediate danger to regional peace and security. Conflict over the ethnic Armenian enclave of Nagorno-Karabakh in the western mountains of Azerbaijan had been growing since 1988, with slaughters of civilians and mass flows of refugees on both sides.[19] As independent Armenia and Azerbaijan joined the CSCE and split the assets of the Soviet Army left on their respective territories, there was a serious danger of full-scale war with real armies, rather than poorly armed militias, between two CSCE participating states.

Following the Second CSCE Ministerial Council in Prague in January 1992, the CSCE sent several multilateral mediating missions to the region to attempt to head off the impending conflict. At the March 1992 Ministerial Meeting in Helsinki, the CSCE participating states adopted an American proposal to hold a CSCE-sponsored peace conference on the Nagorno-Karabakh conflict, and they accepted Belarus's offer of Minsk as a venue. In April and May 1992, the CSCE sent advance observer teams to Armenia and Azerbaijan to prepare the expected deployment of some sort of observation force to help implement a peace agreement.[20]

Unfortunately, the Minsk Peace Conference has never been held. Negotiations on modalities with CSCE representatives broke down in Rome during the summer of 1992. Full-scale military operations broke out between Armenia and Azerbaijan in 1993, and by the time massive hostilities halted in early 1994, Armenian forces had occupied significant portions of western Azerbaijan. More than seventeen years later, this remains the situation. The Minsk Conference is now the Minsk Group, with Russia, France, and the United States as cochairs. Although the three major mediators continue to work well together, Armenia and Azerbaijan remain so far apart that they cannot even agree on the name of the conflict, and official OSCE documents refer to "the conflict dealt with by the Minsk Group."[21]

These mediation efforts in the field in Nagorno-Karabakh took the CSCE out of its exclusive engagement in normative negotiations and into active involvement in conflict prevention and resolution on the ground. Other opportunities also were not lacking starting in early 1992. War broke out on April 7, 1992, between the Serb, Croat, and Muslim (Bošnjak) communities in Bosnia-Herzegovina, with no end in sight to the ongoing conflict in Croatia. As fighting seemed to spread from one republic of Yugoslavia to another, many leaders and observers worried that the violence would spread to the Serbian province of Kosovo, where the majority ethnic Albanian population seethed under exceptionally harsh neocolonial rule from Belgrade after Milošević revoked the region's autonomy in 1989. During the course of the 1992 CSCE Helsinki Follow-Up Meeting, the United States proposed an attempt to head off the spread of war to Kosovo by sending a CSCE "good offices" mission to the region. After some reworking to include the Muslim and Hungarian minorities in Sandjak and Vojvodina, the proposal was blessed by the July 1992 CSCE Helsinki Summit and formally adopted by the CSO in August 1992.[22] The initial mission lasted a little less than a year, because Milošević refused to renew its memorandum of understanding in July 1993, but the idea of mounting field operations in the CSCE caught on.

During the summer of 1992, the threat or outbreak of violence in Georgia, Macedonia, and Moldova prompted the CSCE to establish field missions in these countries. Fears that violence from elsewhere in the former Yugoslavia would spread to Macedonia, either through Serbian expansion or unrest in the country's ethnic Albanian minority, led to the establishment in September 1992 of the OSCE Spillover Monitor Mission to Skopje.[23] In short order, in the autumn of 1992 the CSCE also established a field mission in Georgia, which for some time had been beset by conflicts with the breakaway entities of South Ossetia and Abkhazia, along with ongoing fighting with forces loyal to former president Zviad Gamsakhurdia.[24] When hostilities broke out between Moldova and forces from its breakaway Transdniestrian region in June 1992, the country appealed to the UN, CSCE, and a number of countries for assistance. The CSCE was not able to respond immediately to Moldova's appeal, but in December 1992 it sent a senior representative (Adam Rotfeld, later foreign minister of Poland) to assess the effects of the conflict, and it opened a mission in Moldova in April 1993.[25] Finally, in February 1993 the CSCE deployed a mission in Estonia to assist in overcoming tensions attendant upon integrating the ethnic Russian minority into the newly independent Estonian state.[26]

In its book-length final document, *The Challenges of Change,* the 1992 Helsinki CSCE Follow-Up Meeting and Summit put better-defined form and substance on the nascent institutions established by the *Charter of Paris.*[27] The 1992 Helsinki Document is an all-encompassing attempt to carve out and define a key role for the CSCE in the European security architecture. The document defines the CSCE as a regional organization in the sense of Chapter VIII of the UN Charter, by this presuming a broader (if not higher) status than other European international organizations such as NATO, the Western European Union, or the European Community (EC; later the European Union). The Helsinki decisions codify the rules and procedures for CSCE field and rapporteur missions, and envision the possibility of CSCE-mandated peacekeeping operations. At Helsinki, in addition to firming up the roles of the Secretariat, the Conflict Prevention Center, and other institutions, the CSCE also accepted a proposal from the Netherlands to establish the post of high commissioner for national minorities, which signified a clear response to recent events in Southeastern and Eastern Europe.[28] By the time the third Ministerial Council was convened in Stockholm in December 1992, the CSCE seemed poised to assume a leading role, if not the leading role, in European security affairs.

During this same period, the United States and its NATO Allies engaged in a process of self-examination and subsequently made fundamental decisions that had far-reaching effects not only for NATO's future but also eventually for the entire security order in Europe. With the Berlin Wall gone, Germany reunited, the Warsaw Pact dissolved, and Soviet troops returning home from their bases in Central Europe, one might easily have been excused for asking questions such as: Do we need NATO any more? What is its purpose, now that the Soviet threat is gone? Why can we not spend the funds formerly allotted to NATO more usefully?

At the same time that the end of the Cold War called into question the continued existence of competing military alliances in Europe, the end of the East/West divide on the continent offered unparalleled opportunity to visionaries and advocates of European economic and political integration within the EC, which during the 1980s added Greece, Spain, and Portugal to its ranks and through the Single European Act and Schengen Agreement embarked on a long-term process of internal integration, removing internal barriers to the movement of people, capital, goods, and services and adopting common institutions and standards of governance. With the reunification of Germany, the disappearance of the Warsaw Pact, and the preparation of the Maastricht Treaty that would transform the EC into the European Union, a number of European states—Germany and France in particular—contemplated how Europe could expand its institutions to include its former foes to the east and provide for its own security.[29] Germany showed particular concern for integrating the former Soviet Warsaw Pact satellites and the USSR (later the former Soviet states) into common European institutions, and it provided much of the initial impetus for institutionalizing the CSCE.[30] France, with its long history of ambivalence toward NATO and the American political-military presence in Europe, was the most vocal in voicing fears that with the end of the Cold War, the United States would abandon its commitment to Europe, and in calling for European states to find some sort of wholly European institution to serve as a successor to NATO in providing military security for the continent.[31]

At the conclusion of the Gulf War and the end of the Cold War, President George H. W. Bush spoke about a "new world order," but he never really articulated what this concept entailed.[32] Instead, the post–Cold War Euro-Atlantic security architecture was constructed during the next few years as an amalgam and compromise of the interests and desires of the Euro-Atlantic states, in particular the major powers participating in the process, rather than as the product of some unified grand plan or strategy. The leading figures in the Bush administration's national security team, including the president himself, were all committed Atlanticists, and the U.S. approach on their watch was to preserve America's ties with and presence in Europe through the preservation and adaptation of the North Atlantic Alliance. The major European powers were generally more concerned with building European institutions, although Britain stressed the importance of the transatlantic relationship, France looked more for independent European foreign policy and defense capabilities, and Germany showed relatively more concern about how the East, including Russia, would fit into the new Europe. Given their particular and often less than pleasant histories with Russia, Central and Eastern European states like Poland, Hungary, the Czech Republic, Slovakia, Estonia, Latvia, Lithuania, Romania, and Bulgaria were all interested in association with NATO almost from the moment the Warsaw Pact and then the Soviet Union dissolved. Finally, the Yeltsin administration believed that Russia had played an essential role in the end of the Cold War and democratic reform in Eastern Europe, and expected Russia to become a full partner, most likely through the institutionalized CSCE, in the post–Cold War councils of European security.[33]

The processes of making the key decisions on NATO and the European Union were intertwined during the crucial period from 1990 to 1992. During the 1980s, continuous debates were waged within the EC on whether it should become "deeper," through a closer integration of the sovereign governmental functions of the member states, or "wider," by extension of membership to a larger number of European states. The debates over the "ever closer union" to be established by the Maastricht Treaty during the process of negotiation and ratification of the document launched the EU on the basic path of deepening economic integration, closer political union, and expansion to include most of the states of the continent that it follows to this day.[34] While discussing the terms of the Maastricht Treaty, prodded in particular by France, the Europeans speculated on ways that the nascent union might acquire or develop its own military security capability.[35] One of the most intriguing proposals was to revive the Western European Union, a relic of the early days of NATO and the Cold War, which had lain dormant in its headquarters in London for several decades. Simultaneously, the deeper-versus-wider debate was resolved by attempting to do both, with the adoption in 1993 of the Copenhagen criteria for new EU members; the addition of Finland, Sweden, and Austria to the EU in 1995; and the launch of practical preparations for a far more extensive enlargement in the next decade.

NATO and the EU: Changing Roles, Growing Reach

Meanwhile, the United States and the United Kingdom led efforts within the Alliance to adapt to the tectonic shift in political and security conditions in Europe.[36] At the June 1990 London NATO Summit, the Allies agreed to fundamental changes in the Alliance, including the drafting of a new Strategic Concept, the first restatement of NATO's basic purpose since the 1960s.[37] The London meeting also resulted in development of the North Atlantic Cooperation Council, which was designed to establish a formal political relationship and structure for NATO's cooperation with the countries of the former Warsaw Pact. The debates within NATO between the London Summit and the November 1991 Rome Summit centered on the argument chiefly between the United States and France over whether NATO or a "European pillar" should be the primary provider of security in post–Cold War Europe. The compromise, set forth in the November 1991 Rome Declaration, determined that a European capability should be developed under an overall NATO umbrella, but the details of how this would work in practice continued to be debated within the Alliance for at least another decade.[38] Meanwhile, the new Strategic Concept adopted at Rome reaffirmed the U.S. and European commitments to NATO, and began the transformation of the Alliance from primarily an instrument of collective defense to a collective security structure capable of "out of area" operations.[39]

NATO and EU members had no sooner made these fundamental decisions about their organizations' futures when both were severely tested in practice by the growing crisis in Southeastern Europe. During the years 1992–93, the wars in the former Yugoslavia continued to expand, and external efforts to halt the fighting or contain the effects were largely ineffective. The fighting in Croatia subsided a bit toward the end of 1991, following the deployment of the EC Monitoring Mission (ECMM) and the United Nations Protective Force (UNPROFOR). However, this may have had more to do with the fact that Serb forces had captured most territories inhabited by their co-ethnics rather than the EC and UN intervention, as fighting renewed once temperatures climbed in 1992. The UNPROFOR's mandate was not sufficient to restrain determined combatants, and some observers joked that the ECMM's white uniforms simply made mission personnel better targets.[40]

The fighting spread to Bosnia-Herzegovina immediately after recognition by the United States and the EU member states on April 6 and 7, 1992. The Balkan wars might have spread anyway, but the haste to recognize first Slovenia and Croatia, and then Bosnia, pushed especially by German foreign minister Hans-Dietrich Genscher, arguably gave Miloševic even more reason to grab territory when and where he could.[41] Although the Serb bombardment of Vukovar and gratuitous shelling of

Dubrovnik in 1991 attracted considerable international opprobrium, this was nothing compared with the hue and cry prompted by ethnic cleansing and the Serbian concentration camps discovered in Bosnia and shown by international broadcast news media in the summer of 1992. The international reaction was swift, loud, and yet still ineffective. The UN extended coverage by UNPROFOR from Croatia alone also to Bosnia-Herzegovina, but with a mandate largely to protect civilians and deliver humanitarian aid. Following the mass killing of civilians by a mortar shell in a Sarajevo market in May 1992, the United States led a successful push for the imposition of UN economic sanctions on Serbia. After a personal appeal from President Bush to President Yeltsin, Russia went along with both these sanctions and the exclusion of Serbia-Montenegro (the Federal Republic of Yugoslavia) from the CSCE. The revelation of the war crimes and concentration camps prompted the first steps in the establishment of the eventual International Criminal Tribunal on Yugoslavia, which functions to this day in The Hague.

Diplomatic efforts at intervention and mediation also fared little better. An international conference in London in August 1992 assembled representatives of the belligerents (including one of Radovan Karadzic's last appearances in Western Europe until his arrest in Belgrade and transfer to The Hague in 2008), the EU, UN, and the United States. The ensuing peace process led by UN special representative Cyrus Vance and EU special representative Robert Owen (the former U.K. foreign secretary), produced a plan for a loose confederation of Serb, Croat, and Muslim areas, which was torpedoed by the incoming Bill Clinton administration. Secretary of State Warren Christopher's trip to the region in mid-1993 and subsequent multilateral efforts in the UN did no better. The UN Security Council solemnly established six UN-protected areas for Muslim enclaves in Bosnia, but the UN's member states were unwilling to provide sufficient troops or rules of engagement to defend these areas militarily. As the fighting and slaughter continued (and were gruesomely chronicled by CNN and the BBC) and the flow of refugees to Western Europe mounted, cries for intervention intensified.[42]

It is not the purpose of this volume to relate the whole sad story of the Balkan wars of the 1990s and the failed attempts at international intervention. For this account, it is sufficient to note the quick demonstration of the insufficiency of EU foreign policy and defense capabilities to manage the Yugoslav crisis, and the longer, more agonizing process of the failure of UN intervention. By late 1993, public pressure to "do something" had grown enormously in many European states and the United States. The Clinton administration was still not interested in direct intervention in the Balkans, especially following the October 1993 "Blackhawk Down" debacle in Mogadishu, and thought more and more of NATO as a possible instrument with which to respond. The discussion that had begun at London and Rome over the provision of security by NATO in areas near but not in the territory of member states still continued, and it was galvanized by another Serb mortar slaughter of Muslim civilians in Sarajevo in February 1994. Within days, encouraged particularly by the United States and Secretary-General Manfred Woerner, NATO agreed upon and deployed to enforce a zone around Sarajevo that would exclude Serbian heavy weapons. Russia agreed and joined in the enforcement of the Sarajevo exclusion zone.[43]

For a while, the NATO intervention in Sarajevo halted the Serb shelling, and no-fly zones over the protected areas with NATO participation had some effect. But the infamous UN dual-key authorization system soon proved spectacularly ineffective, as Serb forces attacked Muslims in Gorazde, Bihać, and elsewhere. Through 1994 and 1995, Serb forces pushed the envelope, until the infamous capture of Srebrenica (over the ineffectual resistance of the hapless Dutch UNPROFOR detachment) and slaughter of roughly 7,000 Muslim civilians. This time the United States and NATO took decisive military action, conducting an effective air campaign against Serbian forces in Bosnia and lending support to Croat forces that recaptured territories in Croatia and Bosnia long held by Serbian troops and separatist authorities.[44]

It was U.S. and NATO action that brought Milošević to Dayton and obtained the opportunity for peace in Croatia and Bosnia-Herzegovina. Once the terms of the peace were determined, the Clinton administration was determined that they would not be implemented by what Washington saw as a thoroughly ineffective, discredited UN headed by the weak and waffling Secretary-General Boutros Boutros Ghali. The United States and its Allies agreed to divide the civilian administration of the peace in Bosnia-Herzegovina between a high representative and staff from the European Union and a civilian OSCE Mission, headed by an American. Peacekeeping would be provided by the International Force (IFOR) led by NATO countries, with the United States first and foremost. Russia agreed to participate in the implementation of the Dayton Accords, including the peacekeeping forces. However, unlike other national detachments participating in IFOR, the Russians declined to put themselves under the command of the NATO Supreme Allied Commander Europe. Instead, U.S. secretary of defense William Perry reached an agreement with Russian minister of defense Pavel Grachev that Russian troops in IFOR would be under the control of the American commander, wearing his other hat as commander in chief of the U.S. European Command.[45]

NATO Expands and Russia Objects: A Pattern Emerges

By the mid-1990s, then, NATO had clearly established the precedent of going "out of area" to deal with security problems in other areas of Europe. During this time, NATO also settled the question of whether and how to expand the number and territory of its members. From the fall of the Berlin Wall there was little argument from any quarter that NATO (if it survived) should avoid a security vacuum in Central and Eastern Europe left by the dissolution of the Warsaw Pact. The real question was whether this should be done by reaching out to establish political and military-to-military working relationships with the former members of the Warsaw Pact and the former Soviet republics, or by including some or all of these states in NATO itself. We have seen that a firmly Atlanticist Bush administration was determined to preserve NATO; however, it professed no such certainty and unanimity about how to deal with the security void in Central and Eastern Europe. In the end, the Bush administration came down in favor of outreach through the North Atlantic Cooperation Council.[46]

The first real push for NATO expansion came from a number of former Soviet Warsaw Pact allies and some former Soviet republics, in particular Poland, Czechoslovakia, and the Baltic states. Many Eastern European leaders were not confident about the long-term prospects for democratic reforms and cooperative foreign policy in Russia, and they looked instead to NATO's continued existence and expansion as a hedge against Russian, or neo-Soviet, backsliding on democracy and neo-imperialism.[47] Many contemporary observers claim that the abortive coup against Gorbachev in August 1991 did a great deal to push Central and Eastern European leaders toward NATO and away from the CSCE as a guarantor of security against a possible conservative Soviet resurgence.[48] During the process of German reunification, Gorbachev showed concern that NATO not take advantage to expand its territory or military capabilities. However, Yeltsin and in particular his Westwardleaning foreign minister, Andrei Kozyrev, at first entertained the notion that NATO might expand to even include Russia, in a grand partnership of East and West.[49] Domestic political developments, in particular Yeltsin's struggle with his nationalist critics leading up to the October 1993 attack on the Russian Parliament, soon made such a pro-Western policy line untenable. However, at least until the mid-1990s and sometimes even beyond, Yeltsin maintained a relatively cooperative posture with the West on major issues of European security, as shown, for example, by Russian's participation in IFOR.

The push to extend NATO membership to the former Warsaw Pact and Soviet countries in Central and Eastern Europe was led within NATO by the United States, with Germany (arguably) its greatest supporter.[50] Incidental discussion of the proposition began among a few U.S. government officials and some prominent nongovernmental organization policy experts as early as 1991–92, but really took flight in the first year of the Clinton presidency.[51] Without going into the details of the first tranche of NATO expansion, from the basic decision by Clinton in late 1993 to the 1997 Madrid Summit, where the official decision on the first new members was made, it is worth emphasizing three basic points about the process. First, though the United States led the push for enlargement within the Alliance, inside the U.S. government there was a sharp debate between those who favored expansion as a means of bringing democracy and stability to the former socialist countries in Eastern Europe and those who put the relationship with and democratic reforms in Russia as their foremost concern. Second, the greatest advocates in Europe of NATO expansion were the prospective members from Central and Eastern Europe themselves. Their recent Soviet experiences—and for some, their long, unpleasant national historical experiences with Russia—led them to favor their own security against a possible threat from the east over the possible integration of wider Europe including Russia. Third, after an initial honeymoon with Yeltsin and Kozyrev, the prospect of NATO's expansion to the east became one of the most contentious points in Russia's relations with the major powers of Western Europe and the United States. Moscow claimed bad faith, pointing to alleged promises from President Bush and Secretary Baker during negotiations on German reunification that NATO would not move "one inch to the east."[52]

The Clinton administration made a number of attempts to bridge the difference with Russia vis-à-vis NATO enlargement. The first serious such effort was the Partnership for Peace (PfP), which would bring participants serious political and military collaboration with NATO, in fact, many important aspects of membership. Boris Yeltsin welcomed PfP, apparently because he presumed it would substitute for and prevent NATO's expansion to the east; but his nationalist critics in the Russian legislature were hostile to the initiative from the start. These critics received fodder for their denunciations as advocates of the program such as then–U.S. ambassador to the UN Madeleine Albright were widely quoted to the effect that PfP was the best vehicle for aspirants to gain membership in the Alliance.[53] After an anti-NATO outburst from Yeltsin at the December 1994 Budapest OSCE Summit, Clinton and Deputy Secretary of State Strobe Talbott spent much of 1995 on a dual-track approach, seeking to mend relations and assuage Russian objections while proceeding ahead with NATO's enlargement.[54] Finally, the Clinton administration negotiated a special relationship between Russia and NATO, enshrined in the Russia-NATO Founding Act, which was signed in Madrid in May 1997, at the same time that NATO leaders adopted the decision to offer membership in the Alliance to Poland, Hungary, and the Czech Republic. The NATO-Russia Charter gave Russia a special status and added prestige in its relationship with the Alliance. In negotiations with NATO secretary-general Javier Solana (but basically masterminded from Washington), Russian foreign minister Primakov received a political commitment that NATO did not envision substantial facilities or permanent deployments on the territory of its prospective new members.[55]

Moscow and Washington:
Both Cooperating and Sparring Partners

Although relations between Moscow and Washington grew increasingly more complicated and at times adversarial throughout the 1990s, the majority of practitioners and observers during this period generally perceived the cooperative, collaborative elements of the relationship to outweigh in number and importance those that divided Russia and the United States (as the leader of the West).[56] Part of the seeming calm and cooperativeness of this relationship may be explained by Russia's relative weakness. Although there was loud, vituperative criticism from nationalists in the Duma of the close relations of the Yeltsin administration with the West, these critics did not have the political strength or instruments to do a great deal about their anger. In addition, both Yeltsin and his political opponents were preoccupied with domestic issues and developments within Russia: the bitter war with Chechen separatists that ended in 1996 to Moscow's disadvantage, Yeltsin's controversial reelection campaign, and then the economic crisis of 1998. (For more on the wars in Chechnya, see chapter 3.) Overall, Western leaders and analysts mostly had an overly sanguine view during much of the 1990s of domestic developments within Russia and Western relations with Russia. It was thus probably more of a shock than it should have been when Moscow, empowered by a recovering economy and higher oil and gas prices, began after 1999–2000 to assert the nationalist sentiments and policies that had long enjoyed majority support in the Russian legislature and—arguably—in the population at large.

A real turning point came with NATO's war against Serbia in the spring of 1999. In March 1999, Primakov, by then promoted to prime minister, famously turned his plane around over the Atlantic rather than visit Washington after NATO's attack on Milošević's Serbia in defense of the Kosovo Albanians. However, three months later the Yeltsin administration was still prepared to cooperate with the United States and NATO in avoiding longer and wider hostilities in the Balkans, as former prime minister Viktor Chernomyrdin was instrumental in convincing Milošević to accept a cease-fire, the de facto separation of Kosovo from Serbia, and deployment of NATO peacekeepers. Nonetheless, action by other Russian officials demonstrated the split over NATO's intervention among the elite in Moscow and the depth of Russian bitterness, as Russian peacekeeping troops in Bosnia made an undeclared (and perhaps not fully authorized) quick march to the Pristina Airport in an effort to create realities on the ground more favorable to Belgrade and local Kosovo Serbs.[57]

Moscow got relatively little credit or thanks for its key role in bringing Serbia to the table and helping to avoid what otherwise might have become an ugly ground campaign for NATO forces. Instead, other irritants contributed to a steady deterioration in the climate of Russia's dealing with Western Europe and the United States. Most notably, Prime Minister Putin's savage campaign begun in September 1999 against the "terrorist regime" in Chechnya drew a far more critical response from Washington than Clinton's overly tolerant response to Yeltsin's fight against Chechen separatism in the First Chechen War of 1994–96.[58]

In contrast to the testiness of the United States–Russia relationship during the final year of the Clinton administration, George W. Bush's accession to the White House and initial encounter with Russian president Vladimir Putin in Slovenia in 2001 produced a marked warming of ties between Moscow and Washington that lasted well into Bush's first term. After the (in)famous meeting in Slovenia at which President Bush announced that he had looked into Putin's soul, the Russian leader reacted quickly and cooperatively following the September 11, 2001, terrorist attacks on New York and Washington. Moscow shared intelligence and made no objection to American basing in Central Asia in support of operations in Afghanistan. The Russians also rapidly acceded to American desires and accepted the Strategic Offensive Reductions Treaty with significant loopholes for the retirement rather than destruction of weapons systems and absolutely no provisions for verification. Moscow also made minimal objections to the U.S. announcement of unilateral withdrawal from the 1972 Anti–Ballistic Missile Treaty in order to pursue the development and deployment of a ballistic missile defense system to guard against attack from rogue states such as North Korea and Iran.[59]

Russia under Putin, the United States, and the major Western European powers also dealt relatively successfully with the second wave of NATO expansion, including the extension of membership to the Baltic states Estonia, Latvia, and Lithuania, a decision that was formally adopted at the 2002 Prague NATO Summit. The 1999 NATO war against Serbia destroyed whatever goodwill and confidence in NATO that the Founding Act and Permanent Joint Council (PJC) might have built up. After 1999, the PJC worked badly, if at all, and NATO-Russia working ties remained pretty much in the deep freeze. In the preparations for the Prague Summit, a number of Allies were concerned that continued expansion of the Alliance, especially to former Soviet-controlled territory in the Baltics, could lead to further deterioration of relations and greater tensions. In an attempt to mitigate Russian concerns and objections, at a May 2002 NATO summit with Russia in Rome, the PJC was replaced by a NATO-Russia Council, a body composed of all the Allies meeting together with Russia.[60] The NRC was designed to expand and deepen the previous consultative relationship of Russia with the Alliance in the PJC, by providing for the formal adoption and implementation of joint projects and operations. Western officials working in NATO staff structures and the NRC in 2002–3 expressed considerable optimism about the possibilities and initial working relations in the new NATO-Russia relationship.[61]

Despite these cooperative steps, many Russian government officials and analysts claimed that in the end Moscow received relatively little in return in areas that it might have considered important. In particular, though official American criticism of Russian military actions in Chechnya was toned down a bit in the new Bush administration, American diplomats continued, much to the Russians' exasperation, to meet with representatives of the Chechen opposition in exile (whom Putin and his colleagues claimed were terrorists) and Western countries, particularly the United Kingdom and the Scandinavian nations, refused to extradite prominent Chechen exile leaders. In addition, criticism in the West did not abate of Russian backsliding on democratic reforms, in particular steps taken against critics of the administration and independent media. All this notwithstanding, the U.S. attack on Iraq in March 2003, which Putin called a "big political mistake," failed to shake the remarkably warm personal relationship between the American and Russian presidents, and U.S.-Russian cooperation and good relations continued on a number of fronts.[62]

Looking back, through an atmosphere of mistrust and recriminations permeated with the effects of the 2008 war with Georgia, at relations between Moscow and Washington at the beginning of this decade, it is difficult to imagine that ties could once have been even that good, let alone what they were in the early 1990s. As one enumerates the acts and developments that marked the gradual deterioration of the relationship, it is tempting to adopt an attitude of fatalism toward prospects for Russian-American and East-West cooperation and mutual understanding, let alone friendship. Some point to Putin's moves in 2001 against Vladimir Gusinskii's independent media empire, in particular the television network NTV—independent, critical of the Kremlin and highly popular—or to the brutal, casualty-filled 2002 hostage "rescue" at the Moscow theater taken by Chechen terrorists, as early signs of a wide gulf of values between Russia on the one hand and America and Western Europe on the other.[63] The arrest and show trial of the Russian oil magnate Mikhail Khodorkovskii and the cynical dismantling of the Yukos company, in a process heedless of Western investments, were other signs for many that the Putin administration was headed hopelessly in a nondemocratic, authoritarian direction. The 2003 Russian parliamentary elections and Putin's own reelection campaign in 2004 did even more to tarnish his own and Russia's democratic credentials and to give ammunition to foreign critics who warned that the Kremlin could not be trusted.[64]

Throughout 2005 and 2006, Western criticism of Russia's domestic political system mounted as the Putin administration took a number of steps to assert greater control and limit the freedom of action of Russian media, political parties, and nongovernmental organizations. However, Russian concerns and insecurity were inflamed arguably more by the increasing Western interest, presence, and activities in a number of former Soviet states on Russia's immediate borders. For a number of Kremlin leaders, events such as active Western support for the "Orange Revolution" in Ukraine, Western denunciations of the savage repression by the Uzbek authorities of protests in Andijon, and the Western response to the uncertain upheaval of Kyrgyzstan's "Tulip Revolution" were woven together into a common thread running through the post-Soviet space, in the form of Western democracy-building efforts aimed at expanding geopolitical influence and leading eventually to destabilization and regime change in Russia itself. Moscow's increasingly suspicious, fearful, and hostile perception of Western actions and motives finally found full voice in President's Putin's outburst at the February 2007 Munich Wehrkunde (Conference on Security Policy), which signaled the end of the facade of cooperative relations and opened a chapter of more contentious, troubled ties between Washington, Brussels, and Moscow.[65]

Chapter 3

Conflict Resolution in the Former Soviet Union: Russian Mediation, Peacemaking, and Peacekeeping

The so-called near abroad was where the practical effects of the development and direction of the Euro-Atlantic security architecture mattered most to Russia. To be sure, Moscow had opinions on important normative questions in the Organization for Security and Cooperation in Europe (OSCE) and NATO expansion and involvement in the Balkans. However, most Russian leaders were willing to grant the United States and its Western European Allies considerable slack over much of Europe as long as the Russian Federation maintained its relative predominance and de facto freedom of action in areas deemed to be crucial to Russian interests. Most of these sensitive spots were on the territory of the former USSR, and there were plenty of difficult security problems there for Moscow to manage.

The Aftermath of the USSR's Collapse: Disputes on the Periphery

The Soviet Union collapsed with remarkably little violence on the territory of the Russian Federation itself. Even during the August 1991 coup, in Moscow only three prodemocracy demonstrators perished. Other parts of the Soviet Union, particularly in non-Russian republics, were not so lucky. In Russia the major battle with the Soviet authorities was over democratization; in the rest of the USSR, the fight was often for ethnic separation or national self-determination, where Soviet power was customarily seen as synonymous with Russian imperial domination. Additionally, in some cases smaller ethnic groups and nationalities within the Soviet Union took up against one another historical grievances and territorial aspirations that had hitherto been restrained or suppressed by rule from Moscow.

The number and types of local disputes that arose as the USSR disintegrated were large and varied. Local Soviet authorities, in many cases ethnic Russians, employed force in Riga and Vilnius in attempts to prevent Latvia and Lithuania from leaving the Soviet Union.[1] These repressive actions drew widespread international condemnation; they were not supported by Mikhail Gorbachev, and in the end the Baltic states escaped the USSR with minimal violence. Despite tensions among the Crimean Tatars and the ethnic Russian population on that same peninsula, Ukraine declared and achieved its independence from Soviet rule with far fewer casualties than had been inflicted during the 1970s and 1980s by KGB reprisals against ethnic Ukrainian nationalists and separatists.

Other parts of the periphery had a more difficult time of it. In Central Asia, Tajikistan descended into a civil war between political factions (or, as some argue, clans masquerading as political factions) that produced thousands of casualties and took six years to settle.[2] In fact, the war in Tajikistan at times seems almost an anomaly, as the ethnically explosive Fergana Valley produced no conflict among Uzbekistan, Kyrgyzstan, and Tajikistan, and the ethnic Russian minorities in Kazakhstan and Turkmenistan remained quiet. In contrast, in Moldova (to which this narrative will return in much greater detail) ethnic Russians and Russophones mounted an eventually violent separatist movement to remain in the USSR as the republic's Romanian-speaking majority restored Romanian in Latin script as the official language in 1989 and pushed for separation from the Soviet Union (and some for unification with Romania).

The most numerous, difficult, and bloody conflicts were in the Caucasus.[3] As the British departed the area at the end of World War I and the Soviets suppressed the independent Caucasus states and installed regimes loyal to Moscow, Stalin and his colleagues planted the seeds for war between Armenia and Azerbaijan almost a century later by leaving the Nagorno-Karabakh Autonomous Province, which had an ethnic Armenian majority, inside Turkic Azerbaijan. During much of the twentieth century, the Soviet authorities simply suppressed entreaties from

Karabakh to separate from Azerbaijan and join with Armenia. As Gorbachev's glasnost loosened Moscow's control, a popular Armenian national movement in Karabakh took on its own momentum, got out of hand, prompted pogroms by both sides, and resulted in open combat between Armenians and Azeris. Although it was not always clear whether Nagorno-Karabakh was seeking independence for itself from Azerbaijan or a transfer from Azerbaijan to Armenia, by the time the two states obtained independence in late 1991, they were at war with one another.[4]

In Georgia, as Tbilisi sought to break away from seven decades of Soviet rule, within Georgia at least two small ethnic groups sought to escape from Tbilisi. As the Soviet Republic of Georgia was established in the 1920s, the small Ossetian minority was separated into two entities —the North Ossetian Autonomous Republic within the Russian Soviet Republic, and the South Ossetian Autonomous Province just across the border inside Georgia.[5] Meanwhile, the Abkhaz minority, dwelling largely in the mountains along the Black Sea coast between Russia and Georgia, by the 1930s was subordinated to Tbilisi as an autonomous re-public within Georgia.[6] Neither of these small nationalities was happy within Georgia, but a heavy hand from Moscow kept the area quiet dur-ing the Soviet era. However, once glasnost and perestroika opened the gates for Georgian nationalists to seek independence from the Soviet Union, the Ossetian and Abkhaz minorities sought to escape from Tbilisi's control. The ultimate goal of most of the Ossetians was proba-bly to join with their ethnic compatriots across the border in Russia; the Abkhaz more clearly desired independence, even though they were a dis-tinct minority even in their own autonomous Soviet entity.[7]

Moscow's intervention in the growing conflicts in the Caucasus in the twilight of the Soviet Union was inconsistent, ineffective, and at times counterproductive. Gorbachev hesitated for a long time before attempt-ing to step in between Yerevan and Baku over Karabakh. His vacilla-tions allowed time for atrocities to be committed against civilian popula-tions by both Armenians and Azeris, with the result that the conflict was far less susceptible to mediation from the center when the Soviet leader finally made up his mind.[8] The intervention of Soviet troops in Baku may have prevented violence from spreading further at the time, but no long-term benefit was obtained from the military involvement. In fact, as control from Moscow deteriorated from starting in late 1990 and early 1991, detachments of Soviet Army troops, composed largely of ethnic

Russians, were reported to take part in hostilities on behalf of both sides in the growing conflict over Karabakh.

Moscow's approach to the situation in Georgia was no better. As Georgian national mobilization escalated in the late 1980s, similar processes occurred in response in Ossetia and Abkhazia. The brutal action taken by Soviet security forces against Georgian demonstrators in Tbilisi on April 9, 1989, largely discredited any trust or capability that the central authorities might have enjoyed for mediation in Georgia. And the Georgian authorities, in particular the nationalist president Zviad Gamsakhurdia, claimed that Moscow had encouraged Ossetian and Abkhaz resistance to bring pressure on Tbilisi to sign Gorbachev's union treaty.[9] The Georgian charges are probably true (Moscow deputies gave similar support to Transdniestrian separatists in Moldova), but beside the point. Soviet and Russian actors did not create the wave of national feeling in Ossetia and Abkhazia, but rather took advantage of it. Gamsakhurdia proclaimed highly exclusionary linguistic and educational policies and applied force to impose them, thereby practically ensuring internal ethnic conflict as Georgia sought to throw off Soviet rule. Soviet interior troops stationed in Georgia reportedly helped separate and disarm some Ossetian and Georgian militias in the spring of 1991, but the intervention was neither large nor sustained enough to reconcile Tbilisi and Tskhinvali.[10]

The real fighting in the Caucasus began with the disappearance of Soviet authority at the end of 1991. Despite international intervention and an agreement in March 1992 to hold a peace conference between Armenia and Azerbaijan over Nagorno-Karabakh, fighting continued to escalate steadily throughout 1992 between Armenian and Azeri forces in and around the region.[11] This more localized combat escalated in late 1993 into full-scale war between Armenia and Azerbaijan, resulting in a decisive Armenian victory, serious territorial losses for Azerbaijan, and hundreds of thousands of refugees. In Georgia, if anything, the overall situation was even worse. In early 1992, hostilities broke out again between Georgian and Ossetian forces, while at the same time fighting also began in Abkhazia between Georgian and local Abkhaz forces.[12] In December 1991 and January 1992, the Georgian Military Council—a collection of warlords—deposed President Gamsakhurdia, who fled to his native Mingrelia and took up resistance against the collection of military leaders left in charge in Tbilisi. With the country in chaos, in March 1992 the Military Council appealed to former Georgian Communist Party leader and Soviet foreign minister Eduard Shevardnadze to assume leadership of the country and restore order.

Soviet and then Russian forces were inevitably involved in the conflicts in Armenia, Azerbaijan, and Georgia, although it is difficult to find consistent, general patterns in the extent or nature of this involvement. As the situation deteriorated in all three Soviet Caucasus republics, Soviet detachments stationed there for routine missions of border security and national defense remained in place. This was not a conscious plot of someone in Moscow; there was nowhere else for these troops to go, and moving them somewhere else in the USSR might have been more controversial than just leaving them in place as the country fell apart. Because of long-standing Soviet policy that troops serving inside the Soviet Union would not be stationed in their native republic, many (if not most or almost all) of the troops in Armenia, Azerbaijan, and Georgia were ethnic Russians. In addition, the national armies of most of the former Soviet republics were formed partially or wholly from scratch, and not simply from preexisting Soviet military units stationed on their territory.[13] Formal disposition of the personnel and equipment of the Soviet Army among the former Soviet republics was made by agreement in the context of the Treaty on Conventional Armed Forces in Europe (CFE) and other agreements that were reached directly between the newly independent states. In sum, in early 1992 a large number of the units of the former Soviet Army on the territories of various republics remained either formally subordinate to Moscow (and the Russian Ministry of Defense), or de facto loyal to Moscow because they were composed predominantly of ethnic Russians.

Russia got involved in efforts to avert war between Armenia and Azerbaijan even before the dissolution of the Soviet Union, as Russian president Boris Yeltsin and Kazakh president Nursultan Nazarbaev visited the region in September 1991 on an unsuccessful mediation mission. Russia cooperated fully in the process of mediation under the auspices of the Conference on Security and Cooperation in Europe (CSCE), including visits to the area in early 1992, adoption of the decision made at the March 1992 Ministers' Meeting in Helsinki to hold a peace conference in Minsk, and the deployment of advance teams of observers to Armenia and Azerbaijan in April and May 1992.[14] Both Russia and the United States appeared particularly interested in promoting the CSCE's mediation of the Karabakh conflict after an abortive Iranian reconciliation initiative in the spring of 1992. However, Russia also continued a unilateral pursuit of conflict resolution and its own interests in the region through the activities of Ambassador at Large Vladimir Kazimirov, who worked directly with all the belligerents as well as in concert with other CSCE negotiators.

Despite CSCE, Russian, and UN efforts to end the violence over Karabakh, hostilities continued through 1992. Bolstered by a large amount of former Soviet military equipment, Azerbaijani forces at first seemed to have the upper hand. However, during the internal political crisis in Azerbaijan in mid-1993, when the country nearly descended into civil war and President Abulfaz Elcibey's replacement by former Soviet Politburo member Heydar Aliev in October 1993, Armenian forces went on the offensive and captured wide swatches of Azeri territory, including the key Lachin and Kelbajar provinces linking Karabakh with Armenia. A counteroffensive mounted by Aliev in late 1993 and early 1994 was unable to reverse the Armenian gains. On May 12, 1994, Russian mediator Kazimirov brokered a cease-fire between Armenia and Azerbaijan. However, Baku subsequently refused to accept Russian peacekeepers, originally part of the deal cut by Kazimirov. Nonetheless, neither side resumed hostilities, and the task of mediating an eventual settlement fell to the CSCE's Minsk Group.[15]

In the conflicts in Georgia, Russia also pursued a policy of unilateral intervention simultaneously with cooperation with other major external powers, largely through the CSCE and UN. As renewed violence between Georgian, local Ossetian, and Russian forces in the region threatened to get out of hand in May and June 1992, on June 24 President Shevardnadze agreed to a cease-fire with President Yeltsin in the Black Sea resort of Dagomys, near Sochi.[16] The cease-fire was to be enforced by a tripartite peacekeeping operation consisting of Russian, Georgian, and South Ossetian troops. In November 1992 Russia, along with other CSCE participating states, signed on to deployment of a CSCE Mission to Georgia. Once on the ground, in 1994 the CSCE formally joined the Joint Control Commission, which supervised the operation of the peacekeeping force. By 1997, the CSCE—now the Organization for Security and Cooperation in Europe (OSCE)—was able to open a local office in Tskhinvali.[17]

No sooner had hostilities quieted in South Ossetia than full-scale war broke out in Abkhazia in August 1992. The bitter fifteen-month conflict involved not only Abkhaz and Georgian forces but also militias loyal to Gamsakhurdia (who was killed only in late 1993) and Russian military units.[18] The region was devastated, with tens of thousands of refugees (mostly ethnic Georgians) driven out, leaving a legacy of deep inter-ethnic bitterness on both sides. The Russians were apparently at least as interested in pressuring Shevardnadze as they were in supporting the Abkhaz. The price of the October 1993 Sochi cease-fire was Georgia's agreement to join the Commonwealth of Independent States (CIS), a step Tbilisi had avoided until then. Russian minister of defense Pavel Grachev was eager to keep Russian troops in the region. A CIS peace-keeping operation—composed entirely of Russian troops—was formally established in 1994 and in the same year received a UN mandate.[19] While insisting on the lead in Abkhazia, Moscow was nonetheless willing to accept involvement from other major states. The UN Mission in Georgia included a small number of international observers, including some U.S. military officers. Political settlement negotiations on Abkhazia were conducted in the context of the UN "Friends of Georgia" group, which included most major Western powers, with a special representative of the UN secretary-general on the ground in Georgia. The OSCE did not join the settlement negotiations for Abkhazia, but the OSCE Mission to Georgia established a formal relationship with the UN to monitor and promote human rights in the region.[20]

Russia's Cooperation with the OSCE on Conflict Resolution

During the fighting and the initial stages of the cease-fires and settlement negotiations in all these conflicts, Russia considered it natural to play the leading role in addressing the conflicts, but did not reject the involvement and collaboration of other external parties. Indeed, many Russian officials—politicians, diplomats, and military—considered the CSCE/OSCE as a convenient vehicle for providing international legitimacy for Moscow's CIS peacekeeping operations already in training or in contemplation.[21] To be sure, in each case Moscow showed a desire to insert or keep Russian military forces in the conflict areas, usually on a unilateral basis, and in several cases these troops provided indirect or direct aid to the separatist forces. From Moscow's point of view, how-ever, Russian forces were employed largely to quell the violence already under way, or to prevent the outbreak of violence, in either case in re-gions not too far from Russia's borders where significant Russian inter-ests were likely to be affected.[22] Russian officials often interpreted their support for separatist movements as defense of oppressed or endangered minorities against real or intended persecution at the hands of the titular nationality in the newly independent states. There were sufficient grains of truth in some of these arguments to produce international tolerance, and at times even support for Russian actions. Despite loud warnings from some political and academic critics that Moscow was seeking to restore neo-Soviet imperial presence and control, many Western European states, and even the United States, accepted and at times welcomed Russian actions to stop the fighting and try to manage the conflicts on its periphery. The NATO Allies were, after all, almost wholly preoccupied in the early to middle 1990s with the wars in the former Yugoslavia, and Russia was cooperating actively, if not always effectively, in peacekeeping efforts in the Balkans.[23]

During the 1990s, as active hostilities in Georgia, Armenia, Azerbaijan, and Moldova grew more distant in the rearview mirror, Russia, the United States, and leading Western European states used the OSCE as the primary vehicle for conducting political dialogue and operational cooperation in addressing what soon came to be called the "frozen conflicts."[24] The OSCE's Minsk Group handled the negotiations in search of peace between Armenia and Azerbaijan and agreement on an agreed-on status for Nagorno-Karabakh. In 1996, Russia, France, and the United States became cochairs of the Minsk Group, an arrangement marked by surprisingly consistent and harmonious cooperation and that stands to this day. In Georgia and Moldova, relatively small OSCE missions maintained political contact and participated in the Russian-dominated security institutions aimed at conflict prevention and postconflict settlement in both countries.[25] On an annual basis, OSCE foreign ministers (and occasionally heads of state at summits) discussed the four conflicts and almost without fail—until 2003—were able to produce agreed-on political statements on the situation on the ground and to recommend political steps for each conflict.[26] Although there were often significant disagreements in this process, in comparison with the rancor in U.S.-Russian and EU-Russian contacts and exchanges during much of the next decade, the activity of the OSCE in the 1990s seems almost like a golden era.

Three major security-related currents ran through Moscow's interaction with the West in the OSCE framework in the 1990s. First, Russia's former Warsaw Pact and former Soviet neighbors, in particular Georgia and Moldova, called with increasing frequency and urgency for all

Russian troops deployed abroad, without true host country consent, to be returned to Russian national territory. Second, Russia and other CFE states parties conducted a lengthy, difficult negotiation to update the CFE regime, both to adapt it to the post-Soviet nonbloc security environment in Europe, but also to meet Russian concerns about restrictions on moving troops within Russian territory to meet internal threats (i.e., Chechnya) and to cover states not included in the original treaty (in particular the Baltics). Third, Russia and its OSCE partners worked during much of the second half of the decade to produce a comprehensive program for European security, which was embodied in the *Charter on European Security,* adopted along with the Adapted CFE Treaty at the OSCE Istanbul Summit in November 1999.[27]

These two documents, along with the 1999 Vienna Document on Confidence-Building and Security Measures, provided the prescription for a comprehensive normative, diplomatic, and conventional military security system for Europe, all under the umbrella of the universal membership of the OSCE. Notwithstanding deep differences with other OSCE states on some individual policy issues, Russia was apparently willing to work cooperatively with other OSCE states, including the United States, even on the territory of the former USSR. Moscow seemingly understood (or at least presumed) that the conduct of such cooperation and such operations in the framework of the OSCE in the end did not challenge or undermine its claim for the primacy of Russian interests and the leading role in addressing key security issues in the near abroad. Russia's acceptance at the Istanbul Summit of formal commitments to withdraw its military forces from Georgia and Moldova (in line with political declarations that Moscow had consistently accepted through the 1990s) appears to reflect Russia's basic belief, still extant in 1999, that as an equal with all other participating states, using the principle of consensus, it could ensure that OSCE decisions or actions could never threaten its fundamental security interests.

By late 1999, however, the handwriting was already on the wall for these Russian aspirations and assumptions. The Platform for Cooperative Security and the *Charter for European Security,* adopted at the Istanbul Summit, marked the culmination of a decade-long process within the OSCE to construct a "common and comprehensive security model for Europe" that would produce a "common security space free of dividing lines."[28] The *Charter* gave the impression that the OSCE would be increasingly active in areas such as providing peacekeeping, expert rapid reaction forces, and police assistance.[29] In the preparation for Istanbul and in the years immediately following the summit, at least some senior Russian officials took provisions of the document seriously.[30] In contrast, NATO's response to the crisis in Kosovo and its war against Serbia in the first half of the year were clear portents of the direction in which important Western OSCE participating states were moving. In particular, when it came to questions of so-called hard security, NATO was clearly the preferred instrument of the United States and its chief Allies.

Growing Disagreements, the Wars in Chechnya, and Other Conflicts

Starting in 1999, Russia and its major Western interlocutors experienced increasingly frequent and sharp disagreements over security issues in states from the former USSR. The attempt by Russian peacekeeping troops from Bosnia to seize the airport in Pristina before NATO peacekeepers could deploy went a long way to negating any goodwill Moscow might have earned in Washington and Brussels with former premier Viktor Chernomyrdin's successful effort to convince Miloševic to capitulate. Shortly after this episode, the brutality of the Russian campaign against Chechnya begun in the autumn of 1999 further depressed the Clinton administration's relations with Moscow, which had already been spiraling downward in the wake of the August 1998 financial crisis.[31] There would be no positive references from Washington this time to Putin, as there had been earlier to Yeltsin, comparing the Russian president to Abraham Lincoln facing down rebels seeking to split his country.[32] Never happy with external involvement in its difficulties in the North Caucasus, during the Second Chechen War the Russians first kept the OSCE Assistance Group for Chechnya, which had been founded in 1995, stuck in a small office building in Moscow (citing security risks in the region), and then shut the mission down completely by early 2003.[33]

When the Second Chechen War broke out in the late summer of 1999, some Russian authorities complained that Chechen and other terrorists were seeking refuge in or infiltrating Russia across its mountainous border with Georgia. By December 15, the OSCE Mission in Georgia was authorized to set up a Border Monitoring Operation (BMO) along the frontier with Chechnya, which involved deploying a moderate number of military observers to the rough territory along the frontier to monitor illegal transborder traffic.[34] In subsequent years, the BMO was extended to the border with Dagestan and Ingushetia. Georgia and Western supporters touted the effectiveness of the operation, citing it as an excellent example of innovative conflict prevention. As the war progressed and became even more brutal, and as Moscow's relations with Tbilisi soured, Russia increasingly complained about the ineffectiveness of the BMO and about the continuing presence of Chechens in Georgia's Pankisi Valley and elsewhere. After the September 11, 2001, terrorist attacks on the United States, in 2002 Shevardnadze invited U.S. troops into Georgia as part of the new antiterror train-and-equip program. With the United States in a support role, Georgian troops and police cleaned out the Pankisi Gorge. As the war in Chechnya wound down, Russia broke with the OSCE's consensus and forced the BMO to shut down in 2004. A small detachment of U.S. troops remained in Georgia.[35]

In a sense, the presence of even an insignificant number of American soldiers in Georgia was even worse than massive use by U.S. forces of military facilities in Kyrgyzstan and Uzbekistan in Central Asia to support operations in Afghanistan after the September 11 terrorist attacks. After all, the Americans were in Central Asia with Putin's consent, even if that might have been to a considerable extent an action taken with the hope of obtaining U.S. tolerance for Russian actions elsewhere in the former Soviet Union. In contrast, Shevardnadze had invited U.S. forces into his country, even if in limited numbers for a limited mission, on a bilateral basis, without any reference to Moscow's desires or interests. The miniscule U.S presence in Georgia had a symbolic significance far greater than was warranted by its size, and presaged a trend that became increasingly visible during the decade and increasingly worrisome to Moscow.

During the 1990s, there was a constant Western presence and involvement in Russia's near abroad, but this presence was largely through international bodies of which Russia was a full member with an effective veto, in particular the OSCE. With the NATO and EU expansions of 2002–4, these organizations and their individual member states began to show an interest and to mount an involvement on the ground in the former Russian republics of the near abroad that had simply not existed during the 1990s.[36] NATO, the EU, the United Kingdom, France, Germany, and other states began visiting more often, opening embassies, missions, offices, and sponsoring greater presence and activity by nongovernmental organizations (NGOs) from their countries, as well as local NGOs. This was all done bilaterally or through organizations of which Russia was not a member, and in which Russia therefore had no voice. These contacts and activities were generally welcomed by the authorities in Ukraine, Moldova, Georgia, Armenia, Azerbaijan, and other states. In and of themselves, they posed no apparent threat to Russia or its standing and influence in the region. However, many Russian officials clearly perceived the presence and activities of representatives of other states and organizations to be a threat to Moscow's primacy in the region. Something like this might have happened even without the deterioration of Russian democracy and the increasing disagreement over values between Moscow and major Western capitals. But with the growing "values gap," Moscow more and more perceived an increased U.S. and EU presence as a de facto attempt to reduce Russia's influence in the region or to push it out entirely.

The "color revolutions" in Georgia, Ukraine, and Kyrgyzstan, the increasing activity of Western democracy-promotion NGOs, the ever harsher evaluation of Russian elections by the OSCE's Office for Democratic Institutions and Human Rights (ODIHR), and the failure of any Western government to ratify the Adapted CFE Treaty while calling for modification or elimination of the Russian-led peacekeeping operations in Georgia and Moldova all persuaded officials in Moscow that their worst suspicions and fears about Western intentions were indeed true.[37] As late as 2002, Moscow still seemed to be operating in a cooperative mode with Western partners in the near abroad. Agreement on establishing the NATO-Russia Council considerably blunted the effect of the decision to admit the three Baltic states to the Alliance. Meanwhile, Russia received general credit for working to fulfill its Istanbul Summit commitments to withdraw its military forces from Moldova and Georgia, which would presumably lead to quick ratification of the Adapted CFE Treaty. At the OSCE Ministerial Meeting in Porto, Portugal, in December 2002, Moscow received a one-year extension of the deadline for its evacuation from Moldova, citing difficulties with resistance from local separatist authorities.[38] On a broader scale, the Porto OSCE Ministerial was the last high-level meeting at which Russia, the United States, and the EU member states were able to reach a comprehensive consensus statement on the full range of issues in European security. Although several states added interpretative statements to the ministerial declaration, Porto was also the last time that all European and North American states were able to agree on common statements on all the conflicts in Nagorno-Karabakh, Georgia, and Moldova.[39] By the time OSCE foreign ministers gathered in Maastricht a year later, comity and consensus on these issues between Russia, the United States, and most EU states had vanished. Despite all efforts, it has yet to reappear.

By early 2004, after the "Rose Revolution" in Georgia and the failure of the Kozak *Memorandum* in Moldova, Moscow was increasingly mistrustful of Western involvement in security questions in the states and conflicts on its periphery, and even more inclined to unilateralism than before. Critical ODIHR reports on the 2003 parliamentary elections and in particular the 2004 presidential elections prompted Russian complaints about failure to obtain a consensus before releasing such evaluations, and some in Moscow voiced suspicions that the intent of some OSCE states was to use the ODIHR to weaken the ruling regime in Russia.[40] Putin's bitter overreaction blaming external forces in the aftermath of the September 2004 Beslan tragedy reflected a deep resentment and suspicion that major Western powers like the United States, whom he had assisted in the fight against terrorist foes, were unwilling to reciprocate in the struggle against insurgents in the North Caucasus, and instead concentrated on activities that weakened the government in Russia.[41] No matter how unfounded one might deem such an attitude, there is no mistaking the sense of grievance and unfair treatment in Putin's statements.

The "Orange Revolution" and Moscow's Response

The 2004 presidential elections in Ukraine were clearly the most important event in the sequence that inflated Russian paranoia and hostility with respect to Western motives and actions in the former Soviet space. The whole history of the "Orange Revolution" was all the more galling because it was intensely personal. After Putin's unwise journey to eastern Ukraine to make campaign appearances in support of Party of Regions candidate Viktor Yanukovych, any outcome besides a victory for the "Blues" in Ukraine would clearly be a personal defeat for the Russian leader. The near-unanimous support from Western states for a determination of fraud in Yanukovych's initial victory and for Yushchenko's subsequent triumph in a repeat ballot was too strong for Moscow to oppose, but the whole affair left the Kremlin incredibly bit-

ter. The self-congratulation and self-promotion of a number of prominent Western NGOs (as much as their activities themselves during the
Orange Revolution) went a long way toward convincing the Kremlin
that the West was intent on using nongovernmental "political technol-
ogy" as a means of promoting its own interests and influence at Moscow's
expense in the near abroad. Moscow's response was to redouble its own
efforts in promoting loyal domestic NGOs—such as Nashi, the pro-
Putin youth group—and to Russian Presidential Administration staff
member Modest Kolerov's sponsorship of pro-Russian youth groups
such as Proryv in Crimea and Transdniestria.[42]

Russian suspicions of and hostility to the Western presence in the
near abroad reached full bloom in 2005 in the wake of Ukraine's Orange
Revolution. Western reactions to Kyrgyzstan's "Tulip Revolution" and
Uzbekistan's violent suppression of opposition demonstrations in
Andijon reinforced those in Moscow who saw Western aims in the near
abroad as regime change to facilitate the elimination of the historically
dominant Russian influence and presence.[43] The Kremlin was clearly
pleased at Tashkent's decision to oust U.S. forces from the K-2 airbase
in response to harsh criticism from Washington of the government's actions in Andijon. Moscow also took an increasingly critical stance toward a long-term U.S. presence at Manas Airbase in Kyrgyzstan.

Responding to what it perceived as growing challenges from the West
to Russia's predominant position in the post-Soviet space, Moscow spent
greater and greater effort and placed increasing emphasis on the alternative security and economic organizations that it had founded or pushed
as competitors to NATO and the EU. President Yeltsin had hoped that
the CIS would serve as the organizational framework to preserve Russian
political, economic, and security influence in the territory of the former
Soviet Union. However, most of the newly independent former Soviet
republics declined to participate or imbue the CIS with any military security content. By 2000, it had become clear that the CIS was going nowhere, and served chiefly as a forum for periodic semiformal gatherings
of heads of state and government in the former Soviet area. At the turn of
the century, with NATO and the EU encroaching on what had hitherto
been exclusively Russian turf (at least in Moscow's view), Putin in 2001–2
expanded the membership and role of the Shanghai Five into the Shanghai
Cooperation Organization (SCO). And in October 2002, Russia established the Collective Security Treaty Organization (CSTO), a formal military alliance of six former Soviet republics (seven, after Uzbekistan

joined in 2006), which was widely seen as a Moscow-led alternative and rival to NATO.[44] Moscow has sought to emphasize military antiterrorist cooperation in the SCO, and it has pushed an increasingly ambitious program of exercises in the CSTO. Although the SCO has to an extent become a framework for Russo-Chinese competition for influence in Central Asia, the Kremlin's aim in pushing both organizations is clearly also to diminish Western influence in the region.

In the economic sphere, Putin early in his first presidential term pushed to turn the CIS customs union of Belarus, Russia, and Kazakhstan into a broader "common economic space" subsuming most of the former Soviet republics. In October 2000, Putin joined presidents Nazarbaev, Lukashenko, Akayev, and Rakhmonov in signing the treaty establishing the Eurasian Economic Community (EEC).[45] Putin pressed hard on presidents Leonid Kuchma and Vladimir Voronin to bring Ukraine and Moldova into the EEC's common economic space, and successfully convinced Uzbekistan to join in 2005.[46] Like the CIS, however, the EEC has served largely as a framework for holding high-level meetings of leaders from member states; its visible economic results have been minimal. However, Putin apparently remains torn between the economic need to better integrate Russia into the world economy through the World Trade Organization and his political instinct to use economic association with other former Soviet republics as a means of perpetuating Russian political influence.[47]

Russian energy policy under Putin also became an area of increasing disagreement and adversarial relations between Russia and major Western states, including over Russia's alleged use of "energy blackmail" as a means of exerting political influence over its neighbors. During the 1990s, Russia sold natural gas at prices well below world market rates to just about all the former Soviet states, and it fairly frequently cut off gas deliveries to make a political point when the Kremlin had disagreements over the behavior of the recipient country. Whether justified or not, most Russian diplomats saw nothing unusual or inappropriate in employing the economic energy instrument in this manner for political purposes.[48] By far the loudest criticism from abroad of Russian energy policies and practices in the 1990s generally involved the impediment that subsidized energy prices and deliveries posed to real market reforms in the post-Soviet economies. Moldova, like many other former Soviet states, has more than once suffered a reduction or cutoff of deliveries from Gazprom for what seemed to be noneconomic reasons.[49]

Nonetheless, energy-rich states such as Kazakhstan, Turkmenistan, and Azerbaijan (and the Western energy companies eager to benefit from involvement in development of the energy resources of these states) early on began to contemplate how to bring their oil and gas directly to the world market, rather than selling to Russia at a relatively modest price, and watching Moscow receive a premium price for the same oil or gas after transporting it to the West through Russian-owned and -controlled pipelines. One solution was to build other pipelines, which Azerbaijan did, joining the Baku-Tbilisi-Ceyhan pipeline to the Mediterranean at the urging of a number of Western energy companies and states.[50] Another alternative would be for other states (particularly in Central Asia) to use pipelines owned by Russia to deliver their gas to European markets, in accordance with provisions of the European Energy Charter. Although it is a signatory of this charter, Moscow neither ratified nor observed this particular provision.[51] Eventually, as Central Asian natural gas became more essential to Gazprom to fulfill its contractual deliveries to Europe, Moscow began paying prices closer to world levels to Turkmenistan and Kazakhstan.

However, Moscow remained cavalier with respect to the Energy Charter's provisions regarding noninterruption of transit flows of energy. In particular, highly publicized cutoffs of natural gas deliveries to Ukraine in 2006, Belarus in 2007, and Ukraine again in 2009 resulted in widespread interruptions of deliveries to many countries in Western and Central Europe, all in the dead of winter. In each case the Kremlin justified the shutoff with claims that Ukrainian or Belarusan energy companies or officials had not agreed to or were failing to observe contractual terms regarding transit or purchase of gas. In the case of Ukraine, the Russians made widespread, repeated accusations that Ukraine was stealing gas destined for Western European customers. Even if the actions had been clearly motivated solely by economic and financial concerns, there would still have been an enormous hue and cry from freezing customers in Central and Western Europe. However, particularly with the 2006 cutoff of deliveries throughout Europe, it was hard to avoid the perception that Moscow was taking retaliatory action against President Yushchenko and other leaders of the Orange Revolution. The Russian authorities denied any such political motives, and pointed to alleged widespread corruption and mismanagement in Ukraine's energy sector.

Whatever the merits of the arguments on each side, the gas cutoff of January 2006 greatly strengthened the position of those who argued that the Kremlin's actions and policies posed a threat to the energy security of many Central and Western European states. Russian proposals to build pipelines circumventing Ukraine and Belarus only added fuel to charges that the Kremlin was seeking ways to bring political pressure on its neighbors by denying them needed energy. Moscow's claims that it was seeking long-term security of markets and income for itself were not deemed credible, if they were heard at all.

Ultimately, the issues of European energy security and the rights and wrongs of Russian energy policy—in particular, the extent to which the Kremlin used and continues to use energy pricing and deliveries as a means of exerting political pressure—are outside the purview of this volume. However, the widespread perception, especially after 2005, of Moscow's use of the energy weapon as a means of perpetuating its preponderant influence in the post-Soviet space has clearly been an important factor and bone of contention in Moscow's exchanges and relations with major Western and North American capitals with respect to the states of the near abroad since Putin came to power in 1999. In addition, Moscow has increasingly perceived Western responses to its perceived use of the "energy weapon," such as construction of the Baku-Tbilisi-Ceyhan Pipeline, as a geopolitical campaign to reduce or eliminate Russian presence and influence in the near abroad. The result is perceptions and positions on both sides that amount in effect to self-fulfilling prophesies.

Many factors contributed to the gradual deterioration of the relationship between Russia and the United States from the immediate post-Soviet honeymoon to the post-Munich recriminations. However, an increasing Western presence and activity in the Russian "near abroad," the post-Soviet states Russia considers a part of its historical sphere of interest, played a crucial part in sparking Russian suspicion of Western geopolitical motives and fanning the flames of Russian resentment of Western criticism of the exercise of its influence and power at the expense of its neighbors. From the perspective of Kremlin leaders, Moscow had an interest, responsibility, and right far greater than any Western power, including the United States, to ensure peaceful, stable solutions to the major unresolved questions from the breakup of the Soviet Union. Indeed, in the view of many from Moscow, unassisted Russian military force and diplomacy eventually produced a settlement for the civil war of the 1990s in Tajikistan. Furthermore, such disgruntled Russians would note, in the early 1990s Western partners cooperated and even encouraged Moscow to play a major role in conflicts arising in and between Armenia, Azerbaijan, Georgia, and Moldova over the breakaway entities of Nagorno-Karabakh, South Ossetia, Abkhazia, and Transdniestria.[52] Given such historical facts, what was the problem now?

In the aftermath of the Russo-Georgian War of 2008, it is easy to forget the extent to which the nations of the Euro-Atlantic community accepted and relied on Russia in the early 1990s as an important partner and participant in the stabilization and resolution of the trouble spots remaining in Eastern Europe and Eurasia after the Soviet collapse. This is not meant to suggest that Russia's involvement was universally welcomed (it was not) or that Western partners always agreed with the course of action that Moscow proposed or adopted (they did not). However, during the 1990s and even into the present decade, relations between Russia, its neighboring newly independent former Soviet states, and its major Western partners were arguably far more cooperative and far less confrontational or adversarial than they became during the first decade of the twenty-first century. In stark terms, for many of its Western partners and closest neighbors, Russia has gone from being part of the solution to the major source of the problem.

How did this change come about? The dramatic rupture in late 2003 of the efforts of external mediators to find a political settlement for the case of Moldova's breakaway Transdniestrian region was one of the first cases in which Russian and Western ambitions and actions clashed directly, producing a contentious last-minute failure due in great part to Western opposition to a Russian mediation effort, all of which caused great personal embarrassment to President Putin. The last-minute rejection in November 2003 by Moldovan president Voronin of the settlement proposed in the *Memorandum* of the Russian negotiator Dmitri Kozak, Putin's personal representative, received very little attention in Western capitals, and almost none in the Western press, which concentrated on the contemporaneous "Rose Revolution" in Georgia. However, Moscow had invested considerable political capital and energy at the very highest levels in pursuing a political resolution of the Transdniestrian conflict, and the Kremlin bitterly resented both the fact and manner of Western opposition and intervention to block its carefully constructed deal, to be solemnized at a formal signing presided over by Putin the peacemaker. The Western-induced failure of the Kozak *Memorandum* is not the only reason that relations between Russia and the United States and the EU went bad during the past decade. However, the incident came at a crucial time, and helped turn relations from an upward onto a downward path. Russians still recall the case as one of the first in which the West showed its alleged true colors, desirous of weakening Russian and supplanting Russian influence in the near abroad. After November 2003, the gap in mutual perceptions and trust only widened, and—especially with respect to the states immediately neighboring the Russian Federation—has yet to be diminished by recently improved relations in other areas.

Chapter 4

The Soviet Collapse and the Transdniestrian Conflict

Although some broad historical questions may appear to be resolved suddenly and decisively by cataclysmic events, peripheral details and loose ends can often take decades of turmoil and conflict to be decided. The collapse and dissolution of the Soviet Union in December 1991 took place with incredible speed and calm. However, the split produced in the tiny Soviet Republic of Moldova (or Moldavia, as the Soviets called it) by the so-called Transdniestrian conflict still remains unresolved two decades later. The troubles in Moldova arose out of the indigenous Soviet Moldovan Romanophone, or Romanian nationalist, movement for independence that developed in the late 1980s, and which met resistance from the largely Russian speaking, pro-Soviet political-economic elite on the left bank of the Dniestr (Nistru) River.[1]

The Soviet Legacy in Moldova

Soviet forces expelled the Nazis and took Bessarabia back from Romania in 1944, and the USSR then formed the Moldavian Soviet Socialist Republic (MSSR) by joining a thin strip of land on the left bank of the Dniestr River to the central and northern portions of Bessarabia. The left bank, or Transdniestrian (Transnistrian) portion, of the new MSSR comprised a substantial portion of the old MASSR—the Moldavian Autonomous Soviet Socialist Republic—which had been formed by Stalin in 1924 to keep alive Soviet territorial pretensions to the region until the USSR could take Bessarabia back from Romania in 1940 in accordance with the Molotov-Ribbentrop Pact. The Soviet authorities

48

treated the native population harshly, exiling hundreds of thousands of Romanian speakers to Siberia in several mass deportations during the late 1940s.

Moscow governed the post–World War II Moldavian republic much as they did the Baltics. Ethnic Slavs, mostly Russians, were sent from the center to manage affairs in the republic. The Soviet authorities promoted the republic's industrialization, and ethnic Russians and Ukrainians were encouraged to migrate to the MSSR to work in the new factories, most of which were established on the left bank of the Dniestr, in what Moscow considered more reliably pro-Soviet territory.[2] In addition, the Soviet authorities implemented a policy of strong Russification in the MSSR, and the local Communist Party and government cadres were disproportionately filled with Russian speakers. Even more egregiously, official Soviet policy maintained the fiction that the MSSR's native population spoke the Moldovan language, a separate tongue from Romanian, and constituted a wholly different people with an entirely separate history from the Romanians just across the Prut River. The Moldovan, or Moldavian, language was written in Cyrillic characters.

This Soviet policy was enforced strictly from 1944 into the 1960s, but as internal repression throughout the USSR gradually eased, by the 1980s one could detect timid manifestations of a growing national consciousness among the MSSR's Romanian-speaking population. Showing up at first merely as an increase in native Moldovans in government and party cadres, the Moldovan national movement burst forth with the opening up of Soviet society and relaxation of repression accompanying Gorbachev's glasnost and perestroika.[3] By the late 1980s, as in the Soviet Baltic republics, Moldova had a full-blown popular movement, the Moldovan Popular Front, calling for a reversal of the Molotov-Ribbentrop Pact and a return of Bessarabia to Romania. Moldovan nationalists took control of the republic's legislature and government, and in August 1989 voted to make Moldavian in Latin script (i.e., Romanian) the state language of the republic. This new language law might not have provoked such vehement resistance from Russian speakers, if it had not been for a provision of the measure calling for all state employees to pass a written examination in the state language within five years. At the end of the Soviet period, almost all workers in the republic were employees of the state, including all of the Russian-speaking factory managers and officials of the industrial plants along the left bank of the Dniestr. The deputies from the Russian-speaking areas of the left bank and around

Bendery (Tighina) on the right bank attempted to negotiate an autonomous economic zone in which the language law could be applied flexibly.
When they lost, they walked out of the Moldavian Supreme Soviet, and
on September 1, 1990, they proclaimed an independent "Transdniestrian
Moldavian Republic," comprising most of the territories on the left
bank and the Russian-speaking city of Bendery on the right bank, and
declared themselves a separate territorial unit of the Soviet Union.[4]

The Beginnings of the Conflict

After claiming independence from the MSSR, the pro-Moscow leaders
on the left bank of the Dniestr dramatized the possibility of the republic's incorporation into Romania as a means of mobilizing support
among the Russian-speaking population.[5] The Transdniestrian leaders
attracted considerable support from the largely Russian-speaking
Orthodox Turkic population of the region of Gagauzia in the south on
the right bank, which declared its own independence from Chisinau in
August 1990. The Transdniestrian and Gagauz separatists soon found
support from conservative circles in Moscow, especially from the Soiuz
(Union) Group in the Congress of Peoples Deputies, which was bitterly
opposed to Gorbachev and his initiative to reconstitute the USSR on the
basis of a new Union Treaty.[6] As the Soviet Union gradually disintegrated, the nationalist Moldovan leadership in Chisinau first proclaimed
the republic's sovereignty, and then after the August 1991 coup on August
27 declared the country's full independence.[7] In response, the separatist
leaders in Tiraspol took practical steps throughout 1991 to establish police, security, and military forces with which to defend their claims to
independence. The Moldovan authorities in Chisinau then attempted to
assert their control over the territories claimed by the Transdniestrian
separatists, especially key areas such as bridges, crossroads, and other
infrastructure. The result was a steady escalation throughout 1991 of
armed clashes between police and militias from Chisinau and Tiraspol.
   The dissolution of the Soviet Army in December 1991 and the reallo-
cation of its assets at Tashkent in April 1992 gave the right- and left-bank
authorities in Moldova the wherewithal to pursue their conflicting
claims to sovereignty and territorial control in earnest.[8] In the early
months of 1992, the Moldovans formed a national army, equipped it,
and attempted to use it to reassert their authority in the breakaway

areas. The Transdniestrian leaders formed their own armed forces with popular militias and recruits drawn from the massive Soviet Fourteenth Army stationed largely on Moldova's left bank. The Transdniestrian forces obtained arms, either with Russian consent or by stealing them, from Fourteenth Army arms depots.[9] Unreconciled and both armed, Moldova and its self-proclaimed Transdniestrian entity then engaged in a brief but bitter full-scale military struggle in the summer of 1992.

The wild card in the Transdniestrian conflict was the Russian Fourteenth Army. This unit, as the Soviet Fourteenth Army, had been stationed in the MSSR since the end of World War II. Its supply depots included enormous amounts of weapons, equipment, and ammunition, which had been stored there for use on the Southern European front if the need ever arose to fight World War III. The Fourteenth Army included many ethnic Russian troops who came from families resident in Moldova, having moved to the MSSR from the Russian Republic. Many of these ethnic Russian troops were legally registered as citizens of the Russian Soviet Federated Socialist Republic, though resident in Moldova, and thus circumvented the usual Soviet practice that soldiers stationed domestically not serve in their home republic. In any event, the vast majority of the Fourteenth Army troops in Moldova, officers and enlisted men alike, were decidedly sympathetic to the separatist leaders.[10] Yeltsin's decision to keep the Fourteenth Army as a Russian Federation unit, rather than let it devolve entirely to local Moldovan control as part of the redistribution of the Soviet armed forces, was apparently based on his realization of this fact. Moscow was unwilling to risk large amounts of arms and ammunition, including an undetermined number of tactical nuclear-capable systems, falling into the hands of separatist authorities, no matter how much they proclaimed themselves to be pro-Russian. Instead, in the early summer of 1992, General Aleksandr Lebed was dispatched to take command of the unit, replacing General Yury Netkachev, who had been ineffective in staunching the flow of arms and troops to the side of the Transdniestrians.[11]

The Conflict's Military Phase

The history of the military conflict in Moldova in the spring and summer of 1992 is still bitterly disputed by both sides. Each blames the other for attacking first, and estimates of casualties vary enormously. Judging by various accounts, it would seem that a Moldovan attempt to take Bendery in June 1992 at first appeared to be successful, but was stalled and beaten back after the Fourteenth Army intervened. At what point in the fighting the Russian forces actually became involved is still hazy. Some individual soldiers and small units from the Fourteenth Army fought with the Transdniestrian forces from the very start. Others joined as the Moldovan forces approached the Dniestr. What is certain is that eventually Lebed ordered Fourteenth Army armored units across the river to assist the Transdniestrian defenders of Bendery, and threatened to march on Chisinau if the Moldovan forces did not pull back and agree to a cease-fire.[12] This intervention by the Fourteenth Army on the side of the separatist regime effectively stopped the fighting, but it left the country divided largely along the Dniestr River. On the right bank, the Transdniestrians controlled Bendery; on the left, Moldovan forces remained in control of two small, unconnected pockets to the north and south of Dubossary.

With separatist leader Smirnov present in the hall, President Yeltsin signed a cease-fire with Moldovan president Mircea Snegur in Moscow on July 21, 1992.[13] The agreement provided for the establishment of a tripartite Joint Peacekeeping Force, to be composed of equal numbers of Moldovan and Transdniestrian troops, and a considerably larger number of Russian troops. The Russian peacekeepers were drawn from units in the Volgograd Military District, and not from the local Fourteenth Army. The cease-fire pact also established a Joint Control Commission, comprising representatives from the Russian Federation, Moldova, and Transdniestria. The commission was to meet regularly to provide overall direction to the peacekeeping operation and the implementation of terms of the cease-fire. Lebed's last-minute intervention and the fact that the cease-fire was signed by Russia and Moldova to this day are cited by many in Chisinau as proof that the Transdniestrian conflict was engineered by Moscow to enable Russia to retain a foothold in Moldova. This widespread view of the Transdniestrians as nothing more than puppets of Moscow has permeated and conditioned Chisinau's approach to the pursuit of a political settlement of the conflict ever since.

In comparison, for example, with the wars that marked the breakup of the former Yugoslavia, the actual Transdniestrian war was neither particularly long nor bloody. Sustained combat lasted no more than a couple of months, and the total number killed probably did not exceed 1,000.[14] The conflict produced several thousand internally displaced persons, largely Romanian (Moldovan) speakers who fled from the left to the right bank of the Dniestr. Although ethnic and linguistic grievances were employed by leaders of both sides to motivate their troops, the fighting in the Transdniestrian conflict was based more on territorial allegiance than ethnicity, and produced no ethnic or nationally based slaughters (such as the 1995 Srebrenica massacre in Bosnia). However, the fact that the Transdniestrian conflict was not as long, damaging, or ethnically bitter in the end has made it no easier to resolve.

Efforts at a Political Settlement

Despite the apparent brevity and moderation of the military portion of the conflict, the Transdniestrian question has proved particularly stubborn and unsusceptible to resolution during successive decades. The Russian Federation, which unilaterally brokered the 1992 cease-fire, was joined in 1993 by the international community—represented by the Conference on Security and Cooperation in Europe (later, the Organization for Security and Cooperation in Europe, OSCE), which opened a small mission in Chisinau in April 1993—in attempts to reach a negotiated political settlement. In 1995, Ukraine joined the talks as a mediator and guarantor country, and a decade later in 2005 the European Union and the United States joined the process as observers. From the very beginning, no country or organization has recognized the Transdniestrian region's claim to independence. The international community has without exception considered Transdniestria to be a part of the Republic of Moldova, while generally embracing the idea that the region should have some sort of special political status.[15] The political settlement negotiations between Moldova's recognized government and its breakaway Transdniestrian region have been conducted from the beginning almost exclusively under international auspices. Chisinau and Tiraspol participated in the process, but neither has sought to establish a bilateral negotiating process between them.

The first years of the political settlement negotiations were devoted largely to restoring everyday contacts between the two sides, agreeing on general principles that would guide the search for an eventual political settlement, and finding ways to provide everyday services, such as transportation, utilities, food, health care, and education in a country that was divided to a far greater extent politically than physically. For example, a significant portion of the population ended up living on one side but continuing to work in enterprises located on territory controlled by the other side. Transdniestrians came in large numbers to farmers' markets on the right bank, and citizens from both sides traveled regularly by car, bus, or train to the markets in nearby Odessa. Electric power continued to be supplied to Chisinau from the major generating plant in Transdniestrian-controlled Cuciurgan, on the Ukrainian border. Transdniestria retained the best of Moldova's industrial facilities, and wished to use internationally recognized documentation from Chisinau to permit exports of their production. Moldova wished to place its customs officials along the Transdniestrian segment of the border with Ukraine to regulate (and tax) this import-export trade. Agreed-on terms for every single aspect of these everyday actions had to be painfully negotiated in the talks between Tiraspol and Chisinau. The process was very difficult, replete with mutual accusations and steps back, involving blockades, embargoes, cutoffs of service, and the like.

The political settlement talks between Chisinau and Tiraspol have returned constantly to three major themes: (1) a political status for the Transdniestrian region; (2) control over borders and international trade; and (3) withdrawal of Russian troops and arms, which also raised the issue of guarantees against a resumption of fighting once the Russian forces were gone. On Transdniestria's political status, Moldova's approach was that the country must be a unitary state, and Transdniestria must integrate and observe the Moldovan Constitution and legislation of the recognized government in Chisinau. Transdniestrian representatives either demanded full independence and international recognition, citing the right to self-determination, or would agree to no more than a possible loose confederation with Chisinau. In November 1993, after nine months of consultation and study, the CSCE formulated an approach that was subsequently adopted in principle by all the mediators. In its "Report Number 13" of November 1993, the CSCE Mission argued that neither a unitary state nor a confederation would work in Moldova.[16] The report concludes that the Transdniestrian region should enjoy a special political status within Moldova, with autonomy sufficient to guarantee local rights and interests, but not so much as to undermine the viability of the Moldovan national state.

Control of the borders was another vital issue in the settlement talks. With a much more substantial industrial base, the Transdniestrian local economy was significantly more dependent than that of the right bank on exports based on the processing of imports. The economy of Moldova proper was based heavily on raw and processed agricultural products. Right-bank Moldova was almost totally dependent on the Russian market, whereas Transdniestria traded more and more with countries in Central and Western Europe. The Moldovan authorities dreamed of establishing effective control over the Transdniestrian segment of the border with Ukraine, in the hope of instituting an effective embargo and forcing the separatist regime into submission. Tiraspol obviously pushed to keep the border open to its imports and exports, preferably de jure, but de facto if necessary. In early 1996, in connection with progress on other issues in the talks, Moldova signed a landmark customs agreement with Transdniestria, whereby Tiraspol would be allowed to use Moldovan customs seals and stamps to document its trade. A Moldovan customs office (staffed by Transdniestrians) was established in Tiraspol, and the agreement provided for eventual joint Moldovan-Transdniestrian customs and border posts to be set up along the frontier with Ukraine.[17] Bolstered by internationally recognized documentation, Transdniestrian firms greatly expanded their foreign trade during the next five years.

The presence of Russian troops in Moldova was an especially sore point for both the Moldovan government and just about the entire population on the right bank. From the very beginning of the negotiation process, Chisinau demanded withdrawal as soon as possible of the Russian forces, equipment, arms, and ammunition. To a certain extent, the Russians were pleased to oblige. For example, Russian commanders wasted no time in moving whatever tactical nuclear-capable systems and matériel that had been stored in Moldova to the territory of the Russian Federation.[18] Russian military officials were also quite willing to get rid of much of the aging, increasing obsolete equipment and ammunition stored in Moldova. However, the question of peacekeeping guarantees for a region not far removed from active hostilities remained an important issue.

As talks on general principles and the status issue began to move in 1994, negotiations on a Russian withdrawal took on more momentum. In October 1994, Moldova and Russia signed a treaty providing for the withdrawal of Russian forces and military equipment within three years after signature and ratification.[19] There was a catch, however—the treaty called for the "synchronization" of the Russian military withdrawal with the achievement of a political settlement agreement between the two sides. In crude terms: no status, no withdrawal. Yet despite its disappointment over the synchronization provision, the Moldovan Parliament ratified the treaty almost immediately. The Russian Federation, however, at first delayed, and after the 1995 legislative elections, Yeltsin and his advisers withdrew the treaty because they feared the new, more nationalist and conservative Duma would reject it. Although Moscow throughout the rest of the 1990s continued to sign on to OSCE Ministerial and Summit resolutions calling for an "early, orderly, and complete withdrawal" of Russian troops and military equipment from the "Transdniestrian region of the Republic of Moldova," the pact was never resubmitted to the Duma.[20]

The First Serious Try for a Settlement: The *Moscow Memorandum*

The political settlement negotiations first came close to an agreement on Transdniestria's political status in May 1997, when Chisinau and Tiraspol signed the so-called *Moscow Memorandum.* Russian foreign minister Primakov persuaded Moldovan president Petr Lucinschi and Transdniestrian leader Smirnov to accept the document, in which Chisinau and Tiraspol pledged to build their relations within the framework of a "common state."[21] Primakov envisioned that Moldovan and Transdniestrian representatives would come together under Moscow's aegis after signing the statement of principles in the *Memorandum* in order to work out the practical details of how they would reunite their two entities and distribute their government functions and competencies. A session of the two sides and mediators from Russia, Ukraine, and the OSCE was scheduled to do just that at the Russian government facility in Meshcherino outside Moscow in September 1997. However, the Transdniestrian negotiators failed to show up, which marked the beginning of a four-year pattern of obstruction, evasion, and delay on the part of Tiraspol. The four years of the settlement negotiations from 1997 to 2001 passed in fruitless debate over the practical meaning and specific implementation of the notorious term "common state" and what might be its concrete manifestations eventually in Moldova.

Ironically, though the progress of the political settlement negotiations after the *Moscow Memorandum*'s adoption was disappointing, the atmosphere of relations at all levels between Tiraspol and Chisinau improved considerably. In December 1996, former Soviet Politburo member Lucinschi defeated the more right-wing, nationalist Mircea Snegur for the Moldovan presidency. Although Lucinschi's behavior in office did not bear out the worst fears of critics who charged that he would be reflexively pro-Moscow, he took a much less confrontational approach than Snegur toward Transdniestria in general and Smirnov in particular. Thus, during Lucinschi's tenure a number of practical cooperation agreements on police, transit, health, and other local matters were reached and to some extent implemented. Periodic provocations and small-scale confrontations continued, as both sides continued to harbor deep bitterness and suspicion, but the danger of a major confrontation seemed to recede considerably.[22]

As tensions eased between Chisinau and Tiraspol during the mid-1990s, Moscow quietly made sizable reductions in its military presence in Moldova. From 1992 to 1995, personnel in both the Fourteenth Army and the peacekeeping force were gradually reduced, not only because the lack of hostilities between the left and right banks required fewer troops but also because of the expense to budget-strapped Russia of maintaining sizable detachments there. In 1995, the Fourteenth Army was further downsized, reorganized, and renamed the Operative Group of Russian Forces (OGRF, or in Russian, OGRV).[23] The high-profile commander Aleksandr Lebed was replaced by General Valerii Yevnevich, who came with a clear mandate to sell, destroy, or withdraw excess stocks of equipment, fuel, and ammunition stored in the four Russian bases in Moldova —Bendery, Tiraspol, Dubossary, and Colbasna. At the same time, the peacekeeping forces were reduced in size and transferred from the Volgograd to the Moscow Military District, which also had authority over the OGRF. A sizable portion of the troop reductions in the OGRF was accomplished simply by on-the-spot discharge of the soldiers, most of whom then enlisted in the Transdniestrian army.[24] By 1998–99, the total troop strength of the OGRF and Russian Federation's peacekeeping units stood at about 2,600 to 3,000 men—as opposed to 9,600 in July 1992.

Yevnevich came to Moldova with an apparent mandate to get rid of as much excess military property as possible. He destroyed, sold, or otherwise disposed of large quantities of fuel, pesticides, and other toxic materials (e.g., an unspecified quantity of napalm) stored on the Russian bases. The OGRF, the Russian Ministry of Defense, and the Russian arms sales agency (at that time called Rozvooruzhenie—now Rosoboroneksport) attempted to peddle a good deal of the other matériel—heavy weapons, ammunition, and nonlethal equipment—on the international market. In 1997, the Russian Federation's OSCE delegation privately circulated to other delegations in Vienna a detailed list of arms, ammunition, and equipment in their stores in Moldova, and asked for assistance in selling them.

There were no takers at that time. In 1999, Russian officials told me that they had offered these stocks to at least twenty-seven different countries; the only potential buyers were two unnamed African states to which Moscow deemed arms sales unacceptable.[25]

At the same time that Moscow was hoping to get some financial reward or at least to defray some of the costs while getting rid of its vast military stocks in Transdniestria, Smirnov and his cronies dug in their heels in opposition to a withdrawal of Russian arms or equipment. There were many accusations, especially from right-wing circles in Chisinau, that Smirnov and the Russians were selling arms from the depots in Transdniestria to separatists, insurgents, and other undesirables in the region and around the globe. Though we looked hard, the OSCE Mission never found any convincing evidence of such arms trafficking. However, it was clear that from 1995 on Smirnov stubbornly blocked the withdrawal or disposal of any Russian arms or military equipment for which he (i.e., Transdniestria) did not receive compensation. Hoping to overcome obstruction from Tiraspol, at a March 1998 Transdniestrian settlement process summit in Odessa, Russian prime minister Chernomyrdin agreed with Smirnov in a secret protocol that Russia would share with Tiraspol half of any proceeds realized from the sale or disposal of Russian military equipment located in Transdniestria.[26] The substance and text of the protocol soon became known and caused a furor on the right bank. Unfortunately, it did not end Smirnov's obstructionism, and Transdniestrian opposition and active resistance to the Russian military withdrawal continued well into the next decade.

Despite a lack of cooperation from Tiraspol, the OGRF eliminated an enormous stock of heavy weapons (tanks, armored personnel carriers, and artillery), ammunition, and nonlethal military equipment (trucks, construction equipment, communications gear, field kitchens, etc.) between 1999 and 2001. Yevnevich blew up at least 100 outdated tanks, armored personnel carriers, and artillery pieces and sold them for scrap to steel plants in the region, using the proceeds to fund the OGRF's operating expenses.[27] In addition, immediately following the OSCE Istanbul Summit, in December 1999 the OSCE established a Voluntary Fund for contributions from participating states, to be administered by the OSCE Mission to Moldova, to defray costs incurred by the Russian Federation in the withdrawal or destruction of military equipment in Transdniestria. Despite continuous Transdniestrian obstructionism (Yevnevich and I were hanged and burned in effigy by Transdniestrian protesters in front of the OGRF Headquarters in Tiraspol in the summer of 2001), by late

2001 Yevnevich had overseen the destruction or withdrawal to Russia of more than 500 pieces of Conventional Armed Forces in Europe (CFE) Treaty-Limited Equipment (TLE) and tons of other equipment, in fulfillment of the first of the two deadlines agreed at the Istanbul Summit.[28] At the same time, the OSCE and Russian Federation came up with a plan—presented in October 2001—for the destruction or withdrawal of the 42,000 metric tons of ammunition stored in the Colbasna depot, the last massive collection of Russian military stores left in the country.[29]

The Transdniestrian settlement process, the Russian military withdrawal, and the search for an effective border regime along the frontier between Ukraine and the Transdniestrian region all continued throughout President Lucinschi's term, with mixed results. However, the Moldovan economy and the state of Moldovan domestic politics deteriorated significantly. The short-lived center-right reform government of Prime Minister Ion Sturza was ousted in November 1999 by an alliance of right- and left-wing parties (the Partidul Popular Creştin Democrat, the Popular Party of Christian Democrats; and Partidul Comuniştilor din Republica Moldova, PCRM, the Party of Communists of the Republic of Moldova). As the time for presidential elections in 2000 approached, a beleaguered Lucinschi was the object of an almost unanimous parliamentary attack, as more than 90 of the 101 deputies voted in July 2000 to amend the Moldovan Constitution to provide for the election of the president by Parliament, rather than as before by popular vote in a general election. By that time, Lucinschi enjoyed almost no support in the legislature, although he still had remnants of a substantial popular following. The move was led by Democratic Party head and speaker of Parliament, Dumitru Diacov, who most assumed would in due time be chosen by the legislature to succeed Lucinschi. Events proved otherwise, as Communist Party chief Vladimir Voronin deserted Diacov (after supporting his amendment in July), Parliament deadlocked in the attempted vote in December 2000, and by the terms of the new procedure had to be dissolved and a new general parliamentary election held.[30]

President Voronin and Settlement of the Conflict through Federalization

These elections took place in February 2001, and Voronin's PCRM swept into power with slightly more than 50 percent of the popular vote, and 71 seats out of the 101-seat Parliament. Severe economic difficulties and post-Soviet nostalgia were probably the most important factors behind the stunning Communist victory, the first of its kind in a post-Soviet republic. However, newly elected President Voronin made the achievement of a Transdniestrian settlement and reunification of the country a political priority for personal reasons—he had been born and raised on the left bank, not far from Dubossary.[31] Having run on a strongly pro-Russian platform (e.g., calling for Moldova to join the Russia-Belarus Union), Voronin also presumed that he might have some support from the Kremlin in inducing Smirnov to adopt a more accommodating line in the settlement process.

For six months in the middle of 2001, Voronin conducted intensive, whirlwind negotiations with Smirnov. A number of specific working agreements were signed for cooperation between Chisinau and Tiraspol. Then, just as suddenly, in September 2001, the political settlement negotiations broke down over Voronin's introduction of new customs documentation that he refused to share with the Transdniestrian agencies. Since the 1996 customs agreement, Transdniestrian enterprises had enjoyed significant success in penetrating EU markets with the use of Moldovan documentation. This abrupt change, which apparently was designed to pressure Transdniestria's business and political elite, produced short-term economic dislocation and considerable resentment. After several one-to-one meetings with the Transdniestrian leader, Voronin apparently decided that "one cannot work with Smirnov" and decided to try other tactics instead.[32] Accusations and epithets flew across the Dniestr between the two leaders, as the settlement negotiations remained in limbo through the first half of 2002.[33]

From September 2001 to June 2002, the three mediators—Russia, Ukraine, and the OSCE—spent considerable time and effort in trying to put the political settlement talks back on track. Without apparent warning, in July 2002 Voronin did another volte-face and welcomed an initiative (ostensibly) of the three mediators proposing settlement of the Transdniestrian conflict by creating a federation between Tiraspol and Chisinau. The so-called Kiev Document (named because it was tabled in Kiev on July 3–4, 2002) became the subject of a revitalized political negotiation process during the remainder of 2002. The Kiev Document's proposed federal solution provoked great controversy and noisy opposition on the right bank, in particular from the center and right-wing political opposition and the Romanophone elements of civil society. The major objection was in essence that a federal solution with Tiraspol would offer Moscow a Trojan horse to undermine Moldova's independence and orientation toward European integration.[34]

The basic argument of the Moldovan opponents of federalization (as I understood it) was that it would be a step back from Moldova's declaration of independence and separation from the Soviet Union. The Republic of Moldova was established in 1991 as a unitary state for the Moldovan (or Romanian) population of Bessarabia that had been forcibly subjugated and incorporated into the Russian-dominated Soviet empire in 1940 (and again in 1944). In the minds of the more nationalist Romanophone intellectual circles in Chisinau, the establishment of any subordinate ethnic-based political entity would constitute a danger to the full sovereignty of the state of Moldovans, which could be fully guaranteed only by a unitary political structure. Almost all of civil society in Chisinau had severe misgivings about granting nearly equal political status within the Moldovan policy to an entity that was widely perceived as an agent of Moscow, from whose fifty-year rule Moldova had just freed itself. Whether right or wrong, for a substantial portion of Moldova's educated elite, and perhaps the population as a whole, the issue of federalization was not just a question of adopting a particular political system. It also involved Moldova's independence from Russia and very survival. If President Voronin hoped to reunite his country through the establishment of a federal system, he would have to deal at some point with this fundamental domestic political reality.

The federalization initiative of the Kiev Document was also not particularly welcome among the members of certain circles in Transdniestria who had grown accustomed to de facto independence. Although the settlement negotiations at first appeared promising, by early autumn it was apparent that the initial impetus from the Kiev initiative had been exhausted. The Transdniestrian negotiators, in a behavior pattern that had become all too familiar after the *Moscow Memorandum,* at first seemed to negotiate seriously but soon began quibbling over every word and punctuation mark, clearly doing their best to block progress. In private, left-bank contacts blamed the leadership of Transdniestria's (and Russia's) security organs for the shift.[35]

Western European and U.S. hopes for a Transdniestrian settlement were raised significantly by the initial positive responses and flurry of negotiating activity after the introduction of the Kiev Document. When the negotiations stalled, the Western mediators overwhelmingly blamed the leadership in Tiraspol and began to contemplate coercive measures against the Transdniestrians to induce a more cooperative approach. From the standpoint of both the need for rapid practical applicability and for the achievement of a consensus within the European Union, restrictions on visas and travel by the Transdniestrian representatives seemed the easiest choice.

Along with the means to pressure the leadership in Tiraspol, the United States and EU member countries debated how to revitalize the Transdniestrian settlement process. One important factor was the possible boost a success with this "frozen conflict" might give to relations with Russia. The OSCE Ministerial Meeting at Porto, Portugal, was widely seen as a disaster, in particular with respect to Moldova. After meeting the initial 2001 deadline for elimination of CFE TLE, Russia failed to meet the overall deadline, which had been agreed on at the 1999 OSCE Istanbul Summit, for a complete withdrawal of its military forces from the Transdniestrian region by the end of 2002. With some empirical justification, the Russians pointed to increased Transdniestrian obstructionism since the breakdown in the political settlement talks as the main reason for their failure. The OSCE's participating states agreed at Porto to grant Moscow a one-year extension of this deadline, together with an invidious escape clause "providing the necessary conditions are present." Even worse, Moldova's beleaguered delegation was pressed to accept this unpopular step by Western, in particular U.S., diplomats.[36]

Returning from the Porto debacle, the U.S. and Western European representatives publicly rationalized the need to keep Russia on board in the settlement process. In private, many of them vowed never again to press a small state like Moldova to accept Russia's failure to make good on promises to restore its sovereignty and territorial integrity. Assuming the rotating OSCE Chairmanship in 2003, the Dutch decided to make a political priority of reaching a Transdniestrian settlement, and they appointed former Ministry of Foreign Affairs political director Adriaan Jacobovits de Szeged as their special representative. By good fortune, a degree of high-level U.S. attention remained focused on Moldova as President Voronin made a previously scheduled visit to Washington in December 2002. Thus the pursuit of a negotiated settlement to the Transdniestrian conflict, the reunification of the Moldovan state, and a completion of the withdrawal of foreign (i.e., Russian) military forces remained a significant political objective for the United States and its closest Western European allies as the new year began.[37]

Chapter 5

The Voronin Constitutional Initiative

The Kozak *Memorandum*—or, more precisely, the process that produced it—grew out of an initiative of Moldovan president Vladimir Voronin in early 2003. I had just returned to the Transdniestrian political settlement process for my second term as head of the Organization for Security and Cooperation in Europe (OSCE) Mission to Moldova, when the Netherlands OSCE Chairmanship's special representative, Adriaan Jacobovits, and I met with President Voronin in Chisinau in early February 2003. Jacobovits and I were in the midst of the current round of the five-sided Transdniestrian settlement talks, which at that time included representatives from the two parties to the conflict, Moldova and Transdniestria, and the three mediators, the Russian Federation, Ukraine, and the OSCE. The momentary boost to the process from the July 2002 Kiev Document, proposing a federal solution to the unresolved question of Transdniestria's status within a united Moldova, had clearly dissipated.

While the Kiev Document raised great expectations for an early settlement, the bitter opposition it provoked, particularly in more nationalist Romanophone circles on the right bank in Moldova, was in full flower by early 2003. As I returned to Chisinau in January 2003, I found that hopes were fast dimming among its supporters that the Kiev initiative would produce a solution. The Transdniestrian leadership had reverted to its usual policy of delay and obfuscation, while Moldovan negotiators' resolve flagged under persistent right-wing criticism of the proposed federal solution.

At our first meeting with the president in early February, Voronin told Jacobovits and me that he placed considerable blame on the Russian

Foreign Ministry and its negotiators for the slowdown in the talks and the failure of the Kiev initiative. Voronin was scheduled to travel to Moscow the next week, and he said that he intended to ask President Putin to appoint a special Russian representative or negotiator on Transdniestria from his own personal administration, in order to overcome what Voronin saw as either incompetence or resistance from the Ministry of Foreign Affairs in Moscow.[1]

President Voronin also described to Jacobovits and me a new initiative he had in mind to break the current deadlock in the settlement talks. Considering that the proposed federal resolution of the Transdniestrian question would require extensive amendment of Moldova's current Constitution, Voronin told us that he intended to propose to the leadership of the left bank that representatives of Chisinau and Tiraspol together draft a new, federal Constitution for a united Moldova. This joint effort would become the basis for a comprehensive political settlement of the Transdniestrian issue. Voronin said he wanted the OSCE's reaction to such a proposal before he made it to President Putin. Jacobovits and I duly checked with the OSCE Chair in The Hague, and we relayed to Voronin that the OSCE would be prepared to support such an initiative.[2]

Voronin's February meeting with Putin went well. The Moldovan authorities were particularly excited that the Russian president visited their new embassy on Kuznetsky Most in the center of Moscow. I was in the embassy shortly before the meeting, where I saw almost 200 meters of thick red carpet being prepared for Putin's arrival—this would take him all the way from the street up some two floors on a long staircase to the embassy's main receiving hall. Putin apparently enjoyed the Moldovan hospitality. The discussions reportedly went smoothly, but they did not produce any announcement on the appointment of a new special representative for the Transdniestrian question.[3]

In the second week of February 2003, President Voronin formally announced his "constitutional initiative," which consisted of an invitation to the Transdniestrian authorities to join Moldovan representatives in writing a new federal Constitution for a united Moldovan state. I happened to have a meeting scheduled in Tiraspol with Transdniestrian president Smirnov shortly after Voronin's constitutional proposal was presented to the left-bank leaders and made public. Smirnov used the occasion to give me his formal written—affirmative—answer to Voronin's proposal. I drove at once to Chisinau for an immediate meeting with the president to relay to him Smirnov's response. Voronin seemed less enthused than I expected by Smirnov's acceptance of his proposal, a fact that in retrospect assumed for me greater significance.[4]

Smirnov's acceptance of Voronin's constitutional initiative of necessity was followed by a period of several weeks to work out details of the proposal in the five-sided talks, adoption of the proposal by the legislative bodies in Chisinau and Tiraspol, and formation of the Joint Constitutional Commission (JCC). There were numerous hitches in this process, which took considerably longer than initially expected. Personal relations between the two leaders deteriorated from their already-poor state when the EU and United States imposed a visa ban on seventeen leading Transdniestrian officials. The Transdniestrians responded by barring fourteen senior Moldovan officials from the left bank, in particular preventing President Voronin from visiting his mother in his native village of Corjevo, on the left bank near Dubossary. The JCC did not meet until early July, when I dissuaded the Moldovans from their insistence that the new body meet only in Chisinau by opening a new OSCE Mission office almost solely for that purpose in Bendery/Tighina.

From relatively early in the process of developing the constitutional initiative, it seemed to me that neither President Voronin nor Smirnov (nor many of their chief aides) really had their hearts in the process. Having made and having accepted the proposal to draft a new joint Constitution, neither Voronin nor Smirnov felt that they could afford the political fallout from appearing to make it fail. However, their personal relationship and views of each other remained exceedingly hostile, and the level of mutual mistrust between the political elites across the Dniestr remained exceedingly high throughout 2003. This mistrust persisted despite frequent and often productive contacts between the working levels on both sides.

We began the process of establishing the JCC at the February 27–28 negotiating round. Despite the approval in principle of the initiative by both leaders, it proved extremely difficult to draft language on the issue acceptable to both negotiators. During the first day of the round, in Tiraspol, we hammered out a general outline of how the process of writing a new, joint Constitution would work. The key document was the "Protocol on Establishing a Mechanism for the Drafting and Approval of the Constitution of the Federal State," in which the two sides agreed to form the JCC.[5] We obtained Transdniestrian approval only after the Transdniestrian negotiator Valeriy Litskai left the other negotiators in the OSCE office and went to Smirnov's office, less than a mile away, to get the nod from the top. The new Moldovan negotiator, Minister of Reintegration Vasile Şova, also accepted the text. However, Şova cautioned that he would need to obtain final approval from President Voronin, who at the time was traveling in China and Vietnam. Şova said he did not anticipate any real problems.

There is a cliché in Southeastern Europe that when your local interlocutor tells you there is no problem is precisely the moment you should expect a problem, most likely a big one. President Voronin returned from China and Vietnam over the weekend, looked at the protocol agreed at the end of the most recent round of talks, and disagreed with the reference in the title to the "Constitution of the Federal State." Voronin objected that this phrase could be interpreted as meaning that Moldova and Transdniestria were combining to form a new state. Voronin's unyielding position (and the OSCE's understanding) was that the Republic of Moldova would become a federal state—Transdniestria remained a part of the Republic of Moldova, and no new state was being formed.[6]

Şova reported to me on March 3 that President Voronin would not authorize Şova to confirm his (Şova's) provisional signature on the document. I pointed out to Şova that it would be an enormous public disaster if Chisinau rejected a document, after initially accepting it, that registered agreement on a proposal originally made by President Voronin. I asked and received an emergency meeting with the president the evening of March 4 to work out some sort of solution.

President Voronin had returned from the Orient with a nasty upper respiratory infection, so our meeting was punctuated by hot tea, juice, and sneezes. The president understood the problem with failing to accept the protocol of the most recent round, but he also had a real concern that the language could be misused, presumably by Tiraspol or Moscow, to suggest that it recognized Transdniestria as a separate, independent entity. He also feared an outburst of criticism and demonstrations by right-wing nationalist forces if (or when, as he expected) Tiraspol published the text of the protocol. Together with his chief political adviser, Mark Tkachuk, Voronin came up with the idea that Moldova would append an interpretative footnote in signing the protocol. He and Tkachuk worked out language that made clear Chisinau's position, without (in my judgment) affecting the substance of the document as a whole. I thanked the president for this elegant solution, commenting only that

I suspected the action would provoke a footnote from the Transdniestrians in the next negotiating round.[7] I was correct, but neither footnote disrupted or blocked the process as a whole.

The U.S.-EU Visa Ban

We ran into another bump in the road during the second and final day of the round, Friday, February 28, in Chisinau. Overnight, on February 27–28, the United States and the European Union had finally announced their decision to impose a visa ban on seventeen of the most senior officials of the Transdniestrian leadership.[8] This coercive measure was motivated by a desire to induce Smirnov and his colleagues to negotiate seriously, and was conceived in the autumn of 2002, as the high hopes aroused by the flurry of negotiations on the Kiev Document began to fade. The slowdown in the settlement talks in late 2002 was clearly due to Transdniestrian resistance, and it was obviously crucial to find some means of overcoming this opposition to a settlement from the left bank.

The idea of the visa ban was a good one, and it might have been more effective if it had been applied in a timely fashion. Unfortunately, the bureaucratic politics of coordinating sensitive actions among sixteen sovereign nations (actually almost thirty, because all the EU candidate countries acceded to the action) sometimes goes too slowly. By the time the move was agreed on and the targets had been chosen, it was mid-February and the Transdniestrians had already accepted Voronin's constitutional initiative. A senior EU official called me the evening of February 12 to inform that the measure was ready and ask whether I thought it should be taken. I did not consider the action particularly well timed, given the recent movement in the settlement process. Conversely, I presumed that if the action were canceled, that would eventually leak, and the leaders in Tiraspol would conclude that the international community would never be able to agree on any sort of sanctions against their dilatory tactics in the negotiations. Therefore I somewhat reluctantly offered the opinion that it was probably better to go ahead with the ban.[9]

Near the end of the Friday, February 28, session, Jacobovits and I took Litskai aside and informed him of the joint U.S.-EU action, so that he would not hear of it first through the press. We were prepared for the worst—that he would berate us for the action and perhaps even retract

Tiraspol's agreement to the language hammered out earlier in the round on Voronin's constitutional initiative. Litskai was indeed stunned by the news. He clearly did not expect Western sanctions of any sort, however mild. It was not entirely clear whether his astonishment was occasioned more by the fact that Western states were able to agree on any sort of measures or that the action came at such an obviously inappropriate time (especially in light of the formal explanation of the move). Instead of denouncing us, in a shaken tone Litskai asked immediately: "What else is there? Are there any economic sanctions?" When we responded that the measure included visas only, he was obviously relieved.

The leaders in Chisinau and Tiraspol reacted predictably to imposition of the U.S.-EU visa ban. The measure was generally welcomed on the right bank, although some commentators called it too little and pushed for further sanctions. The Transdniestrian leaders just as predictably denounced the action as one-sided and unjustified.[10] Our Russian negotiating colleagues lamented in public and in private that the step was ill timed and unjustified in the current context of the negotiations. My chief Russian colleagues expressed the fear that the ban would make the Transdniestrians less rather than more cooperative in the political settlement talks. For their part, the Transdniestrians took about two weeks to draft and adopt a decision banning fourteen top Moldovan officials, including President Voronin, from traveling to or through any of the territory under de facto Transdniestrian control.[11] Meanwhile, the negotiations went on.

The question of coercive diplomacy was to reappear frequently during 2003. Many if not most of my Moldovan interlocutors of all political leanings believed that the Transdniestrian regime survived only because it was propped up by the Russians and Ukrainians. The political settlement process was punctuated from the very beginning in the 1990s by Moldovan attempts to convince Ukraine to close its southwestern border to Transdniestrian imports and exports. Voronin was among those who thought that the leaders in Tiraspol would crumble and accept a settlement on Moldova's terms, if only he could find the right kind of pressure to exert on Transdniestria and Russia. The clearest example of this approach came in the summer of 2001, when after negotiating with Smirnov and his administration for only a matter of weeks, Voronin decided to abandon the carrot for the stick, ending Tiraspol's right to use Moldova's customs seals and export documentation in the hope of strangling the left bank's economy.

Periodically, Voronin sought Russia's assistance in coercing Smirnov to negotiate seriously. He was usually disappointed at the failure of his appeals to Moscow to produce results. At other times, he targeted bilateral coercive measures at the regime in Tiraspol, steps that often restricted travel, commerce, or contacts between the two banks. The U.S.-EU visa ban was in part a response to Voronin's constant complaints and agitation. When Ukraine proved repeatedly to be reluctant to close or control better its stretch of border with the Transdniestrian region, Voronin began to plug the notion of deploying an international presence along that frontier. The justification was that the presence of an international border mission would help to end Transdniestria's alleged massive smuggling of cash, people, and weapons. President Voronin's constant attempts to pressure Tiraspol and Smirnov's retaliations became a constant background theme woven through the political settlement negotiations during 2003.

The Withdrawal of Russian Troops and Military Equipment

In the first week of March, there was a major breakthrough on the security front, as the Transdniestrian authorities formally adopted a decision to authorize renewal of the withdrawal of Russian military equipment. When I returned to Moldova in early 2003, the removal or destruction of the remaining Russian arms and ammunition in the Transdniestrian region remained stalled, as it had been through 2002. Although they had met the first OSCE Istanbul Summit deadline, for the withdrawal of the Treaty on Conventional Armed Forces in Europe–limited heavy weaponry, early in the autumn of 2001, my Russian Federation contacts in Moldova and the Operative Group of Russian Forces (OGRF) were not pleased with the failure to meet the overall 2002 deadline and the need for the controversial one-year extension at the Porto Ministerial Meeting.[12]

The Russian authorities blamed the delays in the military withdrawal on Transdniestrian resistance. These Russian assertions were generally met with incredulity and derision in Chisinau and the West; in my personal experience and observation, they were not entirely without some basis in fact. Although Moscow had (and still has) overwhelming influence in Moldova's Transdniestrian region, the authorities in Tiraspol have their own bases of power and their interests did not always coincide completely with official Russian Federation policy. Smirnov and his cohorts had an independent military force of about 6,000 troops and internal police and security forces of about equal numbers under their direct command. I personally witnessed cases in which these local forces made it impossible for the OGRF to carry out operations to move or destroy military property, in particular arms or ammunition.

The reader should not take this to mean that the Russians could not have overcome the Transdniestrians, if they had wished to. The problem was (and is) that Russian forces and representatives resident in Moldova have little desire or motivation for confrontation to overcome Transdniestrian resistance. The Transdniestrian military and security troops are almost all veterans of Soviet forces; many of them simply retired from the Russian Fourteenth Army (the predecessor of the OGRF) and put on a Transdniestrian uniform. Also, because of their common Soviet background, Transdniestrian officials had (and have) many close contacts in the Russian military, security forces, diplomatic corps, and Parliament. For example, former Russian vice president Alexander Rutskoi was a longtime, ardent supporter of Transdniestrian independence.

Conversely, Russian political and military leaders in Moscow in early 2003 in my estimation still desired to complete the withdrawal of their military forces from Moldova's Transdniestrian region—if not completely, at least in some fashion satisfactory to their major Western interlocutors. At the time Moscow still attached great importance to Western ratification and the entry into force of the Adapted Treaty on Conventional Armed Forces in Europe, and in particular accession to this treaty by the three Baltic states. In early 2003 Estonia, Latvia, and Lithuania were not yet formally members of NATO, and the Russians still hoped to obtain a treaty-based restraint on possible Western military deployments to the Baltics before they became members of the Alliance. In addition, from my personal interaction with them, I judged that most Russian military officials had a real concern with securing the large stores of conventional weapons, ammunition, and military equipment stored in Transdniestria and guarded by troops under Russian command, which were thus unavailable to Smirnov and his cronies to use or to sell. The latter concern did not seem to me to be shared in equal measure by civilian Russian officials.

The Russian approach to withdrawing the arms, ammunition, and military equipment from the left bank in Moldova was generally to try to buy the Transdniestrians off. Smirnov did his best to resist the Russian withdrawal. As he explained at one point to former Russian foreign minister and then prime minister Primakov: "If you [Russia] withdraw all your military equipment, then you will leave!"[13] Smirnov clearly saw the Russian military presence as a shield and de facto guarantee of Transdniestrian independence. Smirnov's main argument was that the arms and ammunition located on the left bank were the product of the labor throughout the Soviet period of Transdniestria's population and therefore the property of the Transdniestrian people. Anyone wishing to remove these arms must therefore pay for them.

For good or for ill, Moscow apparently judged it would be easier to pay Smirnov off than to coerce him. Chernomyrdin's agreement at the summit in Odessa in March 1998 that Russia would split with Transdniestria fifty/fifty any proceeds from the sale or disposal of Russia arms and equipment from the Transdniestrian region merely gave Smirnov further justification for obstruction and delay.[14] Smirnov repeatedly cited this agreement, contained in a secret protocol not formally revealed to other participants in the negotiations for several years, as justification for his intransigent behavior. When the OSCE in 1999 established its Voluntary Fund to assist the Russian Federation with the expenses involved in the withdrawal or destruction of military equipment from Moldova, we were not able to use the funds to overcome Tiraspol's resistance. OSCE representatives were authorized to pay for transportation to Russia or destruction of the OGRF's arms and ammunition. Smirnov wanted us to purchase the items, at vastly inflated, unrealistic prices.

When he was presumably given direct indication from Moscow that Russia needed to do something, Smirnov would generally comply. However, the process whereby Moscow obtained Smirnov's cooperation was not transparent, and we in the OSCE could only speculate as to how it was done. For example, in the summer of 2001, as the OGRF prepared to destroy all the tanks and armored personnel carriers remaining on its base in Tiraspol, the Transdniestrian media denounced Russian commander general Valerii Yevnevich and me, and demonstrators burned effigies of both of us on the public square in front of OGRF headquarters.[15] However, by September the Transdniestrian resistance had abated, as the OSCE, Russia, and Transdniestria formed a tripartite working group to discuss how to use OSCE assistance to support the removal and destruction of the roughly 42,000 metric tons of Soviet-era ammunition stored on the left bank. Perhaps the Transdniestrians hoped to get some money out of the process; we never knew for sure.

As Transdniestrian resistance stiffened again in 2002, negotiators in Moscow came up with the idea of offering Smirnov a $100 million credit against the enormous debt for natural gas that the left bank had been accumulating with Gazprom since 1994. Provision of this credit was to be linked directly with Smirnov's explicit agreement to cooperate with Russian efforts to remove or destroy its remaining military equipment in the region, in particular the vast stores of ammunition. The proposal was discussed with both Chisinau (the Russians later announced their intention to transfer the money through the National Bank of Moldova) and Tiraspol off and on for the remainder of 2002, without apparent progress. While in Moscow in early February 2003, I was briefed by my Russian counterparts on the initiative, but I did not receive the impression that a breakthrough was imminent.

On Wednesday, March 5, 2003, less than a week after the visa ban was announced, and after the successful completion of the most recent negotiating round, the Transdniestrian Supreme Soviet, the separatist region's legislative organ, unexpectedly adopted a resolution calling upon Smirnov to ensure completion of the removal and destruction of Russian military equipment from the region.[16] The resolution referred to Russia's obligation to meet the December 31, 2003, deadline established at the Porto Ministerial Meeting. On March 7, in a long meeting in Tiraspol, Litskai explained to me the significance of the Supreme Soviet's action. He claimed that it had been taken after successful negotiations with a delegation from Gazprom visiting Tiraspol that week. Without giving me the details, he indicated that some sort of deal had been reached on rescheduling the Transdniestrian gas debt, although the issue of the $100 million credit was still up in the air. He recounted that Russian experts seemed eager to get started in particular on the removal of ammunition, perhaps to ensure completion by the end of 2003, or perhaps just to create a better political background for Putin's celebration of Saint Petersburg's 300th anniversary two months hence. In any case, Litskai indicated, all the political obstacles to the withdrawal had now been removed, and ammunition trains bound for Russia would be loaded and start rolling almost immediately.[17]

And indeed they did. By the middle of the month, trains loaded with ammunition were departing at the rate of almost two per week from the small village of Colbasna at the northeastern edge of the Transdniestrian region. OSCE Military Mission members traveled to Colbasna almost daily to inspect and verify the loading and departure of the ammunition. By the middle of the year, the process was working so well that the military officers in my mission had become close working acquaintances, even friends, with the Russian officers stationed and working in Colbasna. Some of my staff even stayed overnight in the bachelor officers' quarters in Colbasna. To expedite the process, the Moldovan authorities quietly entrusted the mission with the authority to prepare customs documentation, to be verified by Moldovan officials on the right bank, for each departing train. During 2003, almost half the 40,000 metric tons of ammunition stored on the base in Colbasna was safely, verifiably, and successfully removed to the territory of the Russian Federation.[18]

Many Western press accounts attributed the sudden Transdniestrian acquiescence to the renewal of Russian military withdrawal to the U.S.-EU visa ban, announced only a few days before. Much as I would like to believe in the efficacy of Western pressure, I suspect this would be a case of falling into the logical fallacy—post hoc, ergo propter hoc. My conversations with Litskai (in particular), other Transdniestrian officials, and Russian colleagues lead me (and led me at the time) to conclude that Transdniestrian cooperation was obtained primarily as a result of negotiations with and promises by Moscow. As the rest of this narrative will show, I speculate that Moscow's blandishments very likely included assurances of some sort of continuing Russian military presence, no matter what the pace of withdrawals of military equipment or the twists and turns of the negotiations.

Establishing the Constitutional Commission

As the negotiators prepared in mid-March 2003, for the next round of the political settlement talks, prospects for real progress seemed to be looking up. The main task facing participants was to implement the steps agreed to in the protocol on the Joint Constitutional Commission at the previous round. Laying out recommendations for the OSCE Chair in the immediate future, I described the contradictions and pitfalls hidden in the apparently rosy situation:

President Voronin's February 2003 constitutional initiative and the recent willingness of Transdniestrian negotiators to sign on have led the Moldova-Transdniestria political settlement talks into uncharted territory. Mutual acceptance of federalization as a solution and agreement to draft a new constitution jointly appear to have brought the sides closer to an overall settlement than ever before. However, other aspects of their behavior make me wonder just how much either side wants a settlement. After a decade of efforts, the Moldovans have succeeded beyond their wildest dreams in soliciting external, international pressure on the Tiraspol regime. This very success may have revived the chimera that just a little more pressure will force Transdniestria to knuckle under to whatever (i.e., however little) Chisinau proposes. Meanwhile, Tiraspol's behavior seems to be the most reasonable in years (perhaps ever). However, while accommodating the mediators' proposals, Transdniestrian leaders nurture the hope that when push comes to shove Moldova will not be able to stomach a federation, and the negotiations will fall apart. Though the sides are very close on many points of substance, suspicion runs deep in the leadership on both sides, and powerful opponents of a settlement on both sides are mobilizing to derail the negotiation process.[19]

It seemed to me that the circumstances in the political settlement process presented an historic opportunity. However, to take advantage of this opening would require high-level attention on the part of the West, along with carefully calibrated collaboration with the Russian authorities:

This year may be our best chance in a generation of reaching a political settlement of the Transdniestrian conflict. However, I do not think the parties to the conflict will reach agreement on their own. The leaders and negotiators on both sides must be kept pointed toward the general goal they have all agreed to embrace—reunification of Moldova in a federal state. There will be constant, strong temptations to hedge, turn aside, or misuse the negotiation process for partisan or personal advantage. Recurrent Moldovan dreams that international pressure will finally reward them with a unitary state must be regularly doused with doses of realpolitik. Pressure must be maintained on the Transdniestrians for real actions, no matter how much they beg for relief and promise constructive participation in the negotiations. Strong, consistent guidance from the mediators can help avert these pitfalls. This consistency and guidance will have to come from the OSCE. Despite their status as mediators, Russia and Ukraine are involved in the conflict, with often competing interests. The possibility cannot be excluded that one or both of our mediator colleagues will backslide and provide de facto support for one or another of the parties.[20]

Notwithstanding my personal doubts, Chisinau and Tiraspol continued more or less on course for the first weeks of March. The two negotiators, Şova and Litskai, met on a weekly basis, usually in the OSCE Mission offices, and hammered out an understanding on the protocol establishing the Joint Constitutional Commission. We had agreed to hold the next round of negotiations on March 18–19, which ended up coinciding with a visit by Russian deputy foreign minister Viacheslav Trubnikov to the region. At the negotiating round, the participants formally approved the protocol on the JCC. Tiraspol insisted on the original title ("Constitution of the Federal State"), so Şova inserted a footnote for Chisinau, indicating their understanding that the federal state in question was the Republic of Moldova. Trubnikov met separately with the participants in the talks, to get a firsthand report on progress, and also with local Russian and Transdniestrian military commanders. By that time two ammunition trains had already been loaded and departed from Colbasna for Russia. Things seemed to be going well.[21]

The three mediators—Russia, Ukraine, and the OSCE—were already looking beyond the March 18–19 round to the practical details of the formation and initial work of the JCC. We recommended that Chisinau and Tiraspol work out a plan for implementing the protocol they had just approved, and proposed that we organize an introductory meeting for the members of the newly constituted JCC with participants in the political settlement negotiations. The mediators also proposed organizing a seminar for members of the new organ on contemporary varieties of federalism, with the participation of suitable international experts. As we finished the round, it was not clear whether the protocol would simply be signed formally by the heads of the respective executive branches or whether legislative involvement and approval would be necessary.[22]

No sooner had the March negotiating round finished than the Transdniestrians struck back at Moldova, the United States, and the EU for the visa ban. On Friday, March 21, the Transdniestrian "Foreign Ministry" announced that fourteen Moldovan senior officials—including President Voronin, his son Oleg, and most of the senior ministers in the government—would henceforth not be permitted to enter or transit Transdniestrian controlled territory. The measure was especially designed to inconvenience and irritate Voronin, who frequently visited his aged, ailing mother at the family home in the small village of Corjevo, near Dubossary on the left bank.[23]

The Transdniestrian entry ban also affected the upcoming visit of Chairman in Office (CiO) de Hoop Scheffer to Moldova. The Dutch

Chairmanship and the OSCE Mission to Moldova wanted to schedule an early trip by the CiO to Chisinau to demonstrate the priority attached to reaching a Transdniestrian settlement. When the sports enthusiasts among us learned that the Dutch national football team would be playing a "friendly" match against the Moldovan national team on April 2 in Moldova, it seemed natural to time the visit to coincide. De Hoop Scheffer was (and is) a dedicated football fan, and he welcomed the chance to watch his national team play while at the same time conducting some informal OSCE business by inviting Voronin and Smirnov to join him in viewing the contest.[24]

The only problem was that the Moldova-Netherlands contest was to be played in Tiraspol. Transdniestria's major retail firm (and football champion of the entire Commonwealth of Independent States), Sheriff, had just finished a massive, state-of-the-art stadium on the edge of the Transdniestrian region's major city. Meanwhile, due to a lack of funds and attention, Chisinau's Republican Stadium had deteriorated to the point that the Union des Associations Européennes de Football declared it unfit for major international competitions. To receive the union's blessing for holding the "friendly" match in Tiraspol, the Transdniestrian authorities agreed to fly the Moldovan flag, play the Moldovan national anthem, and not to display any Transdniestrian symbols. However, the authorities were not obliged, and they had no intention to permit President Voronin to attend the game.

During the week before the visit, I was obliged to engage in several rounds of "football diplomacy." The Dutch Chairmanship scheduled and made public the CiO's visit before the Transdniestrians announced their entry ban for the Moldovan leaders. It thereby fell to my lot to convince Smirnov not to block Voronin's travel to the game and to attend the contest together with the CiO and Voronin. It would probably have been easier to convince Smirnov to jump out of an airplane without a parachute. In conversations over the weekend before the visit, President Voronin agreed, with visible distaste, to attend the game with the CiO and Smirnov. The latter clearly had no intention of agreeing to Voronin's presence, and appeared to relish the president's predicament. Smirnov claimed that he was prepared to meet and do business with Voronin, but in a serious venue, not in a football stadium. Smirnov tried to justify his position with the claim that Voronin was exploiting the CiO's interest in football for political purposes—as if he, Smirnov, was not doing the same thing.[25]

In the midst of this football diplomacy, a seemingly chance flap over Transdniestrian security preparations also almost derailed both the political settlement process and the CiO's impending visit. On February 27 the Transdniestrian "Security Council" (composed of the leading police, security, and military figures in the separatist entity) in a secret meeting discussed and adopted a contingency plan for meeting possible emergency situations, up to and including a declaration of martial law. At a later date, when we obtained a copy and read the text of the decree, my mission colleagues and I interpreted the document as a contingency measure drawn up in the context of the just-announced U.S.-EU visa ban and the impending renewal of Russian military withdrawal operations. The document did not call for any immediate operational steps, and no implementing actions of any sort were taken by the Tiraspol authorities in the ensuing four weeks.[26]

The document was shared with deputies of the Transdniestrian Supreme Soviet in early March, as they deliberated their decree charging Smirnov with facilitation of the Russian withdrawal. The lone opposition deputy in the body, an ally of President Voronin, somewhat later showed the document to the authorities in Chisinau. Within days, almost immediately after the Transdniestrian leaders announced their travel ban on Moldovan officials, our contacts in the Moldovan government in Chisinau warned in alarm that the Transdniestrian authorities were preparing to declare martial law and preparing to renew military activities, perhaps even mounting an attack on the right bank. OSCE Mission members, including professional Western military officers and trained observers, were traveling daily along the length and breadth of the Transdniestrian region, and were as near to absolutely certain as one could be that the authorities in Tiraspol were not making any security or military preparations for any unusual action. Moldovan authorities made a loud public outcry about the Transdniestrian decree, and it proved a lengthy and touchy process to convince President Voronin and his colleagues that the document, while repugnant in its substance and what it reflected of the mindset of the Tiraspol leadership, did not constitute a real threat.[27]

Meanwhile, the hullabaloo over the decree effectively brought to a halt any progress on implementing the decisions of the last negotiating round on constituting the JCC. On March 28, Transdniestrian Supreme Soviet speaker Grigorii Maracuţa sent a proposal to Moldovan speaker Ostapciuc to meet and sign an agreement on forming a JCC. President

Voronin rejected Maracuţa's initiative, saying he wished to keep the negotiations between the executive branches in Chisinau and Tiraspol, and to include the legislatures only when it was time to approve a final agreement. However, according to most of our Moldovan colleagues, some sort of parliamentary action was necessary for the Moldovan executive to establish a formal commission to rewrite the Constitution. Despite President Voronin's promises to me, as CiO de Hoop Scheffer's arrival approached, no activity on this score was visible in the Parliament in Chisinau.[28]

The CiO spent about ten hours on the ground in Moldova on April 2, 2003, in meetings with Voronin, Smirnov, their top advisers, the leaders of Moldova's five largest political parties, and a group of Chisinau intellectuals and activists representing civil society in Moldova. The CiO discussed with officials in both Chisinau and Tiraspol possible security guarantees (i.e., peacekeeping) of a political settlement and the possible monitoring by international observers of the Transdniestrian segment of the Moldova-Ukrainian border. (I will return to these issues in greater detail later below in this narrative.) However, de Hoop Scheffer's main concern was to push for progress in the process of working out a political settlement, in particular approving and implementing the protocol on forming the JCC and beginning its work.[29]

The CiO heard emotional pleas from some of Moldova's leading politicians and most of the representatives of civil society to reject any proposal on the table for the federalization of Moldova. The arguments were not new to anyone who had been following the issue, but the noise and fervor of the opponents could not help but make an impression on any spectator at the gathering. De Hoop Scheffer responded to one direct inquiry that the proposal for a mutually acceptable federal system was a position adopted by the OSCE after careful deliberation, consistent with international norms, and therefore not one we were likely to change. He did not add (though he could have) that the proposal seemed to have the full support of Moldova's top leadership, and thus was not an idea being forced on Moldova by the CiO or the OSCE. However, it was clear to us that President Voronin and his colleagues in the government had a lot of work to do with the Moldovan public if they were to have any hope that a settlement involving the federalization of the country would be approved by voters in a popular referendum.

The most pressing and arguably the most important issue on the CiO's plate was to get Chisinau and Tiraspol moving on the joint drafting of the new Constitution. Although the negotiators for both sides had formally signed the protocol on formation of the JCC at the March negotiating round, neither side had moved forward on the issue since that time. De Hoop Scheffer urged both leaders to take all necessary steps to send their representatives to the JCC and to ensure that the body began its work.[30]

Apparently in response to the CiO's demarche, on April 4 Moldovan negotiator Şova spent the day at the Parliament building in a concerted effort by the Voronin administration to have the legislature formally endorse the document approved at the March 18 negotiating session. Members of the two parliamentary opposition parties bitterly denounced the proposed legislative action on both procedural and substantive grounds. However, with a 71 to 30 majority, the ruling Party of Communists easily carried the day. For the first time in the ten-year history of the Transdniestrian political settlement negotiations, the Moldovan Parliament gave formal approval to an agreement reached in the process.[31] As our contacts in Tiraspol promised at the time they delivered Maracuţa's letter to Ostapciuc, the Transdniestrian Supreme Soviet formally approved the March 18 protocol five days after the Moldovan parliamentary action, on April 9.[32] The two sides were now ready to appoint the members of their delegations to the JCC. The March 18 document allowed them six months to complete their work on a joint draft of a new, common Constitution. Things seemed to be back on track.

Unfortunately, difficulties began in the work of the JCC almost before the ink was dry on the legislative acts on its establishment. The first disagreement arose over its size and composition. The Transdniestrians wanted a large body with leading legislators and politicians from each side. The Moldovans desired a small body composed of academic legal and constitutional experts. The Moldovans also wanted the two delegations to be of equal size, not wanting to be outvoted. Litskai and Şova sparred over the question for a week, before compromising on formal delegations of three each, with the possibility of each side enlarging its delegation later. In practice, the agreement was that three Moldovans and seven Transdniestrians would sit at the table, but votes would be three each.[33]

And indeed, on April 17 the Moldovan Parliament approved the appointment of Ion Creanga, chief of the legislature's legal department, as head of the Moldovan JCC delegation. The other members were a retired judge from the Constitutional Court and a senior law professor from Chisinau State University. On April 23 (waiting until the last minute), the Supreme Soviet in Tiraspol announced a seven-person Transdniestrian delegation to the JCC. The group was headed by Deputy Speaker Yevgeniy Shevchuk, and included two legislative deputies, two members of the executive (including Litskai), the chief justice of the local "Supreme Court," and two senior professors from Tiraspol University. Transdniestrian representatives complained privately that the composition of their delegation demonstrated substantial political will behind their participation in the constitutional initiative. Conversely, they charged, the Moldovan delegation—a low-level staff member and two elderly retirees—demonstrated Voronin's lack of commitment to his own proposal.[34]

As the April round of negotiations rolled around, domestic and international interest in the settlement process was at a new high. On Thursday, April 24, in the Chisinau office of the OSCE Mission, we held a brief meeting of the negotiators, followed by an expanded session at which the newly appointed members of the JCC were introduced to the mediators, political representatives of Chisinau and Tiraspol, and to each other. The session—mostly nonsubstantive—was followed by a large press conference and extensive briefings for all the Western ambassadors resident in Chisinau.[35]

As the representatives of Chisinau, Tiraspol, Russia, and Ukraine dispersed for the traditional, lengthy holiday period at the beginning of May, hopes and expectations of the political settlement negotiations were still quite high. The European Union, the Council of Europe's Venice Commission, and the United States were all prepared and eager to provide constitutional experts to assist the new JCC in its work. Critics of the process within and outside Moldova, in particular those who opposed a federal solution for reuniting the two sides, appeared to interpret the formal designation of both delegations to the JCC as a sign that success in drafting a new Constitution appeared to be likely. However, those of us on the inside knew that this was only a first, and exceedingly modest, step. The two sides still needed to reach agreement on how (and where) the JCC would conduct its work. Only then would the most difficult part of the process begin: drafting the articles of the new Constitution that would decide the division of powers between Chisinau and Tiraspol and Transdniestria's actual status within Moldova.

Chapter 6

The Joint Constitutional Commission: Buyers' Remorse?

Work in most countries in the former Soviet Union and Eastern Europe generally comes to a complete halt during the first ten days in May. Almost all the countries in Europe celebrate May 1 as the workers' holiday, or labor day. May 8–9 are devoted to celebrating the end of World War II, or Victory Day. (Conveniently for some, May 9 is now also an EU holiday—the Day of Europe.) Finally, most of the branches of the Eastern Orthodox Church around this time of year celebrate a post-Easter holiday on which believers visit the graves of their parents and relatives. In most of the countries with a significant Eastern Slavic population, almost without exception, everyone simply leaves work on April 29–30 and returns on May 10 or 11.

So it was in Moldova in 2003. The Moldovan and Transdniestrian negotiators and the members of the Joint Constitutional Commission (JCC) were scheduled to return to work on May 12, when the Organization for Security and Cooperation in Europe (OSCE) Mission and the OSCE Parliamentary Assembly Group on Moldova had scheduled a two-day seminar on federalism to be held in Chisinau and Tiraspol. We had invited a number of foreign experts. For example, while on consultations in Brussels during the previous week, I met with a lawyer from the EU Council who would attend and serve as one of the chief EU expert consultants for the work of the JCC. I had also been in touch with the permanent staff of the Council of Europe's Venice Commission, whom I knew well from collaboration on the Moldova-Transdniestria issue in previous years. They would contribute experts to our work with the JCC. Finally, in addition to the deputies from various European parliaments who constituted our Parliamentary Assembly Group for Moldova,

Bruce George, British member of Parliament and president of the OSCE Parliamentary Assembly, came to Chisinau for our May 2003 seminar.

On May 11, on the eve of our seminar, I attended a dinner for George hosted by the Moldova Parliament speaker, Eugenia Ostapciuc, and attended by the parliamentary leadership and deputies working on the Transdniestria question. George gave one of the best ex tempore speeches I have ever heard on the difficulty of resolving ethnic or communal conflicts. He explained the British experience in Northern Ireland and what steps and concessions had been necessary from all sides in order to reach and implement the Good Friday Accords. He related his own personal experiences, including his own difficulty in accepting the release from prison of a terrorist accused of blowing up his—George's—office. His remarks were a moving illustration in human terms of the need for reconciliation, dialogue, and mutual compromise. Alas, his eloquence seemed to wash over my Moldovan friends without visible effect, like water off the proverbial duck's back.

The OSCE Parliamentary Assembly seminar took place successfully May 12–13, with many fine speeches and erudite expert commentary on the varieties of federalism, the relations of the federal entities to the center, and so forth. Administratively, the sessions went without hitches, because the Moldovan and Transdniestrian police and security authorities permitted representatives from the other side to travel without hindrance and attend sessions in the Moldovan Parliament and Transdniestrian legislative organ. Deputies and members of the JCC delegations made their initial working contacts with the international experts that the OSCE had recruited to advise the body in its work. In sum, hopes were higher than they had ever been for a political settlement:

> Successful agreement and ratification by both legislative bodies of the mechanism of the Joint Constitutional Commission (JCC) was a real breakthrough. We now have a forum that both sides have agreed will build the structures of a state reuniting the Transdniestrian region with the rest of Moldova. In addition, we have agreement in principle from both sides that this reunited state shall be on a federal basis. In essence, the past ten years of negotiations between Chisinau and Tiraspol have been about getting to this point. We now have the opportunity actually to write a real settlement.[1]

My OSCE colleagues and I had hoped, if not assumed, that the Moldovan and Transdniestrian JCC delegations would have settled most of the technical aspects of their future work by the time we all returned from the May holidays. I should have known from my considerable experience in the political settlement process that such an assumption was bound to be wrong. In fact, things were worse than I feared. When we discovered that neither side had done anything to formalize working procedures for the JCC, I asked my staff to prepare a draft that could serve as a basis for agreement.

We had assumed that the JCC would probably divide its formal meetings between Chisinau and Tiraspol, just as the OSCE had done with our Parliamentary Assembly seminar. As a precedent, we also had the five-sided negotiations, which for years had alternated meetings between the two cities. We were therefore stunned when Moldovan delegation head Ion Creanga told us on May 13 on the margins of the seminar in Tiraspol that he had strict orders that the JCC should meet only in Chisinau, only in the building of the Moldovan Parliament. In addition, Creanga related, he had instructions that the JCC should use the present Constitution of the Republic of Moldova as the basis for its work, because the JCC was drafting a new Constitution for the Republic of Moldova, not the Constitution of a new state.[2] The Moldovan substantive objection to the February Protocol on the JCC was clearly back in play, and not just as a footnote.

Finally, Creanga announced that Chisinau objected to having all seven members of the Transdniestrian delegation to the JCC attend the meetings of that body. Moldova only had three members in its delegation, and they should not be outnumbered at JCC meetings. Creanga was unmoved by various arguments, such as that Moldova had chosen to limit itself to three members but had not obligated Tiraspol to do so, or that numbers in the respective delegations did not matter, because the JCC would not be deciding questions by majority vote. Creanga eventually made clear that he had rigid instructions on these questions, and no authorization to show flexibility.[3]

At first it was hard to believe that Creanga had not somehow misunderstood or exaggerated his instructions. However, it soon became apparent, both from meetings with Şova and from an unexpected afternoon session with President Voronin at a May 15 local election campaign event, that the Moldovan position had shifted significantly:

President Voronin's constitutional initiative seems to be running out of steam. . . . Developments after the May Day holidays have not been encouraging. The Moldovan side has not been able to agree with their Transdniestrian counterparts about either the number of participants or venue for the JCC's work. The Moldovans were stubborn about not having JCC meetings in Tiraspol, and—more disturbingly—argued that the JCC's work should be consistent with the current Moldovan constitution and legislation. In a two hour meeting with Venice Commission and EU experts, I was told the Moldovan JCC members never uttered the word "federation."[4]

For the rest of May and well into June, my OSCE Mission colleagues and I worked intensively to try to find a compromise that would allow the JCC to begin work in cooperation with the two negotiators, Şova and Litskai; the two heads of the JCC delegations, Creanga and Transdniestrian deputy speaker Yevgeniy Shevchuk; and our colleagues from the Russian and Ukrainian embassies in Chisinau. The two JCC delegation heads met several times at the OSCE Mission offices, usually in the presence of mission members and sometimes also Russian and Ukrainian diplomats. Personal relations between them were cordial, but there was no give in the substantive position of either side.

Those of us working as mediators in the political settlement negotiations searched for explanations of the Voronin administration's change in position. One possible reason for the president and his advisers paying less attention to the negotiations and the JCC might be found in the upcoming countrywide local and municipal elections, scheduled for May 25. Voronin and his Party of Communists mounted a serious effort to unseat the popular Chisinau mayor Serafim Urechean, who increasingly looked and acted as a possible leader around whom Moldova's center and right-wing opposition parties might rally in the next parliamentary elections. The ruling Party of Communists put up the sitting minister of transportation, Viktor Zgardan, who received formal and informal support from the president and other sitting officials that stretched—if not exceeded—Moldovan campaign rules. Urechean was reelected by a resounding margin, which enhanced his credentials as an opposition leader; the Communists had mixed but not unfavorable results throughout the rest of the country.[5]

The Chisinau election campaign may have distracted President Voronin from the Transdniestrian settlement process, but it did not explain why the president had moved to such a hard line and seemingly unproductive position on the JCC. My own conclusion was (and is) that Voronin became more cautious in the face of mounting opposition to federalization of the country from a vocal and significant segment of Moldova's intellectual elite and civil society. From the very beginning of the Transdniestrian conflict, a large portion of the Romanian speaking social and political elite in Moldova favored the establishment of a centralized unitary state in independent Moldova. In late 1993, the newly established Mission of the Conference on Security and Cooperation in Europe (CSCE) recommended granting a special status to the Transdniestrian region as the best chance for settling the conflict, and concluded that a unitary state was not likely to lead to a solution.[6] In 1994, the Romanian-speaking majority in the Moldovan Parliament adopted a Constitution that provided for a highly centralized unitary state, with provisions for some sort of special status for Gagauzia and the "settled points on the left bank of the Nistru River." The national Parliament was to be elected in a single, nationwide electoral district, so that the 70 percent Romanian-speaking portion of the electorate could always outvote the 30 percent of Russian speakers.

During the ten-year course (1992–2002) of the political settlement negotiations, Moldovan representatives resisted any attempt to suggest that Transdniestria had any status other than that of an integral part of a unitary Moldovan state. Moldovan negotiators, and especially Moldovan nationalists, found anathema proposed solutions such as Primakov's infamous *Moscow Memorandum,* which suggested that two separate entities—Chisinau and Tiraspol—would agree to build a third entity, the "common state."[7] The fairly unchanging Moldovan position was that the goal of the negotiations was peacefully to restore legitimate control by Chisinau over those portions of the country that had broken away. This was in stark contrast to Tiraspol's contention that Transdniestria had been part of the Soviet Union, but never a part of an independent Moldovan state.

Moldovan critics of the *Moscow Memorandum* saw the document as an attempt by Primakov to gain acceptance for a Russian Trojan horse inside the Moldovan body politic. To such critics, the *Memorandum* gave too much potential autonomy to Tiraspol; for the Transdniestrian negotiators, it did not provide nearly enough. To many foreign mediators hailing from countries with federal systems, it seemed that a strong federation might be the ideal solution to the Transdniestrian conundrum. However, no one dared propose or even mention the word. A July 1993 CSCE-sponsored seminar in Chisinau designed to help the Moldovans write their new Constitution nearly descended into mayhem in an afternoon session scheduled to discuss varieties of autonomy in federal systems.[8]

In March 2000, the OSCE Mission organized a "working table" in Kiev, with Moldovan and Transdniestrian negotiators and academics and a dozen leading international constitutional experts, to consider possible structural and constitutional aspects of a Transdniestrian political settlement. The Western-led group of participants in the week-long exercise succeeded in constructing a complete settlement document from scratch; the result was facilitated by the fact that it was advisory and nonbinding. The end product of the exercise was in fact a federation in just about every respect; the participants just refrained from using the term when characterizing their handiwork. The seminar provoked fairly widespread interest in Moldova, considerable suspicion, and some criticism from Chisinau civil society.[9] Many Western European and American constitutional experts continued to see creating a federal system as one promising avenue toward a settlement in Moldova.

As of mid-2000, the Moldovan government was not interested in any talk of federation. President Lucinschi had his own worries: externally with former premier Primakov, who tried to force Chisinau and Tiraspol into a quick deal in August 2000; and domestically with the left- and right-wing oppositions, which united in July 2000 to amend the Constitution, creating a parliamentary republic and leading to early elections in February 2001. After the Communists' stunning victory, President Voronin was more willing than his predecessor to entertain innovative ideas for pursuing a political settlement. During the summer of 2001, the Moldovan negotiators embraced a number of the ideas suggested by experts who had participated in the Kiev meeting, such as proposing a bicameral Parliament. However, when I sounded out President Voronin and negotiator Vasile Sturza in September 2001, they were not prepared or interested in proposing any sort of formal federal system as a means of reaching a settlement.[10]

President Voronin clearly changed his mind on the desirability and advisability of proposing a federation sometime during the first half of 2002. The Kiev Document, presented on behalf of the three mediators on July 3, 2002, was drafted in great secrecy. The draft had considerable input from selected Western experts; it was cleared with Russian and Ukrainian mediators in finished form. The proposed document clearly had President Voronin's support, but he also obviously wanted the mediators and not his own negotiators to be the first to place the idea of a federation on the table.

The reaction in Chisinau showed why. The Kiev Document drew a firestorm of criticism from a number of think tanks, nongovernmental organizations, political parties, newspapers, and intellectuals. The critics were largely the same coalition that had mounted massive demonstrations during the winter of 2002 against the Communists' proposal to make Russian a second state language in Moldova. These domestic opponents also enlisted support from several prominent supporters abroad. The basic theme of the criticism was not so much against the insufficiencies of the Kiev Document—and there were many—but against the idea of federalization, which was portrayed as a means of affording Russia the ability for the long-term domination and occupation of all of Moldova.[11]

When I returned to Moldova in January 2003, the momentum behind the Kiev Document had entirely dissipated and it was clear that it afforded no chance of producing a settlement. However, the issue of federalization was very much in debate. One of the first questions posed to me by the press corps in Chisinau was my attitude toward a federal solution. Both to support President Voronin and because I come from a country with a federal system, I replied that I was very much in favor of federalization. Press criticism of my activity stepped up immediately, and many critics sought to portray my actions as pro-Russian.[12] For example, the settlement negotiations from the beginning have been conducted in Russian, with all documents written in Russian. From my time as a student on the U.S.-USSR academic exchange and later service at the U.S. Embassy in Moscow, I was accustomed to writing in Russian and signing my name in Russian on Russian-language documents. (Obviously, I signed English-language documents in English.) During my first term with the OSCE in Moldova, no one paid any attention to this practice. But from the start of my second term, dissident members of the Moldovan negotiating team leaked negotiating documents to the press, which loudly denounced my practice of writing and signing in Russian. Critics also misrepresented other incidents in the negotiating process to portray my colleagues and me as pro-Russian.

Both the Dutch OSCE Chair and the OSCE Mission to Moldova under my leadership offered explicit support for President Voronin's constitutional initiative. This brought us steady, increasing criticism from an important segment of Chisinau's civil, political, and intellectual society. The federalization initiative was often denounced as a pro-Russian ploy, and critics called instead for support for "European values." To no avail we noted in response that the Netherlands (a nonfederal, unitary state) is a key member of the European Union and an exemplary champion of

"European values," and a number of important EU states in fact have federal systems.[13]

The federalization issue posed a real dilemma for the OSCE at all levels in our involvement in the Transdniestrian political settlement process. First of all, the OSCE was in Moldova to assist the government in its pursuit of a negotiated settlement. The Voronin administration, which had won election in 2001 with an absolute majority of the vote, was not only fully behind but was also the initiator of the constitutional initiative. (I have strong reason to believe that the Voronin administration was also the initiator of the Kiev Document, but will let the actual participants speak to that part of the negotiating history.) In any event, in early 2003 the OSCE contemplated a possible solution to the Transdniestrian issue that was strongly supported by the legitimate government of the country and was consistent with accepted state practice and structure in a number of Western European countries. It was difficult not to support the proposal.

Conversely, the opposition to the federalization initiative was clearly deeply held, vehemently expressed, and widely disseminated. The Chisinau institutes, nongovernmental organizations, and newspapers that were most vocal in their opposition to federalization claimed that the vast majority of the Moldovan population shared their views. They produced a number of public opinion polls that appeared to support their case. However, the results of the polls were either confusing—for example, they showed that a vast majority of the population opposed federalization, but also that a vast majority cared little or nothing about the Transdniestrian settlement question—or suspect, either in methodology or political slant. The basic problem was that, no matter how passionately the critics argued, the party now supporting federalization had won a clear victory in a basically free and fair election.[14]

It was nonetheless clear to me and my colleagues in the OSCE Mission that an important segment of Moldovan society was adamantly opposed to any form of federalization of the country, in particular to the initiative currently proposed by President Voronin. Legalities aside, this popular opposition would clearly make it impossible to implement any sort of federal settlement, unless the critics could be won over. As the opponents became more vocal after the JCC's formal establishment in April, it obviously became more urgent to take some sort of action to counter the ever more strident public denunciations of federalization.

My deputy, Neil Brennan, and I came up with a two-pronged approach. First we went directly to the government to note the need to win public support for the president's initiative. At a meeting with Voronin's principal political adviser, Mark Tkachuk, we cited the provision in the president's proposal that the draft of a new Constitution would need to be approved in a nationwide referendum. Pointing to the current criticism in the Chisinau press, we argued that if such a referendum were held at that moment, our guess was that any proposed federal Constitution would probably be voted down. We asked whether the government had any plan for building public support for the constitutional initiative and a political settlement. We said we could offer suggestions, material support, and international expert speakers if the administration desired.

Tkachuk responded cordially, and did not disagree with our assessment of the current standing of the constitutional initiative in Moldovan public opinion. However, he also offered no indication that the government had either any plan or any intention of doing anything to win over public opinion. I inferred that he wanted us—the OSCE—to mount the public opinion campaign, and then the Voronin administration could agree with us. However, this was clearly a domestic Moldovan political issue, for which the Moldovan government had to take responsibility and on which the Moldovan government had to take the first step. I was prepared to support President Voronin and his colleagues in what they had decided to do; I was not prepared to do it for them. We left Tkachuk's office after a couple of hours of friendly conversation, and heard no more of the issue, either from Tkachuk or the president.[15]

Brennan and I also attempted to reach out to Moldovan civil society, including the fiercest critics of federalization. Of course we hoped we might disarm the suspicions and convince some of them. However, we also wanted to maintain a dialogue on the question of a political settlement, as well as the broad range of other questions, such as internal democratization and human rights, that were at the heart of the work of the OSCE Mission. I tried to accept any request for a meeting from any Moldovan representing any legitimate organization, no matter what their point of view. The three leaders of the Christian Democratic Popular Party met with me for almost two hours to express their opposition to Voronin's initiative. So did several sitting and former deputies from the Moldovan Parliament. I sat for one morning with members of the Association to Reverse the Effects of the Molotov-Ribbentrop Pact, one of the first advocates of Moldovan independence during the days of perestroika. I spent a three-hour session one Saturday morning during which Romanian-American journalist Vladimir Socor railed at the errors in the OSCE position, before heading off to a seminar across town to announce that he had "set me straight."[16]

In early June, the OSCE Mission agreed with Victor Ursu, head of the Soros Foundation's office in Chisinau, to hold an all-day seminar of leading politicians and representatives of civil society in Moldova to discuss the federalization proposal and Transdniestrian settlement issues. The discussion was heated, and the denunciations of the federalization proposal from some of the participants were sustained and vitriolic. I still recall one half-hour denunciation, dripping with sarcasm, of the OSCE's support for Voronin's federalization initiative from Christian Democrat deputy head, Vlad Cubreacov. As much as we tried to listen and engage, we were clearly not going to win over the fiercest of the critics. Their positions were too deeply held, and their opposition had been inflamed by emotions aroused during a lengthy political struggle.[17]

If anything, the OSCE's press only got worse over the summer, both in Moldova and abroad. The Christian Democrats, supporters and sympathizers among Chisinau intellectuals, and portions of Moldovan civil society continued their drumbeat of criticism throughout the Moldovan media. Writing for the *Wall Street Journal Europe,* Socor published sharp criticism of the OSCE's role in Moldova. Senior Dutch OSCE officials met with him, but failed to convince him. The United States finally deemed it necessary to weigh in, with a lengthy letter of rebuttal to the *Wall Street Journal* supporting the current direction of the political settlement efforts in Moldova by the ambassador to Moldova, Pamela Smith; the special negotiator for Eurasian conflicts, Ambassador Rudolf Perina; and the ambassador to the OSCE, Stephen Minikes.[18]

From my vantage point in the process, the problem with the opponents of Voronin's constitutional initiative and federalization in Moldova was not so much the fact of their criticism but that they offered no real alternatives to the policies they were denouncing. At our June seminar with the Soros Foundation's Moldova office, one senior centrist politician complained to me afterward: "Those Frontists [Popular Front, now Partidul Popular Creştin Democrat] are idiots! They're against everything, and not for anything!" Without endorsing his characterization, I also found it hard to make out a viable alternative policy line in the criticism offered. We in the OSCE (and all other external actors, like the European Union, UN, or NATO) did not have the physical means of forcing the Transdniestrians to submit to Chisinau's authority. Thus calls for the "restoration of constitutional authority" or "elimination of the illegal separatist regime" make great rhetoric, but are not useful practical guides for peaceful political action. Similarly, we could not exclude Russia from the settlement process, no matter how some participants might wish to. Our task was to persuade Moscow to support a reasonable solution, or—failing that—to prevent the imposition of a bad one.

Against this sociopolitical backdrop, it is easier to interpret President Voronin's actions from April into June 2003. Indeed, the constitutional initiative was his, and he could not disavow it. I suspected more than once that he wished that Smirnov had not agreed to it, so that he could seek more international pressure on the Tiraspol regime. Once the JCC was established and public criticism in Chisinau mounted further, the president ran an increasing risk of collision with influential domestic political groupings. Already under fire and in an election campaign, he was not willing to give the opposition the ability to denounce him for recognizing Transdniestria as a separate entity, even in the context of negotiations for a political settlement that would reunite the country. The fact that he had no trust that Smirnov and his henchmen would do anything but pocket and misuse concessions from Chisinau indubitably could only strengthen Voronin's resolve to hold firmly to the line that he was writing a new federal Constitution of the Republic of Moldova, not for a new federal state.

Chapter 7

Roadblocks over Security Issues

The Russian Military Withdrawal:
"Yes, but You Don't Go!"

In one of the later scenes of Gilbert and Sullivan's *Pirates of Penzance,* British constables who have come to rescue Major General Stanley and his daughters from the pirates boldly sing "forward to the foe" while not moving. The frustrated Major General interjects repeatedly into their determined refrain the impatient exhortation "Yes, but you don't go!"

As I watched the Russian withdrawal of the vast stores of ammunition from the Colbasna depot gather speed during the spring of 2003, I had a similar feeling of frustration, as the outward signs of success in the physical process were not matched by progress on negotiating what would come after. General Vladimir Isakov, the Russian deputy minister of defense and head of the Logistics Directorate (Upravlenie Tyla), called off a scheduled visit to Chisinau and Tiraspol in mid-April because Russia had not yet completed an internal review process on how to provide the $100 million natural gas debt relief credit promised to Tiraspol in mid-2002.[1] Nonetheless, the ammunition inspection and removal operations taking place in the northern part of the Transdniestrian region were increasingly active. Isakov and I were both pleased with the speed and efficiency of the work; the local Russian officers and my mission members had established excellent working and personal relationships. At the rate that ammunition trains were being loaded, inspected, and dispatched for Russia, it seemed possible that the Colbasna depot might actually be emptied by the end of the year, thus meeting the revised December 31, 2003, deadline established at the 2002 Porto

Ministerial Meeting of the Organization for Security and Cooperation in Europe (OSCE).

Against this background of renewed operations and expectations that the Porto deadline might actually be met, the participants in the five-sided negotiations paid increasing attention to the question of guarantees of a political settlement during both the March and April rounds. All the participants agreed that to achieve a comprehensive agreement some sort of umbrella political document would be needed in addition to whatever sort of product the Joint Constitutional Commission would be able to draft. The most important provisions of this political document, we believed, would concern the military and security aspects of the settlement—bluntly, what would be the mandate and composition of any peacekeeping force?[2]

Shortly after the end of the April round, I flew to Washington to join the Dutch in extensive consultations with the United States on the status and future of the Transdniestrian settlement process. The Dutch agenda with the U.S. administration included the full range of issues in their OSCE Chairmanship, but questions involving the Russian withdrawal and the nature of any follow-on military presence connected with a political settlement played an important part in their exchanges at the Department of State and the National Security Council (NSC), and on Capitol Hill. The basic message I received from my Washington colleagues at various levels was that the United States would probably be prepared to support a small peacekeeping operation under an OSCE mandate in conjunction with a Transdniestrian political settlement, but would not be able to contribute any troops.[3]

I had a full set of meetings myself, including a session with an old friend and colleague at the NSC. I reviewed the progress we had made recently in Moldova, but expressed the fear that parochial local and Russian interests might still thwart the process of attaining a full Russian withdrawal and a political settlement. Arguing that success in Moldova could be a win-win for both the United States and Russia, I asked that the issued be placed on the agenda for President Bush to raise with Putin at the summit a month hence to celebrate the 300th anniversary of the founding of Saint Petersburg. Noting President Bush's full plate (Iraq!), my friend said he would endeavor to get the issue on the president's agenda, as long as I would undertake that the Department of State prepare the ground by having Secretary Colin Powell raise the subject during his preparatory trip to Russia in a couple of weeks. I passed this message back to my colleagues from State's European Bureau along with a strong plea that they follow through. As far as I could discover what happened, other issues deemed more pressing crowded Moldova/ Transdniestria off the agenda in both cases.[4]

Right after the May Day holiday, I flew to Brussels, where I joined my Dutch OSCE colleagues for consultations with the European Union Council, the staff of EU high representative Javier Solana, and the European Commission. Two items stood out from a set of discussions of the full range of issues involved in seeking a settlement in Moldova. First, the European Union would be prepared to put substantial resources, both money and personnel, into an effort to patrol the Transdniestrian segment of the Moldovan border with Ukraine.[5] Second, a senior EU Council staffer indicated that there was substantial interest and in his view readiness on the part of the EU to undertake a limited peacekeeping role in Moldova to help guarantee a political settlement.[6]

I traveled from Brussels to Vienna, where I reviewed the substantial encouraging progress on the removal of Russian ammunition from Colbasna with representatives of the donor states to the OSCE Voluntary Fund. During my round of meetings in Vienna, a senior Russian representative asked me in private not to raise publicly the idea of an OSCE peacekeeping effort in Moldova. He explained that Smirnov had been convinced not to oppose the withdrawal of Russian military equipment and ammunition by a promise of a Russian "military-guarantee" operation in conjunction with any political settlement. My Russian colleague said he feared talk of an OSCE operation might cause Smirnov to block current withdrawal operations. I rejoined that I had no understanding with Smirnov on this score, and that in any case, OSCE participating states needed to begin contingency discussions of a possible operation in case of a settlement and full withdrawal by the end of the year.[7]

I returned to Moldova in time for the conclusion of the long set of May holidays, V-E or Victory Day, celebrated in Eastern Europe on May 9. For the holiday President Voronin invited me and American ambassador Pamela Smith to Condriţa, his bucolic country retreat 25 kilometers west of Chisinau. As we strolled through a small complex of hills and ponds teeming with fish, ducks, and geese, President Voronin recounted to us the increasing pressure being placed on him by Russia to sign an agreement on a Russian troop presence in Moldova as part of an overall settlement package. He referred to this as a "military-guarantee" operation (i.e., peacekeeping); I was later shown a communication from

President Putin that simply referred to a "Russian troop presence." When I asked Voronin why the Russians were doing this now, he replied that he thought they wanted to get the question settled before NATO expanded to Moldova's borders in 2004.[8]

Voronin complained that Russia was placing "all-around" economic pressure on Moldova, including keeping the price of natural gas higher than for most other members of the Commonwealth of Independent States (CIS). He blamed the Russian Foreign Ministry for most of these actions—in particular Deputy Foreign Minister Viacheslav Trubnikov, for most of his career a KGB official, who Voronin claimed had personal interests and involvement in Transdniestria. Voronin also blamed the Foreign Ministry and longtime Presidential Administration staff member Prikhodko for blocking the appointment of a Russian special negotiator on the Transdniestrian issue, as Putin had promised him last February.

I urged President Voronin not to give in to the pressure, and reported back to The Hague, Vienna, and Washington:

Whatever the real Russian aim, it seems clear that key OSCE states need to raise at the most senior levels with Russia the political settlement process in Moldova, the need for full withdrawal consistent with all OSCE commitments, and the desirability of an international peacekeeping or stabilization force. We cannot stand idle and allow Russia to pressure Moldova into the kind of deal we have been telling Moldova for years that the international community will not accept. I personally believe the OSCE still has the levers to induce Russia to honor its commitments and support a genuine political settlement. But in order to get such a result, we must speak out now clearly and unequivocally.[9]

Friends and contacts in Chisinau continued to tell me about Russian pressure on Moldova to agree to a unilateral Russian peacekeeping operation or long-term troop presence. Trusted colleagues claimed that much of the inspiration for this campaign came from former prime minister Yevgeniy Primakov, whom Putin had appointed head of the Russian State Commission on a Transdniestrian Settlement in 2000 and 2001. Trubnikov was widely believed to be a protégé of Primakov, from the latter's time as chief of the Russian Foreign Intelligence Service. The incoming Russian ambassador to Moldova, Admiral Iurii Zubakov, was also reputed to be a Primakov man, having served in naval intelligence before being sent to Vilnius as Russian ambassador in the mid-1990s.[10]

I reported that Trubnikov was scheduled to visit Moldova on June 3–4, and Voronin was under increasing pressure to sign a bilateral deal with Russia. After our consultations in Brussels at the beginning of May, the Dutch OSCE team had been busy preparing a discussion paper and proposal on a possible OSCE stabilization operation in Moldova as part of an overall settlement. The Dutch Chair instructed me on behalf of Chairman in Office de Hoop Scheffer to inform the Moldovans, President Voronin if possible, of the possibility of an OSCE stabilization or peace-keeping operation in Moldova, and to urge the president not to agree to or sign anything on a bilateral basis at the upcoming CIS meetings and anniversary celebrations in Saint Petersburg. The president was busy with local and municipal elections before leaving for Russia, and I delivered the message only to Vasile Şova and Deputy Foreign Minister Ion Stavila. They both assured me he would sign nothing in Petersburg.[11]

Meanwhile, I continued to plead for high-level attention to the Transdniestrian issue, particularly in contacts with Russia:

> More than anything else, Russia needs to know that this issue is important to its major European and North American partners. If we never mention it to President Putin or his senior aides, he will assume we don't care or have lost interest. In addition, we should tell the Russians we believe a quick and dirty Primakov style bilateral deal will not produce a stable solution in Moldova, and it may have a bad effect on cooperative efforts elsewhere with major Western partners.[12]

Remarkably, when Trubnikov got to Moldova, he asked for my help in convincing Smirnov not to disrupt the schedule of Russian ammunition withdrawals, which up to that date had been proceeding with remarkable speed and smoothness. Trubnikov explained that Smirnov was demanding that Russia provide the $100 million gas debt credit, promised to him in mid-2002, before General Isakov's next visit to the region on June 16. I noted that the OSCE had little in the way of financial or other inducements to offer, although we might seek coercive measures to augment last winter's visa ban. Trubnikov responded that he thought Smirnov responded better to carrots than sticks.[13]

On peacekeeping, Trubnikov explained that as the Russian military withdrawal continued, the issue had become increasingly important to

Tiraspol. He said that President Voronin had just told him that he—Voronin—would personally make the decision for Moldova as to what sort of military guarantees of a settlement to accept. Adriaan Jacobovits asserted than any peacekeeping operation in conjunction with a settlement should be under an OSCE mandate and that no OSCE participating state should provide more than 50 percent of the force, which Trubnikov did not dispute (the latter was an apparent change in position from our previous meeting). He also did not challenge our statements that any peacekeeping operation should be small, because the main task would be preserving and not making peace. Finally, Trubnikov did not seem to share the view expounded by some of the staff members accompanying him that the current Russian peacekeepers in Transdniestria were not part of the contingent covered by the Istanbul/Porto commitments. In retrospect, the disconnect between Trubnikov and his entourage should have but did not set off alarm bells; the same difference in messages from senior Russian officials would be repeated three months later, at a higher level, with more serious consequences.[14]

Plugging the "Black Hole": The Border Issue

Almost from the beginning of the political settlement process, the question of control of the Transdniestrian segment of the Moldova-Ukraine border was a major issue. Tiraspol fought with great determination to keep the border open to imports and exports from industries based on the left bank of the Dniestr. Chisinau pressed doggedly either through its own agents or with the help of Ukrainian personnel to close the border, thus choking Transdniestria's economic lifeline to the rest of the world. The February 1996 deal reached by Moldovan president Mircea Snegur with Smirnov, whereby Transdniestria would be permitted to use Moldovan customs stamps and seals and export documentation, in return was supposed to provide joint Moldovan-Transdniestrian customs posts placed along the Ukrainian border. Smirnov pocketed the right to use Moldovan documentation, but then refused to follow through with the joint posts. Russia and Ukraine ignored Chisinau's howls of protest.[15] By 1999–2000, more than 50 percent of the left-bank region's substantial foreign trade was with EU states and the United States (in contrast to Chisinau and the right bank, which were heavily dependent on the Russian market).[16]

Chisinau fought back by labeling the Transdniestrian region a "black hole," and accusing the left-bank leadership of engaging in massive smuggling of drugs, weapons, persons, and anything else they could think of.[17] The Transdniestrian authorities denied all accusations. Little concrete evidence was provided by either side. To complicate the matter, organized crime in the 1990s was exceptionally strong on both sides of the Dniestr in Moldova, and also in Ukraine's Odessa Oblast. There was little doubt that extensive smuggling was going on; the problem was figuring out who was doing it, what they were smuggling, and who else was profiting. For example, when I first arrived in Moldova in 1999, every day about 10 a.m. on the main highway from Tiraspol to Chisinau, one would meet an armored car with a police escort headed for Chisinau Airport. The cargo was presumably cash and valuables destined for export and laundering. The vehicle never seemed to have any trouble with the authorities on either side of the river, and I never got a straight answer (no matter whom I asked) as to who owned it and what it was doing.

After negotiating for several months with Smirnov and concluding that the Transdniestrian leader was not interested in a settlement, on September 1, 2001, President Voronin revoked Tiraspol's right to use Moldovan documentation and tried to reach an agreement with Kiev to station Moldovan customs agents along the Transdniestrian segment of the border.[18] Smirnov successfully dissuaded Ukrainian president Leonid Kuchma from cooperating, and loudly accused Chisinau of engaging in an economic blockade.[19] Chisinau fired back with renewed accusations of smuggling arms, drugs, and people. After September 11, the local rumor mill sounded alarms that al Qaeda operatives had been seen on the left bank. During much of 2002, the Moldovan and Transdniestrian authorities periodically disrupted or stopped traffic and commerce between the two banks in a spiral of action and retaliation, all the while complaining to external actors about the perfidy of the other side.

All accusations and polemics aside, the border was a key question. The separatist Transdniestrian entity, though subsidized by Moscow, was kept afloat by substantial exports from the significant portion of Soviet Moldova's heavy industrial plant that had been constructed on the left bank. For example, the steel mill—the Moldovan Metallurgical Factory, MMZ in Russian, built in 1985—by 2000 was exporting production worth $150 million annually, including $70 million to the United States.[20] The Moldovan authorities labeled all this trade "smuggling," because it was not properly documented and taxed. These goods, which were exported using the documentation of the Republic of Moldova, showed up in EU and World Trade Organization (WTO) statistics as Moldovan foreign trade. The Moldovan application for WTO membership was significantly delayed because of the disparity, due to Transdniestrian economic activity, between the data supplied to the WTO by Chisinau and the data collected independently by the WTO.

The Moldovan authorities indeed desired to impose a blockade on Transdniestria, both to collect "lost" tax revenue and to pressure Tiraspol into a political settlement. The problem was that Ukraine always declined to go along, in major part because Ukrainian business elites profited enormously from both legal and illegal trade to and through the Transdniestrian region. Especially during the latter part of the 1990s, Ukrainian, Russian, Romanian, and Moldovan businessmen all used Tiraspol as an ostensible partner or shipping destination to avoid taxes in their own countries. The left-bank authorities happily cooperated with these schemes, and profited accordingly. During 2001 and 2002, President Voronin and his colleagues came up with the idea of stationing international personnel of some sort along the border with Ukraine to cut off Tiraspol's "illegal" trade. As the pressure from Chisinau grew, Smirnov came up with the idea of inviting an international mission to prove that Transdniestria was engaged only in "normal" exports and imports, not running guns and drugs.

In November 2002, a multinational assessment team of OSCE representatives visited both Moldova, including the Transdniestrian region, and also Ukraine to investigate the situation along the border. The team traveled extensively along both sides of the frontier and visited a number of crossing posts, including two operated by the Transdniestrian authorities.

In its December 2002 report, the assessment team concluded that the difficulties along this border area have "a direct negative impact on the Moldovan economy and may give rise to a number of security risks related to the possibility of uncontrolled movement of weapons and smuggling in all its forms." Furthermore, the team observed that, given the complexities involved and the limited progress achieved in recent years, the lack of a unified Moldovan customs space was not likely to be resolved without international involvement. The team therefore recommended that, among other things, "consideration should be given to the use of international customs experts, observers and/or trainers, possibly within the framework of an OSCE project building on the experience of joint control procedures established in other OSCE participating States." Noting the work in this subject area that had already been undertaken by the EU, the team suggested that the OSCE liaise with the European Commission to identify areas where joint action would be advantageous.[21]

When Jacobovits and I met with Smirnov on January 31, 2003, he suggested that the OSCE might deploy monitors along the border with Ukraine to monitor customs operations and also might send experts to inspect the Transdniestrian factories that the Moldovan authorities charged were engaged in producing illegal arms and munitions. At first we did not take these proposals very seriously, because they were buried fairly far down in a written set of points that Smirnov gave us, and he did not dwell on them in his oral remarks.[22] But after the Transdniestrian representatives returned to the proposal several times in subsequent meetings, it seemed that they might be serious enough that the idea could have a chance of acceptance. Moldovan negotiators had proposed a somewhat similar border presence to the OSCE Mission in December 2002, so I began sounding out my interlocutors from Chisinau. The initial responses were qualified but positive.

In a February 26 meeting with me and Jacobovits, Smirnov asked for the OSCE's response and expressed frustration when I told him that we were still considering it. I told him I wanted to take time to make a serious proposal with a real chance of success, rather than just go through the motions. I sent the OSCE Chair and the Secretariat a broad overview of our discussions with the Transdniestrians and Moldovans on a possible border monitoring operation, and tasked my deputy, Canadian Neil Brennan, to organize work on a detailed proposal.[23] We decided to concentrate on border monitoring and not factory inspections. We were persuaded by the argument that the Transdniestrian authorities would surely be able to hide or move any illicit operations in the factories designated for inspection. We decided that we did not need to view a large number of Potemkin villages, and we thought that a presence on the border—even if only for observation and not interdiction—would have many positive effects. On March 21, I sent a formal recommendation to that effect to the Dutch OSCE Chair and the OSCE Secretariat.[24]

During the April 2 visit of the chairman in office (CiO) to Moldova, we discussed the proposal with the leaders on both sides of the Dniestr. The CiO noted that the OSCE has substantial experience in border monitoring, and that "border monitoring along the entire Moldovan/ Ukrainian border, including the Transdniestrian section, would be another important element in increasing mutual confidence and, ultimately, in achieving stability and security in the country and the region."[25] With apparent approval from both sides, the OSCE Mission during April developed a comprehensive concept paper, which laid out the purposes, proposed mandate, territorial scope, and operational requirements for a monitoring operation along the Moldovan-Ukrainian border.[26] During a visit to Vienna in the first week in May, I discussed this paper with a number of OSCE delegations and the OSCE Secretariat. A small operational unit within the Secretariat was tasked with working out a far more detailed operational plan, based on the Moldova Mission's paper.[27]

While the OSCE was busy working out and selling to delegations the proposal for an international monitoring presence on the Moldova-Ukraine border, the Moldovan authorities began to move along another track, lured by the perpetual chimera of getting Ukrainian cooperation in closing the border. When I approached President Voronin in mid-May to confirm his support for the border monitoring concept before formally launching the proposal, to my surprise he insisted that only joint posts of Moldovan and Ukrainian customs personnel on Ukrainian territory would be acceptable. In no case would he agree to station either Moldovan customs and border personnel or international experts on Transdniestrian-controlled territory. "They might become hostages," he explained.[28]

At the same time, I discovered, the Moldovan authorities had been negotiating a new agreement with Ukraine on customs controls along its border, including the Transdniestrian segment. On May 15, 2003, Moldova and Ukraine signed a customs protocol in which Kiev agreed, as of May 25, 2003, to allow across the border for transit through Ukraine only goods bearing the new, post-2001 Moldovan stamps, seals, and export documentation. This agreement was to supersede the prevailing CIS customs regulations, according to which transit goods needed no customs documentation. In reporting the agreement, I noted that Tiraspol would be enraged and would clearly retaliate, given the clear threat to the region's external economic lifeline.[29]

The Moldovan authorities established procedures and locations where Transdniestrian enterprises could register, and Şova duly informed Litskai of these provisions on May 22, three days before the new agreement went into effect.[30] The real problem, of course, was not so much the registration but the fees and taxes that went along with it. Transdniestrian entrepreneurs and the authorities began to complain bitterly about both the new regime and the costs. The June 4–5 negotiation round was punctuated by complaints and recriminations from the Transdniestrian side about the alleged economic blockade. Under pressure from both Russia and Ukraine, which were also receiving a deluge of complaints, the Moldovan government adopted a decree that allowed Transdniestrian enterprises to register as Moldovan economic agents and use Moldovan documentation without additional fees or taxes.[31]

This Moldovan concession should have solved the problem, but it did not. While some negotiators for Chisinau and Tiraspol sought accommodation, zealous or offended partisans enthusiastically exercised or misapplied their authority to retaliate. For example, apparently acting in the opposite direction intended by the June 12 decree, Moldovan agencies limited the number of carnets under the Transports Internationaux Routiers Treaty distributed by the Moldovan Transport Association to trucks transiting Ukraine destined for Transdniestria. Smirnov howled that Moldova was continuing its blockade, and warned me that he would retaliate.[32] When the next round of negotiations began in Tiraspol on July 3, Transdniestrian "border" officials delayed the Moldovan delegation for half an hour. This was followed by news that the Transdniestrian authorities had cut off power to several Moldovan-controlled villages on the left bank near Dubossary and were preventing farmers from some of those villages from visiting their fields in Transdniestrian-controlled territory.[33]

I proposed to both Smirnov and Voronin that the OSCE revive a working group of both sides and mediators on economic issues to try break the cycle of mutual retaliation and escalation. This group, headed at the deputy minister level, began its work on June 28, and was formally endorsed by the negotiators at the July 3–4 round. The three mediators adopted a formal statement requesting Chisinau and Tiraspol not to take any further measures of economic pressure, but discussions between Şova, Litskai, and the members of the working group remained heated and difficult.[34]

The two parties would continue to discuss economic issues through the rest of the summer and autumn, but to no avail. The atmosphere just got tenser, further actions were taken, and mutual distrust deepened. The problem was not so much the issues as the mutual distrust and antipathy between Voronin and Smirnov. When one of the leaders adopted a coercive measure, the other's anger and suspicion were usually aroused so much that rational argument was of little use in heading off retaliation. In addition, I formed the impression that both leaders, even while their subordinates negotiated a fundamental compromise between them, continued to nurture a hope that with a little bit more pressure or resistance, complete victory was still possible. This produced a pattern of sometimes promising negotiations, punctuated by frequent crises and setbacks. The combination of personal factors and internal inconsistencies in the positions of both sides produced a real dilemma for those of us seeking to drive the negotiations to a conclusion:

There is a distressing pattern to all of these economic disputes that reflects the larger dilemma of the political settlement negotiations. The Republic of Moldova understandably insists upon its prerogatives as the sole recognized subject of international law. Unfortunately, this concern of principle has sometimes led Moldovan negotiators to reject compromise solutions of practical, technical questions for fear of compromising the general principle. On the other hand, Transdniestrian entrepreneurs and enterprise managers are often ready to reach practical working compromises with Moldovan authorities over questions like registration and documentation. However, higher political authorities in Tiraspol continue to press their bid for independence and international recognition, and actively prevent left bank economic managers from accepting practical working solutions.[35]

For the remainder of 2003, control of the border remained a potential instrument of pressure, rather than an opportunity for transparency and cooperation. The OSCE Mission and Secretariat's detailed recommendations for an international presence along the border remained on the shelf, unreviewed and undebated. Ultimately, the work proved not entirely in vain, for it served as a starting point and partial basis for the EU Border Assistance Mission, which was finally agreed on between Ukraine and Moldova and deployed in November 2005.

Smirnov: No Money, No Ammo . . .

Bessarabia and Transdniestria may be those regions of the Earth where observers first came up with the adage that troubles never arise singly, but in twos or threes. From mid-March to mid-June, 16,500 metric tons, or 35 percent of the roughly 42,000 tons of ammunition stored at Colbasna, were removed to the territory of the Russian Federation. If work could continue at that pace, the munitions depot would be empty before mid-October. The Porto deadline for the Russian military withdrawal would be met ahead of time.[36]

On June 16, 2003, the OSCE Mission's military members watched Russian soldiers at Colbasna load 790 tons of 125-millimeter tank ammunition onto a train for Russia. To their surprise and dismay, in an end to three months of cooperation, the Transdniestrian "border" troops refused to allow the train to depart the depot. The Russian troops had removed considerably more 125-millimeter tank ammunition from nearby bunkers; these munitions remained sitting on the loading docks while the train remained stuck on the main siding in the Russian base.[37]

I was in the United States when all this occurred, and first got a chance to ask Smirnov directly what was happening on June 26. OSCE Mission staff and diplomats in Chisinau speculated that the move was retaliation on Smirnov's part for the recent Moldovan measures on the border and registration for Transdniestrian enterprises. When I asked Smirnov, he heatedly denied any connection with the border or "embargo" issues, and pointed to Russia's failure to deliver on the $100 million gas debt credit. Smirnov showed me a September 2002 memo from Russian deputy premier and minister of finance Aleksei Kudrin promising the money. He complained that not only was Russia delinquent in delivering the money, but Moscow was also changing the deal's terms, proposing to provide the credit through the Moldovan Ministry of Finance rather than directly. I argued that the Russian commitment to withdraw the ammunition was not conditioned on payment. Smirnov said he did not care what I thought; the Russians had promised him money, and the ammunition would not move until he had it.[38]

The Russian Federation had indeed promised the credit; Smirnov gave me a copy of the memorandum signed at the deputy prime minister level. I learned that on June 9 a Moldovan delegation that included the Transdniestrian "minister of industry," Anatoly Blascu, had gone to Moscow for consultations with the Russians within the framework of the Moldova-Russia November 2001 Base Bilateral Treaty. The story from the Russians was that by terms of this treaty (negotiated with Transdniestrian participation), Moscow was obliged to provide such payments through Moldovan government agencies. The Moldovans maintained that the International Monetary Fund had raised questions about the implications of such a transfer for Moldova's external debt. No one could explain why the Russian government, which at the time owned 39 percent of the shares in Gazprom, could not find some way of transferring the credit directly to its own corporation, avoiding issues of de facto recognition of Transdniestria or increasing Moldova's indebtedness.[39]

Meanwhile, the Russian military withdrawal remained stuck. Eventually, the Russian troops at Colbasna unloaded the train and put all the 125-millimeter ammunition back into the bunkers, lest it be struck by lightning or subject to some other disaster. I returned to the issue repeatedly during the summer of 2003, but I could not get better explanations or produce any change in the Moldovan, Russian, or Transdniestrian positions on this issue. The impasse was doubly frustrating, because the successful operations during the spring had demonstrated that the ammunition withdrawal—once thought to require years—could be completed in a matter of months, if not weeks.

. . . and No Peacekeeping Either

The Dutch 2003 OSCE Chairmanship continued to focus on military guarantees as an essential element of a Transdniestrian settlement, which remained a priority of the OSCE Chair throughout the year. Our colleagues in The Hague relied on the OSCE Mission to take the lead on a number of issues involved in pursuing a political settlement where either local expertise or a presence on the ground might constitute a comparative advantage. However, the question of fashioning a revised peacekeeping operation in Moldova's Transdniestrian region involved the security relationship with Russia along with broader European security issues, and our colleagues in the Dutch Foreign Ministry took the lead on this issue. I also received the impression that the Dutch were interested in how the issue could be used to develop the European Union's foreign policy and security capabilities in a fashion compatible with the transatlantic elements of the Euro-Atlantic security architecture.

While my OSCE Mission colleagues and I were busy with stalled ammunition trains, economic disputes, and the blocked Joint Constitutional Commission, our Dutch colleagues drafted a succinct "food-for-thought" paper to float the idea of an OSCE-mandated, EU-staged peacekeeping operation to guarantee a political settlement of the Transdniestrian question. The Dutch paper proposed a combined military and civilian Peace Consolidation Mission, all under an OSCE mandate, with at least a couple of options for fielding the mission. The paper envisioned a small multinational peacekeeping force to be augmented by an international civilian contingent for monitoring and supporting implementation of a political settlement. The military element, which would replace the tripartite peacekeeping force established by the July 1992 cease-fire agreement, would number no more than several hundred troops and would serve mainly as a deterrent to any outbreak of hostilities. The mandate of the mission would be of unspecified, but limited, duration. The Dutch envisioned two possible ways of mounting the force: (1) The OSCE Permanent Council would subcontract out to another international organization, such as the EU, on a turnkey basis; or (2) the OSCE would mount the operation directly through a coalition of the willing. According to the Dutch proposal, a civilian observer force of 60 to 100 persons should augment the military contingent. In any of the options, the paper envisioned that the OSCE Chair would appoint a special representative to oversee the entire mission, both military and civilian.[40]

The Dutch paper expressed a clear preference for the OSCE to contract out the project. The Dutch noted the lack of experience and a planning capacity in the OSCE; given these conditions, they expressed doubts about whether the OSCE could successfully handle the logistical and administrative requirements of mounting an operation. The Dutch preference seemed to me in any case to be for the OSCE to turn to the EU, as a means of helping develop EU security and defense capabilities. The Dutch paper referred to the recent successful EU experience of Operation Concordia in Macedonia, and argued that the EU also had other instruments that could help support a political settlement in Moldova.[41]

The next round of negotiations was set for July 3–4. During the previous week, the Dutch had quietly shared the paper with a number of OSCE delegations in Vienna, both to obtain substantive comments but also to gauge potential support. No strong objections having arisen, Jacobovits brought the paper to Moldova to present first to our mediator colleagues from Russia and Ukraine, and then to the negotiators for Chisinau and Tiraspol.

The paper could not have been a surprise to Russian negotiator Aleksandr Novozhilov, because for six months the mediators had been discussing the need in principle for security guarantees of any settlement, and the OSCE had raised the subject with Deputy Foreign Minister

Trubnikov during our last meeting just about a month before (see chapter 5). Nevertheless, when Jacobovits informed Novozhilov and Ukrainian ambassador Chaliy of his intention to present the document at the five-sided meeting, Novozhilov took vehement exception, arguing that the issue and the paper should first be coordinated among the mediators. When Jacobovits presented the paper at the full session of the talks, Novozhilov denounced the action, stated that he considered the document to be unofficial and without standing, and announced that Russia reserved the right to present its own paper. In another meeting of the mediators the next day, Novozhilov continued to complain about the OSCE's failure to consult with Russia. When Jacobovits and I expressed readiness for such consultations, Novozhilov stubbornly refused to respond to any proposed date or place. Finally, he refused to sign any record of the negotiating round that even contained a factual record of the paper's distribution, explaining that as far as he was concerned it was not an official negotiating document.[42]

Both Şova and Litskai expressed satisfaction at receiving a substantive proposal. The Moldovan reaction was basically favorable. Chisinau remained ready to discuss the paper in the five-sided negotiations, and supportive of the idea of a multinational peacekeeping force under Western control. From a different angle, Litskai was happy to receive the paper, both because it gave him concrete insight into the OSCE's thinking about security guarantees and also because it would help flush out the Russians. For the time being, Tiraspol took no official position on the paper or the general subject. At a meeting later in July, I had the chance to ask Smirnov about his position on the subject. He inquired: "Mr. Hill, do you know the position of the Russian Federation on this question?" I responded that, as far as I knew, Russia had not yet taken an official stance on the paper or the issue. "You know," he continued, "We are allies of Russia. When the Russian Federation has a position, that will be our position."[43]

The Dutch OSCE Chairmanship kept after the issue. Following the general European break for vacations in August, my Dutch colleagues asked me to join them for consultations in Moscow and Kiev on September 10–12. In Moscow, Daan Everts, head of the Dutch OSCE Task Force, met with Russian deputy foreign minister Vladimir Chizhov, who was charged with overall OSCE matters, while the rest of us met with the ministry's area specialists for Moldova. All of us then met with Trubnikov, with whom we raised the question of security guarantees for a Transdniestrian settlement, the Dutch food-for-thought paper, and the need for consultations. By the end of the discussion, Trubnikov had agreed in principle to try to schedule working-level expert—civilian and military—discussions on security issues involved in the Moldova-Transdniestria settlement process.[44]

It turned out that we had not talked with the right guy. After the Dutch returned home and began the process of arranging what we all thought were the agreed-on consultations, they were informed that Deputy Minister Trubnikov had strayed into unauthorized territory. European security issues, which included the Adapted Conventional Armed Forces in Europe Treaty and peacekeeping in Moldova, fell in the bailiwick of Deputy Minister Chizhov, who did not agree that such working-level consultations were either timely or necessary. The Dutch kept after the Russians for the remainder of their OSCE Chairmanship, but it soon became clear that Chizhov apparently had the last word on this subject. We later learned that Moscow had a very different concept of how to handle peacekeeping for a Transdniestrian settlement.[45]

Chapter 8

The Summer of 2003:
Pressing for a Settlement

The Joint Constitutional Commission
Finally Gets to Work

While work proceeded and then ran into trouble or ground to a halt on the Russian military withdrawal, border monitoring, and peace consolidation mission, the Moldovan and Transdniestrian negotiators labored steadily to seek a formula that would allow the substantive work of the Joint Constitutional Commission (JCC) to get under way. Most of the energy of the three mediators was spent on attempting to find some flexibility in the Moldovan position. The Moldovan insistence on meeting only in Chisinau eroded somewhat, as Ion Creanga eventually allowed that he was authorized to agree to meet in the Organization for Security and Cooperation in Europe (OSCE) Mission office in Chisinau, at the Moldovan government Dniestr River resort at Golercani, or at a mutually agreed-on foreign location. In response, Transdniestrian delegation head Yevgeniy Shevchuk simply repeated his offer to meet on an alternating basis in Chisinau and Tiraspol. Chisinau had no rationale for its stubbornness that was convincing to external observers, so Tiraspol was clearly winning the public relations battle:

The Transdniestrians have largely been content to sit on the sidelines and watch this debacle develop. Transdniestrian deputy speaker and JCC delegation head Shevchuk seems to me genuinely interested in producing a good result, but his preparations and activities are also self-serving, as they make Tiraspol look good to international observers. Transdniestrian negotiator Litskai has been pursuing a separate agenda of establishing direct contact with Venice Commission and EU representatives, the better to counteract Moldovan allegations of Transdniestrian iniquities in various international fora. The current impasse clearly fulfills Transdniestrian hopes that Moldova would not be able to follow through on Voronin's initiative. This will allow Transdniestria to pose as the willing negotiating partner, while Moldova abandons its own proposal.[1]

By mid-June, even though the impasse seemed to work in Tiraspol's favor, Shevchuk was becoming visibly annoyed by Creanga's inability to agree to any proposed compromise on the meeting site and size of delegations. Shevchuk attended a June 16 session at the OSCE Mission in Chisinau only after I sent him a personal appeal. The two chairs again failed to reach agreement on the key disputed points at that session, and adjourned until June 25. However, during the session Shevchuk suggested that the JCC could meet at an office in Bendery furnished by the OSCE Mission, a new element in the now-familiar recitation of the positions of the two sides.[2]

We met again on June 25 with Creanga and Shevchuk in the OSCE Mission office in Chisinau. Consultations with their respective leaders had produced little movement on the two key questions. There was no agreement at all on the site for JCC sessions. On delegation size, both were able to agree on three persons each, but Creanga said he did not have authorization to accept the rotation of Transdniestrian delegation members. All other elements in the proposed JCC procedures were fully agreed upon. I therefore persuaded Creanga and Shevchuk to attend the next scheduled meeting of the five-sided negotiations, which was scheduled for July 3 in Tiraspol. Creanga said he could come, because he would be attending as part of the Moldovan negotiating delegation, and not as head of delegation at a JCC meeting.[3]

To put the pressure on them to agree on procedures and begin substantive JCC work, I noted that international experts were eager to come to Moldova to assist, and proposed inviting them before the end of July, when European vacations traditionally set in. Both agreed to an expert visit. Creanga provided me with a list of six topics he asked the experts to address:

- the legality and legitimacy of a federation,
- bases for the necessity of creating a federation,

- the transformations of unitary states into federal states,
- the division of competencies between the center and subjects in a federation,
- the composition and election of a Senate in a federation, and
- regionalization as a form of resolving the conflicts, status, and competencies of regions.

Shevchuk promised to give me a list of topics of interest at the July 3 negotiating session. I immediately got in touch with my colleagues at the EU and Venice Commission to arrange for an expert visit during the week of July 20.[4]

In the next two days, I had meetings scheduled with Smirnov and Voronin. The June 26 session with Smirnov was largely devoted to other troublesome topics, although in the course of our conversation I made sure he was on board with Shevchuk's suggestion that the JCC could meet at an OSCE office in Bendery. The crucial link was my discussion with President Voronin, which took place on June 27. I told the president bluntly that his initiative was going to fail unless we could find some reasonable compromise on the site for the JCC meetings. I noted that we had tried all sorts of reasonable proposals, and then came around to the suggestion that the OSCE provide a neutral site in Bendery. Voronin sighed deeply, and agreed to my proposed solution so quickly that I was astonished (I hope I hid my surprise). Remembering his days in the 1980s as head of the Bendery City Party Committee, the president began to talk expansively about possible locations in Bendery that the mission could use. He also agreed readily that the Transdniestrians could rotate the composition of their delegation at each meeting, just as long as they only had three delegation members participating in each session. Finally, President Voronin was enthusiastic at the prospect of the early arrival of international experts to assist in the work of the JCC. After a month and a half of pushing against a stone wall, it was almost a surreal feeling to reach agreement so quickly and easily.[5]

At the July 3 negotiating session in the OSCE office in Tiraspol, the Moldovan and Transdniestrian negotiators formally agreed to the compromises I had reached with President Voronin. The two sides agreed that the cochairs of the delegations would meet on July 10 in the OSCE Mission office in Chisinau to sign the agreed-on procedures and to exchange ideas on the basic structure of the new Constitution, and that the JCC's first formal, substantive meeting would take place in Bendery during the week of July 14–18. Both sides assured me that their delegations had been working in private, and that they had outlines and drafts of some sections ready for exchange and discussion.[6]

Representatives of all three mediators were delighted that we had finally resolved the impasse vis-à-vis the JCC. However, our optimism was tempered by the growing economic and administrative quarrels between Chisinau and Tiraspol, which cast a pall over the entire July 3–4 round. At the time, I reported to The Hague with mixed feelings:

> Reaching agreement at last on the procedures for the JCC was welcome, but I expect tough sledding soon after the Commission begins substantive work. Furthermore, the mounting tension in the economic field, with increasingly shrill denunciations and threats of retaliation, cast a threatening pall over the entire negotiation process. Smirnov's limited cutoff of electricity to the Moldovan villages near Dubossary is almost certainly an intentional shot across Chisinau's bow. I interpret the action to imply further such measures if the problems of Transdniestrian enterprises with Moldovan customs and registration are not resolved soon to Tiraspol's liking. On the positive side, we now have agreement from Chisinau and Tiraspol for their economic experts to meet to try to work out solutions to questions such as customs processing, enterprise registration, collection of revenues, and budget allocations. On the negative side, the current tone in their dialogue suggests they will have trouble keeping the economic working group going, let alone getting anything done in it.[7]

On July 10, Creanga and Shevchuk finally signed the JCC procedures at the OSCE Mission office in Chisinau. They also exchanged outlines of the proposed new Constitution. The Moldovan draft duplicated almost exactly the outline of the current constitution of the Republic of Moldova. A chapter was added for the "Autonomous Territorial Entity of Transdniestria." Surprisingly, the Transdniestrian draft did not differ markedly from the Moldovan paper, except for a separate section on federal structures and procedures. Creanga and Shevchuk scheduled the first full meeting of the JCC for July 21 in Bendery, at which they agreed to exchange draft sections of the constitutions on the "Rights and Obligations of Citizens."[8]

The July 21 date was a favor to me and the OSCE Mission. President Voronin had not seen Bendery in a decade and a half, and his memories of suitable real estate in the city no longer matched the lamentable post-

Soviet reality. There was a significant shortage of both residential and office buildings, and most available premises were empty because they were uninhabitable ruins. My resourceful Dutch OSCE Mission administrative chief, Jelle Marseille, scoured the city and finally found a small four-room house near the city center that needed major repairs—including one corner sinking, with two cracked walls—but was otherwise structurally sound and clean enough to fix up in two weeks or less. Marseille hired local contractors and workers, who labored around the clock. We finished the essential repairs, including plastering and painting, sometime between the evening of July 20 and the morning of July 21. We were able to hang the OSCE flag and welcome the delegations, international experts, and hordes of reporters (a large crowd, even for Moldova) for the formal opening.

Once agreement was reached on a place to meet, the JCC engaged in a flurry of activity during July. Constitutional experts from the Council of Europe held a joint seminar and separate meetings with JCC members to provide general and specific advice on the process of drafting a Constitution. From comments and interventions by members of both delegations at that seminar and from individual conversations, it was clear that there was a significant gap between the Moldovan and Transdniestrian approaches to writing a new Constitution. Remarkably, this gap was concentrated almost entirely in the respective understandings of the two sides as to how the federation was to be constructed. The Transdniestrian representatives insisted that the new federation was to be formed by means of an agreement (*dogovor*) between two previously existing state entities, or, as Smirnov was fond of repeating, "on a treaty basis" (*na dogovornoi osnove*). Just as persistently, the Moldovan representatives maintained that a federal state would be formed by the devolution of authority from the central authorities to the authorities of a region within an already-existing Moldovan state. This conceptual difference was the chief and most difficult difference of principle between Chisinau and Tiraspol.[9]

Surprisingly, there were relatively few normative disagreements between the delegations from Chisinau and Tiraspol in most of the other areas to be covered by the new Constitution. Both delegations readily accepted the basic UN and European documents on human rights and political liberties as the bases for the new fundamental law. (This did not necessarily mean, in particular on Tiraspol's part, that they were prepared to observe and implement these documents in reality.) The JCC eventually produced one chapter of the proposed new Constitution, covering human rights and obligations of citizens, which showed a surprising degree of agreement between the two sides. However, the JCC members from Chisinau and Tiraspol were in almost total disagreement over the most important issues in the chapter on state structure and institutions, reflecting the devolution-versus-treaty disparity.

Once started, the work of the JCC continued steadily into August, and beyond. The delegations met regularly, and drafted and exchanged sections of the proposed new Constitution. OSCE Mission members and diplomats from the Russian and Ukrainian embassies in Chisinau usually attended the sessions. However industrious the labor of the individual delegation members, during the rest of 2003 the JCC's overall work sank into an ever-deeper impasse over the chapter on the bases of the structure of the state. In the end, neither domestic nor international constitutional experts were able to overcome the underlying chasm between the political approaches of the left and right banks to the basic character of a political settlement.

This fundamental difference of principle on how to form a federation was apparent to the mediators in the political settlement process from relatively early in the year. Much of the mediators' discussion in their own meetings and in the negotiating rounds was devoted to the need for a "political document" as the basis for a settlement, and what should be in this document. Once the various obstacles were overcome and the JCC started its substantive work, the OSCE Chair, in consultation with a few key OSCE states, decided it might help the process if the OSCE introduced a paper proposing generally acceptable compromise solutions to the key questions of state structure and the division of powers. Given the state of the settlement process at the end of July, OSCE representatives in The Hague, Vienna, and Chisinau generally agreed that this paper should be as comprehensive as possible, to serve as a basis for reaching agreement in the five-sided talks and for guiding the JCC's drafting work. The Dutch OSCE Chair agreed to give the OSCE Mission to Moldova first crack at producing such a draft.[10]

Kozak Enters the Scene

It was against the background of these events in the summer of 2003 that Voronin's earlier initiative with President Putin began to bear fruit. On July 8–9, the head of the Russian Federation's Presidential Administration,

Aleksandr Voloshin, paid an extremely low-key visit to Chisinau. Putin's chief of staff met with President Voronin, but the local and Russian press reported little more than the fact of the meeting.[11] On July 24, President Voronin's press service reported a long conversation with Putin, during which the two chiefs of state discussed the Transdniestrian settlement process and the work of the JCC, as well as an official visit to Moldova by President Putin in November 2003.[12] Then, at the end of July, Dmitri Kozak, Voloshin's deputy and the chief constitutional expert for the Russian Presidential Administration, turned up in Moldova without advance announcement or explanation.

Press reports of Kozak's initial visit to Chisinau and Tiraspol were meager.[13] Subsequent explanations claimed that he was offering advice and assistance to the Moldovan and Transdniestrian participants in drafting the new federal Constitution. The report seemed odd, because a team of constitutional experts, largely from the Council of Europe's Venice Commission but also including constitutional experts from Ukraine and Russia, was in Chisinau and Tiraspol in the latter part of July to meet with the JCC's Moldovan and Transdniestrian members to assist in the negotiation and drafting process.[14] At least a couple of senior diplomats from the Russian Embassy in Chisinau were following the work of the JCC, and they said nothing about the Kozak visit.[15]

From July to August 2003, the work of the JCC was at its most active. The JCC met steadily, and a number of draft sections of the proposed new Constitution were completed by each delegation, exchanged, and distributed to the mediators, and in some cases released to the press. With the assistance of hindsight, it is relatively easy to understand that without external assistance this process was going nowhere. However, at the time hopes were high among the public in both Chisinau and Tiraspol, as well as with a number of the mediators who had not seen representatives of the two sides ever work together so closely and actively.

Yet at the same time, in mid-August I received a strange visit from the chief Moldovan negotiator in the five-sided political settlement talks, Minister of Reintegration Vasile Șova. Without much explanation, Șova gave me a relatively detailed Russian-language draft settlement document. The paper was roughly similar in content and scope to the July 2002 Kiev Document, which prescribed state structures and governmental institutions for a united federal Moldovan state. In response to my questions, Șova intimated that the document had been drafted by a narrow circle of Voronin advisers "together" with Kozak. Șova could not or would not specify for me the nature of Kozak's involvement in the Transdniestrian settlement process, in particular his relationship—if any—with the five-sided talks. Şova was clear only that the whole matter was extremely confidential; I inferred from his remarks that it would be useful for me to have a copy of this draft, but I should not inform anyone that I had it.[16]

The authors of the draft Şova shared with me clearly drew heavily on the 2002 Kiev Document in both style and substance. The paper was in the form of a formal agreement between Moldova and Transdniestria, to be signed by the Moldovan president, the Transdniestrian leader, and the heads of the two legislatures. The document was meant to establish an agreed-on framework for the new Constitution being drafted. The proposal called for the reintegration of Transdniestria into a federal Moldovan state, to consist of three federal entities—Transdniestria, Gagauzia, and the remaining territory of the current Republic of Moldova. There was apparently some doubt or dispute about including Gagauzia in the agreement as a federal entity, because all the references to Gagauzia in the text were in italics.[17]

The August draft specified that the head of the reunited Moldovan state would be the president, to be elected by a direct nationwide ballot (as opposed to the parliamentary system established in the 2000 constitutional amendment). The president would nominate, and the legislature would confirm, the prime minister and the government. There was to be a bicameral legislature, with a lower, 101-seat House of Representatives to be elected from a single nationwide electoral district (as was already the case on the right bank). The upper house, or Senate, was to consist of 25 members, chosen by direct ballot on a geographic basis, with 3 from Gaguzia, 10 from Transdniestria, and 12 from right-bank Moldova. Laws vetoed by the president or rejected by the Senate could be passed with a two-thirds vote of the House of Representatives.[18]

The draft agreement included the right of secession for Transdniestria if Moldova were to become part of another state (i.e., Romania). Both Moldovan (Romanian) and Russian were to be state languages. The proposal reserved defense, foreign relations, monetary policy, energy, citizenship, and borders exclusively for the federal government. There was a long list of other powers, many of them less important governmental powers, to be shared among the federal subjects, including law enforcement, civil and criminal law, environmental protection, federal budget and taxes, and land rights and use. All powers not specified as exclusive federal or joint competencies were to be reserved for the Transdniestrian authorities. The powers left for Tiraspol alone by this draft were relatively inconsequential. The proposed division of powers was muddled even more by indecision on whether to include Gagauzia as a full subject or simply to refer to the existing 1994 law on Gagauz autonomy.[19]

The Genesis of the Mediators' Document

Meanwhile, in August, I was busy with preparation of the OSCE's own proposed settlement document, which we hoped might break the growing deadlock in the five-sided talks and the JCC. It had become clear in the five-sided talks' initial sessions in 2003 that work on the Kiev Document had run out of steam. At the July 3–4 negotiating round, the OSCE Mission presented all the participants with a list of potential provisions of a comprehensive political document that had been agreed on since the introduction of the Kiev Document. Our negotiating partners, without exception, were not impressed.[20]

With the increasing likelihood that the JCC would not be able to reach a consensus on the basic structures and institutions of a federal state, the OSCE Chair and I agreed that by the end of the summer break I would complete a draft document for a comprehensive political settlement in Transdniestria.[21] After agreeing among ourselves (within the OSCE Chair and Mission to Moldova) on the draft, we would coordinate it with our fellow mediators from Russia and Ukraine, before presenting it to Chisinau and Tiraspol as a possible basis for reaching compromise solutions to these key issues.[22]

At the September 4–5, 2003, round of the five-sided negotiations, the OSCE (Adriaan Jacobovits and I), according to plan, noted the lack of progress in the settlement talks and the JCC and offered to try to construct a draft of proposed common elements that could facilitate reaching greater agreement between Chisinau and Tiraspol. All four other participants—Russia, Ukraine, Moldova, and Transdniestria—accepted the OSCE's suggestion. We agreed that the three mediators would meet later in the month somewhere in Europe to finalize an agreed-on draft that could then be presented to the sides.[23]

During the September 4 mediators' meeting, I reviewed the reports we were likely to hear during the full negotiating round from the Moldovan and Transdniestrian economic experts, as well as the contributions of the chief negotiators, Şova and Litskai. I inquired whether there were reports from other contacts or mediation activities, an effort to elicit some explanation from the Russians of Kozak's activities. Russian negotiator Novozhilov speculated about the utility and productivity of including economic experts or JCC members on the agenda of the five-sided talks. He avoided any mention of Kozak.[24]

During the formal negotiating round, both Şova and Litskai, as the mediators had requested at the end of July round, presented written proposals of what their side wished to be included in any framework political settlement document. Both Şova and Litskai indicated they could sign an interim document containing a proposed delimitation of competencies between the federal center and one or more subjects of the federation, which could then be used by the JCC as a basis for drafting the details of a Constitution. Although there was significant overlap between the Moldovan and Transdniestrian positions as iterated by Şova and Litskai, the key differences over state structures remained. Şova insisted that the sides were drafting a new Constitution for the Republic of Moldova, establishing a federation on an asymmetrical basis, with Chisinau the senior partner. Litskai repeated Tiraspol's standard refrain about a federation of two equals *"na dogovornoi osnove* [on a treaty basis]." However, in the final protocol of the round, both supported the modest offer of the mediators to prepare a draft "general political document."[25] I had formal agreement to introduce a document whose preparation was already well under way.

My draft became the eventual "Proposals and Recommendations of the Three Mediators" or so-called Mediators' Document, which was agreed to by Russia, Ukraine, and the OSCE in October 2003 but formally presented to Chisinau and Tiraspol only in February 2004 (for the text of this document, see appendix A).[26] I used a number of previous documents from the Transdniestrian settlement process as templates for the document's structure and scope. To construct an asymmetric federation that might be acceptable to both sides, I drew heavily on structures and practices from Canada and Spain, in particular Catalonia. The initial drafts of the document were seen and critiqued by experts from the Netherlands, the European Union, the United States, and the Venice Commission. By mid-September, the process was far enough along to schedule a meeting at the OSCE Mission to Croatia's office in Zagreb with our colleagues from Ukraine and Russia to work out a coordinated draft for presentation in the five-sided talks.

Chapter 9

The Competing Negotiations

Initial OSCE Encounters with Kozak

On September 22, 2003, I had a meeting scheduled with Smirnov in Tiraspol to go over a long list of outstanding unresolved or disputed issues that were hindering the settlement process. As I waited in Smirnov's outer office, a figure emerged from his inner office who seemed uncannily familiar to me. I wondered to myself "Who can this Transdniestrian be? I thought I knew everyone who works closely with Smirnov." The Transdniestrian negotiator Valeriy Litskai, who was waiting with me, introduced this unfamiliar *pridniestrovets* as Dmitri Kozak, whom I then recalled from a recent photo in the local press.

During our meeting, Smirnov lit into Kozak and Russia for allegedly pushing an unproductive approach in the settlement talks, favorable to Chisinau. Smirnov gave me two documents. The first, he said, was an unbalanced draft that Kozak was allegedly trying to get the Transdniestrians to accept. The second, Smirnov continued, was Tiraspol's preferred solution to the basic questions involved in constructing a united federal Moldovan state. During the conversation, Smirnov did not offer any insight or enlightenment into the relationship of Kozak's work to the five-sided political settlement process.[1]

The first document Smirnov gave me was clearly a reworking of the paper Şova had given me in August, but with a number of changes. From subsequent conversations with Moldovan and Transdniestrian colleagues, we in the Organization for Security and Cooperation in Europe (OSCE) Mission learned that this second draft was the result of at least a month of steady work by Kozak with Voronin, Smirnov, and a small circle of Voronin's most trusted advisers. These included presidential political adviser Mark Tkachuk, deputy speaker and old-line Communist Party leader Vadim Mişin, and parliamentary legal adviser (and later presidential administration adviser) Artur Reşetnikov. Moldovan negotiator Şova apparently took part in this process only intermittently. Kozak and the Moldovan drafters reportedly finished on September 11 the draft that I received on the 22nd. Colleagues in Chisinau also claimed that Mişin and Reşetnikov had accepted this draft on behalf of the Moldovan side.[2]

Like its August 21 predecessor, the September 11 draft was cast in the form of an agreement between Moldova and Transdniestria, to be signed by the leaders of the two sides (not identified as president) and the chairs of the two legislative bodies. The aim was still to assist in drafting a new Constitution of the Republic of Moldova, thus reflecting Chisinau's stand on devolution. The draft refers explicitly to reintegration of a single state based on federal principles. If anything, the September 11 draft had been strengthened to reflect Chisinau's view of Moldova as a single, unified state, with unified defense, customs, and financial structures. Transdniestria was accorded the status of a subject of the federation, with the right to its own Constitution, state property, budget, and tax system. Gagauzia was not explicitly accorded the status of a subject of the federation, although the September 11 draft speaks of strengthening Gagauz status, taking into account the provisions of this memorandum.[3]

The new draft made Moldovan the single state language, and accorded Russian the status of an official language throughout the state. The division of powers between Chisinau and Tiraspol remained much the same as in the August draft. The September draft more clearly reflected the shared and exclusive competencies of the Gagauz Autonomy, which had remained in italics with question marks in the August redaction.[4]

The September draft returned election of the federal president to the Parliament, which was also slightly altered in this variant. The lower house—the House of Representatives—was now to consist of only seventy-one deputies, to be elected in a single nationwide electoral district. The Senate, or upper house, was to include twenty-six senators, with five from Gagauzia and eight from Transdniestria. The House of Representatives could overcome a presidential veto or a veto by the Senate of ordinary legislation by a two-thirds vote. A Senate veto of an organic law was to be absolute. Provisions for the government and the judicial branch remained largely unchanged. The September 11 draft included no references to guarantee a political settlement.[5]

The September 22 Transdniestrian alternate draft that Smirnov gave me was meant to highlight in extreme form the major differences in approach between Chisinau and Tiraspol. The title of the paper referred to the "construction of a federal state formed by the Republic of Moldova and the Transdniestrian Moldovan Republic," an idea that was anathema to Moldovan negotiators. The Transdniestrian draft referred to the new state as the legal successor to the Republic of Moldova. The other major difference in the Tiraspol paper lay in the role of the Senate. The upper house could approve legislation only after approval by both the Moldovan and Transdniestrian legislative organs. The Senate possessed an absolute veto over all federal legislation, which could be overcome only by a new vote of the Senate. The Transdniestrian draft mentioned the need for international guarantees, but it did not specify any.[6]

None of the other negotiators took the Transdniestrian paper seriously, and neither Smirnov nor his negotiators followed up on it after he gave it to me. Although after eight years I am still not sure whether Smirnov meant for me to take it seriously, the paper clearly reflects the basic Transdniestrian desire for a loose confederation. As such, it was dead on arrival with Chisinau, and no Western mediator would have pursued it seriously. The OSCE Mission, after all, had already concluded publicly in November 1993 that a confederation was not a realistic or viable solution to the Transdniestrian problem, and a decade of negotiation and evolution had not altered this assessment.[7]

What I found more interesting and helpful was the line-by-line analysis of the September 11 draft memorandum made by Transdniestrian negotiators and passed to me by Litskai. First of all, the paper was not polemical, but rather a serious effort to highlight points of disagreement and possibly acceptable rephrasings. Among the more important points in Litskai's analysis was Tiraspol's insistence that the settlement involved not the reintegration of a single state but rather the creation of a joint, common state. As such, Litskai called for the new fundamental law to be named the "Constitution of the Federal State of Moldova and Transdniestria." The Tiraspol comments also noted that the September 11 draft singled out only Transdniestria as a subject of the federation. "There cannot be a federation consisting of only one subject" the paper notes, and proposed calling both the Republic of Moldova and Transdniestria subjects of the new federation. The paper's comments on the division of competencies and state structures all grow out of this view of the federation as a new entity, uniting two previously existing state entities.[8]

The September 11 version of the Kozak paper obviously reflected and favored the Moldovan approach to a political settlement. Tiraspol's objections to the draft were clearly fundamental; responding to them was more than a matter of simple horse-trading. Smirnov and his henchmen clearly continued to push for nothing more confining than a loose confederation with Moldova, an idea that would never fly with Chisinau. It was not apparent whether this position bespoke a serious intent to resolve the conflict or simply reflected a cynical desire to preserve the status quo. After more than a decade in power, Smirnov understood full well where Moldovan leaders stood on the question of a confederation; we may never be able to pin down Smirnov's intent. The point is that a real gulf lay between Kozak's September 11 draft and Transdniestria's bottom line. In the end, Kozak had to move closer toward Tiraspol; the question was whether he could persuade Chisinau to move along with him.

The Zagreb Meeting: Progress on the Mediators' Document

The meeting of the mediators followed immediately after my September 22 session with Smirnov. Assembling in Zagreb on September 24–25, we began an article-by-article, line-by-line review of the draft political document that I had distributed to my colleagues a few days after the conclusion of the September 4–5 negotiating round.[9] We made good progress going through the draft but did not finish. We agreed to check with our capitals and to meet in Kiev in early October to continue our work on the document.

The Zagreb mediators' meeting produced one moment of high comedy when I tried to learn from our Russian colleague, Ambassador Aleksandr Novozhilov, what role Kozak was playing in the settlement process. I had traveled straight to Zagreb from Tiraspol, and I had not had a chance to tell most of my colleagues about the papers that Smirnov had given me. After our initial exchanges at the formal meeting, I asked Novozhilov whether the Russian Federation was pursuing a political settlement on a separate, parallel track. When Novozhilov offered a predictable, heated denial, I asked if he was sure that work was not proceeding on another document. Novozhilov replied "What document could you be talking about?" To which I replied "This document," and produced copies for everyone at the table of the latest Kozak draft.

Novozhilov glanced at the paper, and without apparent thought (or discomfiture) replied "Oh, *that* document!" As I recall, I had warned my OSCE colleagues of my intention just before the meeting, so there was relatively little visible reaction from our side. However, in years of close collaboration, I have never seen our Ukrainian colleagues—the ambassador to the OSCE (and later foreign minister), Wolodymir Ohrysko, and the ambassador to Moldova, Petr Chaliy—so wide-eyed and obviously stunned.

Once the incredulity from our Ukrainian colleagues subsided and the understandable recriminations passed, Novozhilov explained that Kozak was offering bilateral consultative assistance to the Moldovan and Transdniestrian Joint Constitutional Commission negotiators at the personal request of Moldovan president Voronin. Adriaan Jacobovits and I complained that Kozak's paper seemed to duplicate our draft and the work of the five-sided negotiations. Novozhilov responded that Kozak's efforts were not meant to supplant our work in the five-sided process, an explanation that none of us in Zagreb found convincing. As the furor from unmasking the Russians' parallel track subsided, we actually made a good bit of progress on my proposed draft, working perhaps 40 to 50 percent of the way through the text. However, we would clearly need more time on the effort, and we agreed to continue at the next mediators' meeting before the next round of negotiations in the first week of October.[10]

An OSCE Parliamentary Assembly Moldova Group seminar with legislators from Moldova and Transdniestria was scheduled in the Moldovan Nistru River resort town Vadul lui Voda early in the week following the Zagreb meeting. On Saturday, September 27, Finnish deputy Kimmo Kiljunen, head of the OSCE Parliamentary Assembly Moldova Group, I, and our wives made an informal visit to Tiraspol. The only working portion of this visit was to be a meeting for Kiljunen and me with Transdniestrian Supreme Soviet chairman Grigori Maracuţa, while our wives were to pass the time seeing the sights of the Transdniestrian "capital."

As we met Maracuţa on the front steps of the government building, I noticed one of the newer Russian Embassy vehicles parked a bit to the side of the main entrance. (I later learned that this was the vehicle used by one of the embassy counselors to chauffeur Kozak around Chisinau and Tiraspol.) With a big smile, Maracuţa inquired whether we would object if all of us were invited to meet their "president." Smirnov proceeded to spend two hours with us in an office call, devoted largely to complaints about Moldovan behavior and Russian pressure on Transdniestria. This meeting was followed by a 90-minute tour of the enormous new Sherrif football complex on the edge of town (which included two outdoor stadiums, one indoor stadium, two hotels, and eleven practice fields). To get to the stadium, Smirnov and Maracuţa piled into a new maroon official Volga sedan that Smirnov drove himself, without escort, at high speed through the weekend Tiraspol traffic. The tour flowed into a two-hour lunch at the official Dom Priemov (House of Receptions), where Smirnov received visiting delegations. After lunch, Smirnov wandered around the enormous fenced gardens next to the facility, greeting several wedding parties there for customary wreath-laying and photographs. The point was not that Smirnov had so much to say to us, but that all the while Kozak was cooling his heels waiting for Smirnov in the main government building.

On the margins of our traveling circus with Smirnov that Saturday, Transdniestrian negotiator Valeriy Litskai told me that the Russians were putting tremendous pressure on Tiraspol to agree to the Kozak draft before October 1, when the next round of five-sided negotiations was scheduled. Litskai said Moscow had threatened to annul the Russian passports of the Transdniestrian leaders and to restrict or prevent their travel to Russia, an especially serious threat after imposition earlier in the year of the U.S.-EU visa ban.

At a September 29 OSCE Mission reception for the OSCE Parliamentary Assembly, I persuaded the Russian Embassy's deputy chief of mission to schedule a meeting for me with Kozak, who remained in Moldova after the weekend. This is how I reported the September meeting with Kozak:

Finally on September 30 Ambassador Jacobovits and I succeeded in meeting with Kozak in the Russian Embassy in Chisinau. Kozak told us his involvement in the constitutional process was President Putin's response to President Voronin's request last spring for help in the negotiations. Kozak said most of his document had been worked out in collaboration with Moldovan negotiators. As such it [was] acceptable to Chisinau but not to Transdniestria. Kozak said the two sides [were] far apart, and expressed skepticism at prospects for bridging the conceptual gap quickly.

I gave Kozak copies of the OSCE draft and the mediators' paper worked out at Zagreb. I noted that although we had worked separately, we had arrived at very similar schemes for the structure of a possible federation in Moldova. I added that we had some differences over how to divide competencies between the center and the federal subjects; his draft had a lot of mixed competencies, while the OSCE draft followed the advice of the Venice Commission experts to eliminate mixed competencies as much as possible. Kozak replied that the high number of mixed competencies came from the Moldovan input, and did not square with his own preferences. I said all this gave me hope that we could work together, and made a pitch for coordination and collaboration. He agreed in principle, and Ambassador Jacobovits exacted from him a further commitment to look over our paper that evening and provide comments to Ambassador Novozhilov prior to our October 1 mediators' session.[11]

Completing the Mediators' Document

The mediators from Russia, Ukraine, and the OSCE held their customary tripartite meeting at the start of the October 1–2 round of five-sided talks. Kozak apparently heeded the OSCE request, as Russian negotiator Novozhilov arrived for the mediators' session with comments from Russian experts on the mediators' draft. We made good progress, and even inserted several changes to the mediators' text suggested by Kozak via Novozhilov. However, we could not finish before our meeting with the Moldovan and Transdniestrian negotiators. As we completed the negotiating round, I provided the following assessment of the situation to the OSCE Chair:

Where does the negotiating process go from here? On the plus side, there are reasonable compromise solutions being worked out among the mediators. Ukrainian representatives have been highly supportive during this process. After a period of freelancing by Russia, it appears that we now may have strong support and cooperation from our Russian colleagues, especially as the Maastricht ministerial meeting approaches. The big question is whether either side will accept the mediators' compromise now being worked out?

We will need strong Russian support and cooperation to convince Tiraspol. Smirnov is still trying to employ his long-established tactics of delay, divide, and evade. His aim appears to be to preserve the status quo as much and as long as possible. [This is unlikely to change] as long as there is no reasonable Moldovan proposal on the table and there is no real pressure from the mediators and the rest of the outside world.[12]

The three mediators agreed to meet again in Kiev on October 8–9, where we would complete the Mediators' Document. The hardest question proved to be one sentence on a postsettlement peacekeeping presence. The Russian negotiators did not wish to call explicitly for ending the current format dominated by Russian military forces. We worked out a rather convoluted compromise that we all accepted ad referendum. It took me a series of phone calls to Moscow and The Hague during the week of October 13–17 before the document was finally approved.[13] As a result, although we completed drafting the Mediators' Document by the end of the day on October 9, we did not reach an understanding on how or when to present it to the Moldovan and Transdniestrian negotiators. This would be a significant omission as the Kozak process developed in October and November.

The OSCE Chairman Seeks to Unite the Negotiating Efforts

The OSCE chairman in office (CiO), Jaap de Hoop Scheffer, tackled the problem created for the Transdniestrian settlement effort by the parallel Kozak process in two meetings with President Voronin in October and November 2003. The CiO attempted to get a clearer picture from Voronin as to the scope of Kozak's mandate, and he urged that the Kozak initiative be coordinated with, if not subsumed into, ongoing OSCE settlement efforts. Voronin's replies to Scheffer's inquiries only increased the confusion about what Kozak was doing and how it related to the five-sided settlement process. Meanwhile, the OSCE Mission obtained information from Moscow that indicated Chisinau and Tiraspol were deeply immersed in a tripartite drafting exercise on a settlement document that appeared to be consciously obscured from the OSCE, European Union, and United States. All efforts, even at the highest level, to convince our Moldovan interlocutors to come clean about what was going on proved in vain.

Adriaan Jacobovits and I traveled directly from Kiev to the Netherlands for an October 11 dinner meeting between CiO de Hoop Scheffer and President Voronin, to be followed by a Moldova-Netherlands football match in Eindhoven. President Voronin flew in with a large (forty persons or more) Moldovan delegation for a Saturday afternoon and evening of talks, food, and football. The Dutch hosted Voronin and his entourage for talks and dinner in an elegantly modern museum constructed in the original nineteenth-century Philips factory building. After a tour of the facility, we sat down to clarify the situation in the Transdniestrian settlement process over dinner.

The exchange between CiO de Hoop Scheffer and President Voronin was strange.[14] Voronin gave a relatively upbeat assessment of the ongoing process of removing the vast stores of aging ammunition stored at the Russian base in Colbasna in the north of the Transdniestrian region.[15] Voronin praised and thanked the Dutch OSCE Chairmanship for its activity, and asserted that we were closer than ever to achieving a political settlement of the Transdniestrian question. He noted that the Joint Constitutional Commission had finished the chapter on human rights of the new Constitution, which all participants had assumed would be the easiest. However, Voronin added, Chisinau had not been able to settle political differences with Tiraspol over other portions of the new Constitution.

Voronin placed Kozak's involvement in this context. The Moldovan president claimed Kozak was working with Chisinau and Tiraspol on the chapter of the new Constitution involving the delimitation of competencies between the center and the federal entities. Voronin related that he had met with Kozak the previous day, there now remained eight points of disagreement between Chisinau and Tiraspol, and the Transdniestrian leaders needed to make decisions on these points. If the two sides were successful in reaching a consensus on all points, they could present the agreed-on package to their respective legislative organs for approval.

CiO de Hoop Scheffer repeatedly asked President Voronin what was the relationship between Kozak's activities and the mediation role currently being played by the OSCE. De Hoop Scheffer noted that in a recent conversation Russian foreign minister Igor Ivanov had agreed that Kozak's and the OSCE's activities aimed at resolving the Transdniestrian conflict should be closely coordinated. The CiO several times made the plea that the OSCE and Kozak should be in close contact, to avoid duplication of effort or working at cross purposes.

In response, President Voronin repeatedly avoided answering the question about any relationship between Kozak and the OSCE. Instead,

Voronin described Kozak as a mediator, a "tough guy," whose task was to help the Moldovan and Transdniestrian sides. Voronin asserted that Kozak was active in Moldova at President Putin's behest, and related in some detail the chronology of his involvement. The president further claimed that there was nothing secret about Kozak's mission; the Moldovans said relatively little in public about his activities only because they feared leaks. At the end of the meeting, under extreme pressure, Voronin agreed that political adviser Tkachuk would brief me in the near future in Chisinau about the eight remaining points of disagreement, thereby bringing the OSCE a bit closer to the Kozak effort. The president did not offer to share with us any text from the Kozak process, nor did he indicate any willingness to include the OSCE in the negotiations between the two sides currently facilitated by Kozak.

On October 12, I flew to Washington for several days of consultations on the current state of the political settlement negotiations and the ongoing process of removing ammunition from the Colbasna depot to the Russian Federation. (The United States had donated more than $15 million to support OSCE assistance for the removal or destruction of Russian arms and ammunition stored in the Transdniestrian region.) During the week of October 13, I was on the phone every day with my negotiating counterparts in The Hague and Moscow to reach agreement on the remaining disputed sentences of the "Mediators' Document," which concerned the transition from the current peacekeeping operation to a multinational force. We settled on a final text by October 17; unfortunately, there was still no understanding among the Russian, Ukrainian, and OSCE representatives on when and how to present the document.

I returned to Chisinau over the weekend of October 18–19, and sought a meeting as soon as possible with the presidential political adviser, Mark Tkachuk. I brought copies of the now informally agreed-on "Mediators' Document," which I thought I might either pass unofficially and informally or quote in some detail during our discussion. In return, I hoped to receive at least the highly touted eight points of remaining disagreement between Chisinau and Tiraspol in the Kozak document. Tkachuk and I had an extremely friendly conversation that lasted well more than two hours and covered the waterfront of issues actively under discussion in the political settlement negotiations and the Joint Constitutional Commission. However, no matter how hard or how inventively I tried to raise the subject, I received neither texts nor substantive oral description of the infamous eight points of disagreement.[16]

Movement on the Kozak Draft

Immediately before my meeting with Tkachuk (October 23), I had a long session with Kozak at the Russian Embassy in Chisinau. I found Kozak friendly and engaging, but either unwilling or unable to provide much substantive information on his talks with the two sides. I gave him a copy of what I hoped was the final redaction of the Mediators' Document, and repeated my plea that we join our two processes. He demurred, claiming that his Moldovan interlocutors were against this. He asserted that there were still great gaps on most of the key substantive issues between Chisinau and Tiraspol.[17]

However unforthcoming my Moldovan and Russian colleagues proved on this subject, I was able to call on friends and contacts in Moscow who possessed and were willing to provide a detailed description of the differences of text and principle between Chisinau and Tiraspol. As of late October, there remained so many difficult, disputed points between the two sides that it was hard to see how they would come to agreement on a comprehensive document.

In a working Russian draft dated October 22, one could discern how many of the disputed provisions of the memorandum had moved toward the overall Transdniestrian position. Characterized for the moment as a joint memorandum of the Moldovan Parliament and the Transdniestrian Supreme Soviet, the draft stated that the settlement would be achieved through the transformation of the state structure of the Republic of Moldova with the aim of building a single federal state.[18] This idea was clearly closer to Tiraspol's concept of the union of two equal state entities. The October 22 draft also introduced for the first time, based on a Transdniestrian proposal, a new name for the federal state—the Federative Republic of Moldova.

The October 22 redaction eliminated specific references to the work of the Joint Constitutional Commission, instead merely asserting that the list of basic principles that followed in the text should be reflected in the Constitution of the united state. The change was especially significant, because it also eliminated specific references to the assistance of international experts from the OSCE, European Union, and Council of Europe's Venice Commission. In short, assisting in the elimination of differences between the sides and development of the new Constitution became de facto a Russian monopoly.

For the first time also issues of military security appeared in the draft memorandum. Immediately after noting that the federation should have unified territory with a single system of government, customs, defense and currency, the draft asserted that the federation was a neutral demilitarized state. Until full demilitarization could be attained, the armed forces should be structured along territorial lines and could not be used to ensure internal order or security.

On the issue of territorial status within the federation, the October 22 draft defined both Transdniestria and Gagauzia as subjects of the federation. The bulk of the right bank currently under Chisinau's control was alternatively defined by Chisinau and Tiraspol as "federal territory" or a "federal district." In addition, Tiraspol wanted to call Transdniestria a "state formation in the composition of the federation," thereby underscoring the region's claim to statehood independent of its union or subordination to Chisinau. On language, Chisinau proposed Moldovan as the state language and Russian as an official language. Tiraspol proposed that there be three state languages throughout the federation—Moldovan, Russian, and Ukrainian.

The division of competencies between the central (or federal) government and the Transdniestrian federal subject had not changed dramatically, except with respect to defense and security. Given the references at the beginning of the draft to the neutrality and demilitarization of the federation, the October 22 draft enumeration of federal competencies removed "defense and security" from the list, leaving only control over the production, sale, and purchase of arms, munitions, and toxic substances. The October 22 list of shared competencies reflected increased Transdniestrian insistence on having greater local control over the administration of civil and criminal justice.

On state structures, the October draft returned to a system of direct election of the president from a nationwide electoral district. The House of Representatives and Senate remained unchanged from the September 11 draft, except that Tiraspol proposed a transition period until 2015, during which a three-fourths majority in the Senate would be required for the passage of all organic laws of the federation. This took on added significance in that legislation affecting all shared competencies was to be adopted via organic laws. Finally, Tiraspol proposed that any amendment of the federal Constitution require a four-fifths vote of the Senate.

Looking back, it is easy to see in the October draft almost all the elements of the completed Kozak *Memorandum* that was almost accepted in late November. At the time, it was not so easy to foresee any convergence of views emerging in any reasonable amount of time out of this disjointed document. In many places, in the text dissenting Moldovan or Transdniestrian variants were noted in italics. However, there were no indications of how far apart the sides were on each particular issue, and no discussion of what trade-offs might be available to persuade one or another of the parties to relent on any particular point. Therefore, judging by the overall appearance of this document and what Kozak told me on October 23, it seemed a reasonable assumption that Chisinau and Tiraspol would not soon reach full agreement on the basic issues essential for a political settlement.

The negotiators had scheduled the next round of the five-sided political settlement talks for the last week of October. Russian negotiator Aleksandr Novozhilov was characteristically unforthcoming (though uncharacteristically tight-lipped) about how things were going in the parallel Kozak process. In their usual preliminary meeting, the mediators went over the final text of their "Proposals and Recommendations," checking the few final points that had been agreed on by phone after the Kiev meeting. However, the mediators (Novozhilov, Chaliy, Ohrysko, Jacobovits, and I) were unable to reach full agreement on how and when to present this document to the Moldovans and Transdniestrians. With continued pressure on this question from the OSCE, the negotiators finally agreed to include in the protocol of the negotiating round a formal request from the mediators to the Moldovan and Transdniestrian negotiators for assistance in arranging meetings to present the document to the leadership in Moldova and Transdniestria.[19]

The rest of the late October negotiating round was discouraging. As had become customary, we heard from representatives of the Joint Constitutional Commission, who had no progress to report. The almost agreed-on draft section of the new Constitution on human rights was still out for comment by international experts at the Venice Commission and the EU. The two delegations had not resolved any important differences about the key section on state structures and institutions.[20]

More distressing, Chisinau and Tiraspol were quarrelling ever more bitterly about almost every aspect of their day-to-day working relations. Local Transdniestrian authorities continued to hamper the work of the Moldovan-administered Romanian-language schools in Transdniestrian-held territory. In particular, the seizure by local authorities of a newly constructed school building in the northern city of Ribniţa remained unresolved. Representatives of both sides continued to challenge and provoke one another in the central portion of the Security Zone around Dubossary, where Chisinau controls two separate small enclaves on the left bank. Transdniestrian police posts, established in violation of the 1992 cease-fire agreement, constantly interfered with daily travel of Moldovan farmers and workers to and from their fields and jobs in Transdniestrian controlled territory. The negotiators invited the cochairs of the Joint Control Commission, which supervised the peacekeeping operation in the Security Zone, to attend our meeting. In a heated discussion, all agreed that the decisions of the commission were not being respected, but no one could come up with an agreeable means of enforcement. The Moldovans called on the Russian peacekeepers to undertake coercive measures; the Russian delegation chief called on Chisinau and Tiraspol to implement decisions to which they had agreed.[21]

The main point of contention was the so-called telephone war. On September 8, 2003, the Moldovan authorities announced that they were beginning tests of a new digital television system from transmitters located about 25 kilometers west of Bendery. Residents of the area, in particular on the left bank, soon discovered that the new Moldovan television system was broadcasting on precisely the frequencies used by the Transdniestrian CDMA mobile telephone network. As long as the Moldovan television towers were transmitting (and that was round the clock), Transdniestrian mobile telephones would not work. After an exchange of inquiries and then recriminations, the Transdniestrian authorities fired up several old Soviet-era radio jamming towers and began interfering with the Moldovan mobile telephone networks. The Moldovan authorities retaliated by altering the land-line exchange stations under their control to block most domestic and international calls into and out of the Transdniestrian region. By the end of September, cell phones on almost any network would not work anywhere in Transdniestria and roughly half the right bank in Moldova. The OSCE Mission hauled out several old satellite phones we kept for emergencies; Moldovan residents just waited for it all to be over.[22]

The telephone situation became bad enough that we all raised it at the October 1–2 negotiating round. The Transdniestrian "minister" of communications, Belyayev, proposed that both sides refrain from interfering with telephone communications and begin talks on how to handle the telecommunications sector. Moldova telecommunications head Stanislav Gordea claimed that Chisinau was simply modernizing its systems in conjunction with new requirements connected with membership in the

World Trade Organization. None of us believed him, but there was no convincing Moldovan negotiators that any compromise on the issue was in their interest. At the October 29–30 round, discussion of the telecommunications conflict was even sharper. Chisinau and Tiraspol agreed to an expert-level meeting on November 3 at the OSCE Mission office in Chisinau to continue discussion of the issues, but Moldovan representatives refused to budge a millimeter.[23]

As we finished the late October round of talks, it seemed to me that President Voronin still thought that he could use economic levers to press Tiraspol into making concessions on the basic political and constitutional issues in the settlement process. It also seemed that Russian representatives were happy to work with the OSCE in tackling these relatively mundane economic and jurisdictional disputes. The OSCE Mission presence in Moldova was active, but nonetheless still small. If we had to get involved in enough working groups on specialized issues, we were that much less able to follow closely the big question of the Kozak mediation. When we did turn our attention to that issue, we got no answers from either Chisinau or Moscow.

A Second Try at Uniting the Two Mediation Efforts

Another high-level opportunity to reunify the disparate efforts at achieving a Transdniestrian settlement presented itself with Foreign Minister de Hoop Scheffer's visit to Chisinau in early November for the Council of Europe's Ministerial Meeting, at which Moldova was passing the council's Chairmanship to the Netherlands. On November 5 de Hoop Scheffer, OSCE Secretary-General Jan Kubis, and I met with President Voronin for a broad review of the state of play with respect to Transdniestria.[24] De Hoop Scheffer made a blunt appeal to Voronin for some return on the political investment made by the Dutch in the Transdniestrian settlement process during their year in the OSCE Chair. The Dutch chairman asked Voronin whether he had endorsed the Kozak document, while also encouraging Voronin to embrace the Mediators' Document, which had been prepared also with Russian participation. De Hoop Scheffer also asked Voronin whether he was willing to meet Smirnov, and explored other possible avenues for closing in on a deal on Transdniestria, such as a "proxy" conference of the two sides, with trusted representatives of the two leaders.

Voronin bobbed, weaved, and dodged in response to the OSCE chairman's questions. In quick succession, he claimed the Kozak document had not been accepted by the Transdniestrians, while Kozak showed no knowledge of the Mediators' Document. With multiple documents, Voronin asserted, the Transdniestrians could accept what they wanted and avoid reaching a comprehensive solution. Voronin also claimed there was no need for him to meet with Smirnov. Instead, the best way forward was to work one step at a time, first tackling the division of powers between the two sides, and then the structure of the future reunited state and the system of guarantees. Any document should be presented simultaneously to the Moldovan and Transdniestrian sides. Voronin likened any other course to putting one's hand inside the mouth of a crocodile, inviting it to be bitten off.

De Hoop Scheffer then pressed Voronin to unite the two Transdniestrian settlement efforts. He pointed out to the president that Kozak had been informed about the Mediators' Document (which was quite true; see above) and claimed that Kozak supported this document (probably an exaggeration, but not untrue, given what Kozak had said to me). The chairman urged Voronin to combine the two documents into one, which he proposed that I then present to the two sides. "If you accept one document," he told Voronin, "then we can all press Smirnov." De Hoop Scheffer added that he would try to meet Kozak and agree to this step forward before the OSCE Maastricht Ministerial Meeting (scheduled for the first week in December). This would give him the opportunity, while still OSCE chairman in office, to urge the Russians to keep the pressure on Smirnov to accept this combined proposal. He wound up his appeal by noting his hope to garner EU support for this effort, explaining that he would soon be meeting EU high representative Javier Solana, and that EU colleagues seemed to think there was some urgency in seeking a settlement.

President Voronin was apparently unmoved by this appeal. He noted that the Kozak document was "drafted here," while not explicitly admitting the original Moldovan authorship. He explained that "we" (presumably those involved in the Kozak process) had studied the constitutions of "all federal governments." Kozak was a "shuttle diplomat"—the document is "ours," Voronin asserted. (It was not clear whether he meant by this the Moldovans or all participants in the Kozak negotiations.) He then claimed that he had learned about the other document—presumably the mediators' draft—from the Transdniestrian mass media.

How could this document not have any differences from the Kozak document, he wondered.

The chairman and I explained the origins of the Mediators' Document. Voronin countered that he feared the two documents—Kozak's and the mediators'—would be different, and Smirnov would exploit this. After further discussion with me, President Voronin suggested that we get together and work out one text. We could only go to the Moldovan Parliament with a single text, he emphasized.

De Hoop Scheffer reiterated his hope to speak with Kozak, stressing his desire to have a document with OSCE backing. The chairman asserted that most OSCE states would need more than a draft prepared unilaterally by Russia. Both De Hoop Scheffer and Secretary-General Kubis repeated the need for a document that the United States and Western European OSCE participating states could back. It was important, they said, for our Russian friends to understand this.

President Voronin quickly and succinctly agreed in principle to the need for a document that could gain Western backing. Winding up the meeting, he called the Transdniestrian question a regional and European security problem that could not be allowed to linger unresolved as NATO and the EU approach the Prut River. He asked for a very strong statement at Maastricht and for further measures against the separatist regime. De Hoop Scheffer reminded the president that it would help if by Maastricht we had succeeded in agreeing on a single document in the settlement process. He repeated his desire for a deliverable on Transdniestria at Maastricht; if Voronin supported an agreed-on single document, it would make it easier for all the OSCE participating states to bring pressure on Smirnov. This plea continued to fall upon apparently deaf ears.

The CiO went right from his conversation with the president to a meeting at the OSCE Mission office in Chisinau with representatives of a broad spectrum of Moldovan civil society, which demonstrated clearly the depth of frustration, suspicion, and opposition to the ongoing efforts at reaching a Transdniestrian settlement. Moldovan intellectuals, journalists, and opposition politicians made three basic points during an impassioned 90-minute exchange. First, they questioned the rationale for establishing a federal system as the basis for a settlement. A clear majority of the speakers saw a federation in Moldova not as a means of achieving an acceptable division of powers between Chisinau and Tiraspol but as a stratagem for Russia to ensure continued domination of the

Moldovan state through its clients in Tiraspol. Arguments along this line were frequently accompanied (although not always illuminated) by expressions of deep resentment against the "criminal" leadership in Transdniestria and unwillingness to accept Transdniestrian interlocutors as equal parties in a negotiation, perhaps not even as real Moldovan citizens.[25]

Second, a number of Moldovan economists and political scientists at the meeting pointed out that whatever the original causes of the conflict along the Nistru, the essence of the current impasse was a conflict between economic and political elites on both sides over property and business activities (which often were partly or wholly illegal). Competition over property and sources of income also gave Russia opportunities for maintaining and extending influence on both sides of the Nistru, many of the participants complained.

Third and finally, many of those present complained about the failure of the political settlement negotiation process to keep the Moldovan public informed or to involve representatives of Moldovan society in the process in any meaningful way. For example, one opposition Parliament deputy noted the existence of a new mediators' draft and asked how it was different from the document all of them knew from the press—that is, the summer 2002 Kiev Document. This deputy, along with other participants, pleaded for more openness in the negotiation process as at the very least a means of dispelling misinformation and misconceptions about what was actually going on.

While recognizing the depth of popular feeling and the real difficulties created by the closed character of the negotiation process, the OSCE—indeed, any external party—was limited in what it could do to answer these concerns. The negotiations were being driven by a president with more than a two-thirds majority in his Parliament, all duly elected in a process recognized as free and fair by almost all Western states. It did not help that the ruling Party of Communists (Partidul Comuniştilor din Republica Moldova) was despised by the opposition right-center and right-wing parties, who were nonetheless utterly powerless to block any Communist initiative in the Parliament. Secure in his ability to obtain legislative approval for any of his initiatives, President Voronin apparently failed to perceive any need to cultivate public opinion or seek support from other quarters of the Moldovan political classes.

After the CiO's visit, in early November I contributed a short draft statement on Moldova for a prospective ministerial document to the

Dutch OSCE delegation in Vienna, which was tasked with the preparation of documents for the Maastricht gathering. There were also other concerns to keep the OSCE Mission in Chisinau busy in the absence of negotiating meetings. I prepared a major speech on the struggle against trafficking in human beings for an OSCE-sponsored antitrafficking conference in Chisinau in mid-November.

The big question, however, remained how and when to present the proposals and recommendations of the mediators to President Voronin and Smirnov. As the fruit of considerable effort, we had explicit agreement in the protocol of the October 29–30 negotiating round to seek a meeting of the mediators with the two leaders to do just that. After the departure of a delegation from the incoming 2004 Bulgarian OSCE Chair, I spent the second week of November attempting to get the agreement of my Ukrainian and Russian colleagues to send a letter to each side with a formal request for a meeting. I quickly obtained assent from Ukrainian ambassador Petr Chaliy, who was himself wrestling with preparations for a visit to Moldova by President Leonid Kuchma. However, my Russian counterpart Novozhilov and the Russian ambassador in Chisinau, Iurii Zubakov, both proved hard to find and hard to pin down—not an encouraging sign.

The days of the Dutch OSCE Chairmanship were drawing to a close. As CiO de Hoop Scheffer made clear to President Voronin at the Council of Europe's summit, he strongly desired some sort of tangible political result from the priority the Dutch Chairmanship had afforded the Transdniestrian issue during the course of the year. As we met continued obfuscation and resistance to joining the two settlement efforts, my Dutch colleagues authorized me to seek agreement once more of my Russian and Ukrainian colleagues to present the Mediators' Document collectively. If one or both demurred, I was instructed to present the document on my own on behalf of the OSCE.[26]

Chapter 10

A Settlement Is at Hand

The Public Announcement of the Kozak *Memorandum*

The Ukrainian ambassador, Petr Chaliy, agreed immediately to sign a cover letter for presenting the Mediators' Document to the two sides. Throughout Friday, November 14, 2003, I sought a meeting with Russian ambassador Zubakov to request his signature on the cover letter. But for most of the day, Zubakov was nowhere to be found. My Ukrainian colleagues told me they were hearing "from the Moldovans" that some sort of "declaration" was imminent from the Kozak process.

Finally, on Friday evening I received an urgent invitation to the Russian Embassy in Chisinau. In the presence of Ambassador Zubakov, Dmitri Kozak greeted me with a draft settlement document, which he stated that both sides had accepted.[1] He claimed that the basic structure of the document had not changed from the September 11 draft that I had seen, although compromises had been worked out between the two sides on a number of specific points. He explained that agreement had been reached very rapidly during the past week. Even a week ago, he claimed, there had been a "chasm" between the two sides. He told me that Russia had used considerable pressure on Smirnov "as you suggested" in order to gain Transdniestrian acceptance. Kozak asked me to keep the document strictly in confidence while operational arrangements for completing the agreement were being made. He asked me, representing the Organization for Security and Cooperation in Europe (OSCE), to join with Russia in supporting this apparent settlement.[2]

I congratulated Kozak on obtaining agreement from both Chisinau and Tiraspol, noting that I knew well from personal experience how dif-

138

ficult it was to accomplish this on almost any subject. Otherwise, I gave Kozak and Zubakov the typical, and expected, diplomatic reply—I promised to send the document and report at once to the OSCE's chairman in office (CiO), who I noted would make the decision whether to support it. I did not have time to read the document during the meeting, but I told Kozak that I would discuss its contents only with a narrow circle around the OSCE Chair. I noted that CiO de Hoop Scheffer had been trying to speak with Kozak by telephone for at least a week, and asked if he would be in his office on Monday. Kozak confirmed his readiness to take the CiO's call; he did not indicate how soon he needed an answer from the OSCE.

Kozak was visibly tired but pleased with the results of his efforts. He appeared satisfied that my initial response was businesslike and not negative. He clearly understood that I would not be the one to accept the document on behalf of OSCE, but seemed happy that I did not have instructions to oppose it.

I found the head of the Dutch Foreign Ministry's OSCE Chairmanship Office, Ambassador Daan Everts, still at work late on a Friday night, and faxed him the text of the Kozak document. We agreed that he and his colleagues would seek appropriate comment on the Kozak draft from European colleagues, while I would find the U.S. special negotiator for conflicts in the former USSR and get American input on the document. I found my U.S. colleagues—ironically—in Moscow on Saturday morning, while I enlisted my two most senior colleagues from the OSCE Mission in Chisinau to give a quick, but exhaustive, analysis of the Kozak text.

The *Memorandum on the Basic Principles of the State Structure of a United State* (hereafter, the Kozak *Memorandum*), which Kozak gave to me the evening of November 14, contained fifteen articles. This fact in itself is important, because the ultimate version of the *Memorandum* published on the Internet consists of eighteen or nineteen articles (depending on the redaction), including those that address guarantees of the agreement and a long-term Russian Federation military presence. Neither of these latter subjects was addressed in the version of the *Memorandum* that was presented to me on November 14 and that was used by the OSCE during subsequent days for consultations to determine our position on the document.

The Kozak *Memorandum* provides for the settlement of the Transdniestrian conflict and the reunification of Moldova in an asymmetric federation with two subjects—Transdniestria and Gagauzia—and federal territory (the remainder of right-bank Moldova).[3] The *Memorandum* incorporated Transdniestria and preserved Gagauzia in the federation without many appreciable changes (so that incumbent local officials would keep their places). The *Memorandum* used the language favored by Transdniestria on achieving a settlement through the transformation of the state structure of the Republic of Moldova and the construction of a federal state. The *Memorandum* used the new name suggested by Tiraspol—"the Federative Republic of Moldova."

As in the earlier redactions, the new federal government would have a bicameral legislature. This redaction called for the proposed lower House of Representatives to have seventy-one members elected for four years by proportional representation from a single national electoral district. The upper chamber, or Senate, would have twenty-six members, with four from Gagauzia, nine from Transdniestria, and thirteen from the House of Representatives of the federal government. One new feature, which we had not seen before, was that the senators would have an imperative mandate; that is, they would be obliged to vote in territorial blocs. There would be no possibility for Chisinau to draw off senators from Transdniestria to its side on measures that might be opposed by the leadership in Tiraspol.

The November 14 text of the *Memorandum* provided for mostly the same distribution of powers between the federal government and the subjects of the federation. As in earlier drafts, some of the most important governmental powers were to be shared between the federal government and its subjects. These included human and minority rights, customs, the National Bank, energy, law enforcement, civil and criminal law, federal budget and taxes, environmental protection, education, social welfare, and electoral law. All these shared competencies were to be exercised according to organic laws, which during a transition period until 2015 could be passed only by a three-fourths majority in the Senate. Thus not only were some of the most important powers of the national government to be shared with the Transdniestrian and Gagauz authorities—because of the introduction of the imperative mandate, until 2015 Transdniestria had an absolute veto over any federal action in these spheres!

By mid-day Saturday, November 15, detailed analyses provided by my American and OSCE Mission colleagues and my own reading of the document led me to doubt that the *Memorandum* provided the basis for a real, just, and lasting settlement of the Transdniestrian question.[4] We were particularly concerned by the provisions of the *Memorandum* for Transdniestrian representation in the upper house (Senate) of the proposed bicameral legislature. Transdniestria would have only slightly more than one-third of the senators, whereas the agreement called for a two-thirds vote in both houses for even the most routine federal legislation to be adopted. In effect, the Transdniestrian representatives would have a veto over almost all the activities of the reunited national government—clearly not a formula for a viable state.

Later, on November 15, I met with Moldova's chief negotiator, Vasile Şova, who told me that President Voronin would likely call me in Monday morning, November 17, to ask for OSCE support for the *Memorandum*. Having read the document carefully by that time, I told Şova that what I had feared apparently had come to pass. Working without the OSCE, the Moldovans, Transdniestrians, and Russians had produced a draft that would be very hard for the OSCE to support. Şova told me that there were some portions of the *Memorandum* that he opposed, but he said the document was a package. To get the overall settlement, one must accept some compromises one dislikes. I responded that for the OSCE to offer support, we would need the Moldovans, in particular President Voronin, to make clear publicly that, first, they had arrived at this deal of their own volition and, second, that this is what they really wanted.[5]

I spent much of Sunday, November 16, with my two most senior colleagues in the OSCE Mission analyzing and discussing the *Memorandum*. At the end of the day, I sent the following comment and recommendation to the Dutch OSCE Chair:

I urge the CiO to voice serious OSCE concerns about the content of some provisions and the omission of others from the document given to me by Kozak. . . . In particular the proposed division of powers undermines the authority of the federal government. In addition, absence of substantive reference to human rights, democratization, free elections, multi-party system, and other key reforms makes it impossible for the OSCE to endorse the document fully. Furthermore, the proposed legislative structure gives Transdniestria a potential veto over all federal actions for at least ten years. My Mission staff and I believe these provisions will be viewed by some as a sell-out and could provoke massive protests and opposition from right bank civil society. Even with both sides reaching agreement on the basic structure of an asymmetric federation, it will be difficult for the OSCE to do much more than welcome this effort in very general, non-committal terms.[6]

In principle, the OSCE during 2003 supported a federal solution to the Transdniestrian conflict. However, we could support only a federal solution that resulted in a viable, independent Moldovan state. We in the OSCE Mission knew that a substantial portion of the Moldovan population opposed a federation of any kind. We were confident that even proponents of a federation would find this agreement unacceptable. "We believe Moldovan society on the right bank will react massively and negatively to this proposed settlement," I reported to my Dutch colleagues.[7] I noted that though the Kozak *Memorandum* might at first glance provide for a federal solution similar to that proposed in the Mediators' Document, the Kozak plan would not produce a viable state; in other words, it would not be a real solution to the problem it was addressing. For the time being, I did not advocate the immediate rejection of the *Memorandum,* but proposed for the CiO's use with Kozak a set of talking points that would make clear we could not accept the document without major revisions.[8]

The first question in reacting to the *Memorandum* was, What did President Voronin think about it? I found out quickly, when he called me in Monday morning, November 17, and announced: "Russia has decided to give up Transdniestria!"[9] Voronin said that Russia would continue to play a role in Transdniestria, in particular in the peacekeeping operation, but he said that he wanted an OSCE mandate for a multinational force. He requested the OSCE to support the document, noting that it gave the OSCE the initiative in time for the Maastricht meeting. He told me that he planned to meet with the diplomatic corps in Chisinau to announce and explain his position. In particular, he requested CiO de Hoop Scheffer to speak with EU high representative Solana and U.S. secretary of state Powell to request their support. He stated that he, Smirnov, and the Gagauz Bashkan (governor) would sign the document, and send it to their respective legislatures for approval. He said Kozak would be arriving in Moldova that night to help iron out the remaining details.

I asked the president whether the text of the document was a done deal, to which no changes could be made. He quickly denied that, so I launched into a string of questions and criticisms that the OSCE Mission had prepared. Some of Voronin's responses puzzled me. For example, when I expressed surprise that the *Memorandum* changed the name of the state (Federative Republic of Moldova), the president denied that he had agreed to that change. I noted the OSCE's unhappiness with the extensive joint competencies, the lack of federal participation in control over foreign economic activity, the vagueness of provisions for defense, the failure to address human rights and democratization, and the lack of mention (or reform) of the Transdniestrian Ministry of State Security (Ministerstvo Gosudarstvennoi Bezopasnosti) and other security organs. Voronin seemed to take my comments on board, but he provided no real substantive reply or commitments.

Western Deliberation and Response

By chance, the Dutch OSCE Chairmanship had previously asked me to come to Vienna on November 18 to join a meeting with the U.S. special negotiator for regional conflicts, Ambassador Rudy Perina, who had been in Moscow over the weekend, in part for bilateral consultations on the Transdniestrian question. After I reported on my meeting with President Voronin, we decided we would use our meetings in Vienna to develop a recommendation on the Kozak *Memorandum* for the CiO, before he called President Voronin with the OSCE response.

The Moldovan and Russian governments announced the proposed settlement on Monday, November 17, and published the text of the *Memorandum* in the state-owned press on Tuesday, November 18.[10] A Moldovan government spokesman asserted that the Kozak document basically coincided with proposals of President Voronin and the OSCE. On Tuesday, President Voronin met with the leaders of the three Parliamentary party delegations—the Party of Communists' Viktor Stepaniuc, former prime minister Dumitru Braghiş, and Christian Democrat Iurie Roşca—to explain the *Memorandum* and seek their support. Voronin also invited Council of Europe resident representative Vladimir Filipov (a Bulgarian) to the meeting. According to press accounts of the meeting, Voronin claimed that the Russian document took into account the OSCE proposals and his own February constitutional initiative.[11]

The representatives of the ruling Party of Communists predictably supported President Voronin and the *Memorandum,* but the reaction of almost all other political forces in Moldova was swift and negative. With limited time before I left for Vienna late Tuesday afternoon, I sought to meet with as many Moldovan political leaders as possible to get a sense of the range of their opinions and advice. I succeeded in finding former premier Braghiş, former speaker Dumitru Diacov, Our Moldova leader Viaceslav Untilla, and Social Liberal Party leader Oleg Serebrian. All of them had extremely negative comments on the *Memorandum,* citing many of the flaws that my mission colleagues had also seen. Their consensus (although I did not meet with all of them at the same time) was that the OSCE should not support the *Memorandum.*

In Vienna on Tuesday evening, over dinner at the residence of the Dutch ambassador, I met with the senior officials of the Dutch OSCE Task Force from The Hague, the Dutch OSCE delegation, and U.S. special negotiator Perina, who had arrived in Vienna earlier that day from Moscow. We all agreed that the Kozak *Memorandum* did not provide a viable settlement for the Transdniestrian conflict, but we had difficulty deciding what would be the best OSCE response, both public and private. On the one hand, we felt there was no way that we could support the *Memorandum* in anything like its present form. I asserted that if the OSCE supported this document, we would have to close the OSCE Mission to Moldova and I would have to leave the country. In addition, I noted that we had no indication that any alterations or edits on our part would be welcome. On the other hand, every meeting and communication with President Voronin seemed to indicate that Moldova was determined to accept the document. If we objected, it occurred to all of us, we might be blamed by both Chisinau and Moscow for torpedoing the long-sought resolution of the Transdniestrian conflict.

We hit upon a solution that pleased no one—we would neither endorse nor publicly oppose the *Memorandum,* citing the inability of the OSCE Chair to find a consensus on the document's substantive provisions. This was true, but begged the real question. At a breakfast meeting held by the Dutch with a number of EU delegation heads on Wednesday morning, which Perina and I attended, the prevailing opinion was highly critical of what they knew of the *Memorandum.* I discerned absolutely no sentiment in favor of supporting the document.

Kozak called me Wednesday morning, while I was still in Vienna, to try to wrap up another loose end connected with an impending Transdniestrian settlement. He reported that the International Monetary Fund was preventing Chisinau from agreeing to Moscow's provision of the by-now-infamous $100 million credit to Tiraspol to reduce its outstanding debt to Gazprom for past natural gas deliveries. I called the IMF representative in Chisinau, who asserted that the IMF had only advised Moldova not to assume any new debt in conjunction with the initiative, not to oppose it entirely. When I called him back with this information, Kozak promised to work on the issue and said he looked forward to hearing the results of my consultations later that day.

Back in Chisinau by dinnertime Wednesday, I gave Kozak the news of what the OSCE Chair's decision would be at an evening session at the Russian Embassy. He inquired what objections we had to the *Memorandum*. I cited what I called the two chief substantive problems we saw in the document. First, there were simply too many shared competencies between the federal government in Chisinau and the federal entity in Tiraspol. Kozak said he understood, noting that "we have too many shared competencies in the Russian Federation" and that he had been trying to reduce their number in his work on constitutional reform in Russia. Second, I pointed to the ability of the Transdniestrian bloc in the upper house of the Parliament to veto almost any action by the federal government. Kozak acknowledged that this was bad, but said the arrangement in the *Memorandum* was the best he had been able to get both sides to accept. He expressed the hope that, after they had worked together for a couple of years in a joint legislature, perhaps such a broad veto would become seen as unnecessary and could be removed.

I told Kozak that CiO de Hoop Scheffer would be calling President Voronin as soon as possible with this decision, after which we would make it public. I expressed my regret to Kozak that we had not been able to work together during the course of the summer and fall in a truly collaborative fashion, and wished him well. We parted amicably.

On Thursday, November 20, President Voronin met formally with the diplomatic corps resident in Chisinau to announce the Kozak *Memorandum* and to request the support of their countries for the settlement.[12] Voronin reviewed the history of the OSCE's Kiev Document and his February 2003 constitutional initiative, and said that Russia had now—in the form of the Kozak *Memorandum*—come forward with its own plan for a Transdniestrian settlement, which Voronin claimed was largely based on the initial Moldovan initiative. He claimed that he and his administration had consulted widely within Moldovan society. Although there was much criticism and opposition to the plan, and signing the *Memorandum* was a big risk, he said it would be a big mistake not to take advantage of this opportunity.

Continuing in a vein that in retrospect seems ominously prescient, Voronin related that Smirnov that day had advanced further demands, especially with respect to peacekeeping. The president said he appreciated the current Russian peacekeeping effort, but that any Russian peacekeeping mission must be transparent to the EU, OSCE, and Ukraine. When questioned closely on this by the foreign diplomats, he explained that Smirnov's demand was that Russia offer a unilateral peacekeeping guarantee for an interim period (he said perhaps until 2010). Moldova had no objections in principle to such a proposal, he added, as long as it was coordinated with key European institutions, in particular the EU and OSCE.

Voronin also promised that if Tiraspol continued to act in a constructive fashion, Moldova would recommend lifting the visa ban against key Transdniestrian leaders. He pointed to a number of conciliatory measures he had already taken, such as ending the jamming of Transdniestrian cellular telephones and a broad amnesty for left-bank fighters in the 1992 conflict. Voronin said the new Constitution, which he hoped could be adopted by 2005, would preclude the possibility of further conflict within the country.

New Iterations of an "Agreed" Document

President Voronin's remarks at this meeting showed clearly—despite what Kozak and Zubakov had told me—that the *Memorandum* was not a finished document. Negotiations between the right and left banks were continuing, and the OSCE was completely excluded from the process. I spent a good part of Thursday and Friday, November 20 and 21, attempting to find a time when CiO de Hoop Scheffer could speak with President Voronin on the telephone, both to deliver the message agreed on at Tuesday's Vienna consultations and (we hoped) to find out what had occurred in the process of negotiation after we received our copy of the *Memorandum* on November 14. It proved extraordinarily difficult to find a mutually convenient time. When we finally thought we had, the Dutch phoned the president in Chisinau (with de Hoop Scheffer waiting in his office), but were told by a staff member from the Protocol Office that President Voronin was at lunch and could not be disturbed.

(Sheepish Moldovan colleagues later explained to me that Voronin had been in a meeting with Parliamentary Speaker Ostapciuc, and with the chief of protocol absent, no one there had dared to interrupt the president.) Frustrated with the OSCE Mission in Chisinau and his staff in The Hague, the CiO went off to other pressing business, and we lost our chance to get through to Voronin for the rest of the week.

Our Russian colleagues were no more forthcoming than the Moldovans with respect to what was going on with the negotiations. My counterpart from the Russian Ministry of Defense, Deputy Minister General Vladimir Isakov, met with me Friday in Chisinau to discuss our most recent accomplishments and further plans for the withdrawal of the remaining stores of ammunition at the Russian military depot near Colbasna. At least we were heartened by the fact that during November, ammunition trains continued to depart the Transdniestrian region for Russia, irrespective of the lack of OSCE involvement in the Kozak negotiations.

Russia was pushing for a quick resolution—signature of the Kozak *Memorandum,* settlement of the Transdniestrian conflict, and a triumphant report on the successful Russian mediation at the December 1–2 OSCE Ministerial Meeting in Maastricht. By the end of the week, Moldovan and Russian contacts informed me and my staff at the OSCE Mission that President Putin would in all probability visit Moldova at the start of the next week for a formal signing of the *Memorandum.* With all apparent avenues of appeal having been temporarily exhausted, I joined my wife in Bucharest for a welcome interlude at the U.S. Embassy's Marine Ball on Saturday evening, November 22.

I know from subsequent conversations that my Russian, Moldovan, and Transdniestrian colleagues were not idle over the weekend. Hard bargaining continued, and the text of the document continued to evolve. My own part of the story resumes at about 4:00 p.m. on Sunday afternoon, November 23. As I drove through the Moldovan border town of Leuşeni in the fading autumn twilight, one of my Moldovan negotiating colleagues called me. "Where are you?" he asked me frantically. "We have to see you." We agreed to meet in an hour in my office in Chisinau, where he showed me a new redaction of the *Memorandum* (for the text of this document, see appendix C).[13] The document contained three articles at the end—numbered 17–19—that I had never seen before and that concerned guarantees for the settlement. Article 18 provided for a security guarantee in the form of a bilateral treaty between Moldova and Russia for a Russian peacekeeping presence of up to 2,000 troops during a transitional period until 2020. The European Union, the OSCE, and Ukraine could join as co-guarantors only with the consent of both Moldova and Russia.

I photocopied the next-to-last page of the *Memorandum,* which contained part of the additional text. At my colleague's request, I copied the final page of the new redaction longhand—rather than making a photocopy—because the text was followed by two signatures, which I recognized as resembling those of Smirnov and President Voronin. I asked a few questions, but the text (and its implications) was clear. My colleague indicated that President Putin would be coming to Chisinau Tuesday to preside over the formal signing of the document. I said that Western capitals would be very upset when they saw these additions to the *Memorandum.* I would be reporting to the OSCE Chair immediately, and I expected President Voronin would be hearing a strong, negative reaction in the very near future.

During the course of Sunday evening, I hunted down my colleagues in Europe and North America to make an oral report and to ensure that policymakers were found and alerted that evening to the new, unwelcome situation in Moldova. I eventually found a key member of the Dutch delegation in Vienna and the U.S. negotiator at home in suburban Virginia, to whom I related my incredulity, dismay, anger, and sense of urgency. I translated the offending articles into English, and sent messages to Vienna, The Hague, and Washington, so that responses could be formulated on the text, not just on my say-so.

My own oral message and recommendation was clear. The new provisions of the *Memorandum* for security guarantees constituted an obvious attempt to exclude other actors and ensure unilateral Russian control of security arrangements, in particular the peacekeeping operation, through a fait accompli. I also considered the action a violation of both the spirit and the letter of the agreements that had been reached with respect to Moldova, in particular the withdrawal of Russian military forces, at the 1999 OSCE Istanbul Summit. If allowed to go forward, this agreement would most likely preclude ratification of the Adapted Conventional Armed Forces in Europe Treaty by a number of Western states, most certainly by the U.S. Senate. From my conversation Sunday afternoon, I did not judge that the Moldovans were entering into this agreement either happily or voluntarily.

Chapter 11

The Dénouement

Chisinau awoke on Monday, November 24, 2003, to the news that Russian president Vladimir Putin would make a short visit to Moldova the next day to witness the signing of the Kozak *Memorandum*.[1] Kozak and Zubakov had indicated to me as early as November 14 that they hoped the settlement would be signed in Putin's presence. By the end of the week, the OSCE Mission's Russian contacts indicated that this would likely happen during the week of November 24. Now the news was public. By mid-afternoon, a Moldovan military band, dressed in full formal regalia, was rehearsing for the upcoming visit in front of the Presidency Building on Chisinau's main street, Boulevard Stefan cel Mare. In the late afternoon, mission members reported to me that a large advance party from the Russian Federation's Presidential Administration had checked into Chisinau's Hotel Dedeman (now the Leogrande), not far from the government, Parliament, and Presidency buildings.

As news of the impending visit and settlement spread, almost all of Moldova's opposition political parties and independent nongovernmental organizations joined to form a Committee to Defend the Independence and Constitution of Moldova. In its founding statement, the committee claimed that the Kozak *Memorandum* would "tear up the [Moldovan] Constitution, and replace it with complete political control by Russia and its Trans-Dniester proxies." The committee referred pointedly to a statement by Russian minister of defense Sergei Ivanov in conjunction with the proposed settlement that Russia would keep its troops in federalized Moldova "for another twenty years." The committee appealed to the United States, European Union, Romania, and Ukraine to join in the settlement process, and called on Russia to fulfill its commitment to withdraw its troops from Moldova. Finally, the committee urged the public to begin assembling in the center of Chisinau on Wednesday, and said they would demand President Voronin's resignation if he signed the settlement.[2]

Political figures of all kinds and ranks in Moldova, including President Voronin, arrived to work that Monday with recent television images from Tbilisi still running through their minds. On Sunday, November 23, most of the broadcast and cable TV channels available in Chisinau (in particular, Russian-language programming) carried lengthy, sometimes live coverage of the crisis in Georgia. Fascinated viewers watched as President Eduard Shevardnadze was carried out of the Georgian Parliament and spirited away to safety—and private life—as mobs of angry Georgians protested the alleged theft of the recent elections.[3] As of Monday morning, the situation in Georgia was still without a final resolution, but the dramatic, forced exit of President Shevardnadze had clearly made a profound impression on Moldova's political elite.

Although the Committee to Defend the Independence and Constitution had called for crowds to assemble only on Wednesday at 10:00 a.m., by mid-day Monday small groups of anti-*Memorandum* demonstrators were already in evidence around the center of the city.[4] Their numbers would swell through the next 48 hours until they jammed Boulevard Stefan cel Mare, between the Parliament and Presidency buildings. The Moldovan press reported that local students joined demonstrators in front of the Presidency by early evening on Monday, and chanted slogans against the *Memorandum,* Putin, and Voronin through the night.[5]

My first meeting Monday morning was with American ambassador Heather Hodges, who briefed me on the instructions she had received overnight from Washington to seek a meeting with President Voronin to urge him not to sign the *Memorandum,* particularly in light of the additional provisions we had seen over the weekend. Ambassador Hodges met the president later that morning, while I was in contact with the Dutch OSCE Chairmanship in The Hague to arrange a phone call to Voronin from Chairman in Office (CiO) de Hoop Scheffer, new talking points for the CiO, and a public statement following the telephone call.[6]

De Hoop Scheffer got through to Voronin in the middle of the day, and delivered a clear message that the Kozak document—especially in its new, expanded form—was not acceptable to the vast majority of OSCE states, including the Chair. The CiO's statement that the OSCE would not support the *Memorandum* reportedly was not only unwelcome but also a bit of a surprise to the president. His associates subsequently claimed to me that the Russian negotiators—including Kozak—had repeatedly assured Voronin during the final stages of the negotiations that the OSCE was already on board with the document. In private, my closest Moldovan contacts similarly repeated to me alleged Russian assurances that President George W. Bush had been informed and approved of the basic deal embodied in the *Memorandum*. My heated protests that there could never have been any such approval remained unconvincing to them, until the United States and the OSCE formally weighed in.

The OSCE Mission and the Dutch Chairmanship worked out a statement, which we released as soon as the CiO's phone conversation with President Voronin was over. The text read:

The Hague / Chisinau, 24 November 2003—There is no consensus among OSCE participating states to support a new proposal by the Russian Federation for resolving the Moldovan/Transdniestrian problem, the OSCE Chairman-in-Office, Netherlands Foreign Minister Jaap de Hoop Scheffer, told Moldovan President Vladimir Voronin.

. . . "If indeed the parties come to an agreement on this Memorandum, we shall have to take a neutral stance," the OSCE Chairman-in-Office said in a telephone conversation with President Voronin on Monday. "This means we will leave it to the Moldovan people to decide on the agreement."

The Chairman-in-Office informed President Voronin that several participating states had expressed serious reservations regarding some provisions of the Memorandum, such as the lack of clarity on the proposed division of powers between the central and regional authorities, the de facto veto power of Transdniestria in the Senate until at least 2015, and the absence of a satisfactory multinational guarantee system.

"Our consultations with participating states show there is no consensus to support this document," the CiO told President Voronin.

At the same time, the Chairman-in-Office assured the Moldovan President that if the parties reach an agreement, the OSCE is ready to continue work with both sides in the process of elaborating a new Constitution.

The OSCE is also prepared to assist in organizing and conducting a nationwide democratic referendum so that the Moldovan people may express their will on the future of their divided country. As always, OSCE principles and commitments will guide these efforts.[7]

My Dutch colleagues told me the CiO's actual words to President Voronin were considerably sharper and blunter than the somewhat veiled message of this public statement. By all accounts, the intent was for Voronin to understand that he should not agree to the *Memorandum,* but that the OSCE would not abandon him. Despite the indirect language of the statement, the headlines in the Chisinau newspaper showed that the message had been understood: "OSCE Rejects the Russian Draft on Federalization of the Republic of Moldova."[8]

Colleagues from other international organizations told me that on Monday the 24th President Voronin also received telephone calls about the *Memorandum* from Council of Europe secretary-general Walter Schwimmer and European Union high representative Javier Solana. The message from Solana was particularly harsh, as staffers related that he told Voronin: "If you sign this *Memorandum,* you can say good-bye to your hopes for European integration!"[9]

The rest of the day was a blur for most of us even peripherally involved. The entire workforce of the enormous Russian Embassy was preparing for a presidential visit. OSCE Chair and Secretariat staffers were in constant contact from The Hague and Vienna, not only to inquire about the latest developments but also to consult about preparations for the Maastricht OSCE Ministerial Meeting, which was now just a week away. Dmitri Kozak flew into Kiev and visited Ukrainian president Leonid Kuchma in the latter's hospital room to obtain his endorsement of the *Memorandum.* Kuchma obliged, expressing his "full support" for the proposed Russian settlement plan. The Ukrainian negotiators subsequently complained bitterly that Kozak had misled the Ukrainian leader about both the content of the plan and the extent of Moldovan and Western support for the *Memorandum.*[10]

Preparing to depart the office at about 10:00 p.m., I received a call from Moldovan negotiator Şova, who said he was with a small group in the president's office. He asked about the OSCE statement on the CiO's phone conversation with Voronin, and I faxed him a copy, with a written apology that I had it only in English. I asked him whether the Putin visit was still on, and how things were going. "It's hanging by a thread," he replied enigmatically. I went home and went to sleep.

The insistent ringing of my cellphone awakened me about 6:30 a.m. on Tuesday, November 25. I barely succeeded in mumbling something into the instrument when Şova's excited voice announced: "There will be no signing! There will be no visit!" Sometime in the early morning—various Moldovan accounts put the time anywhere from 4:00 to 6:00 a.m.—President Voronin called President Putin to state that he—Voronin—could not sign the *Memorandum*. The Russian presidential airplane was already preparing for departure in Moscow. The press corps in Moscow reportedly had already boarded their plane. Suddenly a brief announcement was made that President Putin's visit would not take place.[11]

Somewhat later on November 25, President Voronin issued a declaration explaining his decision not to sign the *Memorandum* (and beginning the process of trying to escape from the political hole he had dug for himself).[12] He noted the priority he attached to the country's reintegration and asserted that a real settlement of the Transdniestrian question had never been closer, largely due to the "constructive and balanced position of the Russian Federation." He cited a number of elements from the *Memorandum*—asymmetric federation, multilingualism, mechanisms of democratic institutions—as fully in accord with Moldovan interests. However, he added, "a document of such strategic importance cannot be adopted in a situation when there is resistance from one side or another." Acknowledging domestic critics of the *Memorandum,* he also cited international actors and aspirations for European integration as factors in his decision. He concluded: "The leadership of the Republic of Moldova considers it premature to sign the [*Memorandum*] before coordinating the text with European institutes."

However, by November 25 it was already too late (although we did not know it then) to unite the negotiating tracks and reconcile the documents. Visibly exhausted and furious, Kozak made a long, bitter denunciation of President Voronin's "political irresponsibility" in a press conference later that day in the departure lounge of the Chisinau Airport.[13] In a discourse shown in its entirety on Russian TV broadcasts, Kozak asserted that Voronin had failed at the last moment to sign a document that he had already agreed to and initialed. Kozak dismissed Moldovan popular opposition to the *Memorandum,* noting that every letter could be explained and justified. Instead, he charged, the Moldovan leadership had demonstrated "an absence of political courage, a lack of desire for open dialogue, and a fear that they might be criticized."

By all accounts, President Putin was furious with Voronin and anyone else who might have been involved in the failure of the *Memorandum*.

Mission members reported to me later in the week that Russian Embassy colleagues had been warned by the Ministry of Foreign Affairs in Moscow not to be seen having anything to do with the OSCE, in particular with me personally, lest Putin's Presidential Administration find out and have them fired. A week later, at the OSCE Maastricht Ministerial Meeting, Russian foreign minister Igor Ivanov complained to Western colleagues that Russia had gone along and not interfered with their actions in the Balkans (i.e., Kosovo), even though Moscow disapproved. Now, when Russia had brokered a settlement of a conflict in their back yard, Ivanov raged, the Western countries had intervened and torpedoed this agreement.[14] More important, over four days of continuous negotiations in Maastricht, the Western and Russian representatives were unable to find common ground on a number of contentious issues, in particular the situation in Moldova/Transdniestria. In a December 1 phone conversation with President Bush, Putin reportedly complained of U.S. participation in derailing the Transdniestrian settlement, even singling out some U.S. diplomats by name for particular blame.[15]

The Aftermath and Recriminations

In his November 25 press conference, Kozak asserted that the *Memorandum* remained on the table and offered to return if both sides were prepared for serious dialogue. He also asserted that President Putin remained ready to come to Moldova for the signing of the *Memorandum.* However, the mass popular opposition in Moldova to the document and the almost unanimous criticism of the document and the process from the United States and Western Europe had a deep and, in the end, apparently irreversible effect on President Voronin. Although his negotiators worked for the first half of 2004 with a Moldovan redraft of much of the *Memorandum,* Voronin's heart and mind were already clearly occupied in concocting other approaches and proposals that might move him toward his unswerving goal: reunification of the country.

On the second anniversary of President Voronin's rejection of the Kozak *Memorandum,* Moldovan-Russian relations were approaching their nadir. Ostensibly in response to recent Moldovan statements on the subject, on November 25, 2005, Kozak, by then President Putin's plenipotentiary representative in the North Caucasus, disputed the idea that Voronin and his Moldovan colleagues had somehow been misled on the

Memorandum's contents and provisions. In an interview in the Moscow newspaper *Kommersant*, Kozak claimed that a November 14 redaction of the *Memorandum*, every page of which he asserted had been initialed by the Moldovan president, contained the subsequently disputed provisions on Russia's peacekeeping presence.[16] Kozak continued that Voronin had known of and approved Transdniestria's desire for a Russian military guarantee of a settlement since the September 2003 Yalta Summit of the Commonwealth of Independent States.

Kozak asserted that Voronin made known his decision not to sign the *Memorandum* only after Kozak's return to Chisinau from Kiev the evening of November 24. The action, Kozak claimed, was a complete shock. Between November 14 and 24, the text of the *Memorandum* was changed a number of times, most of those at Moldova's request. Not once did Voronin show any doubts about signing, Kozak charged. He attributed Voronin's turnaround to a November 24 visit from an unnamed diplomat (most readers would probably assume this to be the U.S. ambassador) and to his failure to obtain support and political cover from the OSCE. Mostly, however, Kozak attributed Voronin's action to the president's alleged duplicity and weakness of character.

Moldova chose to answer Kozak a week later in the same forum with an article by the president's adviser on domestic politics, Mark Tkachuk.[17] To no one's surprise, Tkachuk's reply was a blast at both Kozak's and Russia's credibility. Tkachuk claimed that throughout the final stages of the negotiations, the president had repeatedly queried Kozak about U.S., EU, OSCE, and Council of Europe views on the *Memorandum*. In each case, according to Tkachuk, Kozak had replied that Russia was working with these parties and either had or would obtain their support for the terms of the settlement. Tkachuk also accused Kozak of misleading President Voronin about the terms and duration of the Russian peacekeeping presence by implying that this was just a ploy to win Transdniestrian agreement.

Tkachuk's account makes clear that Moldovan negotiators hoped for broad international support for the proposed settlement in order to counter expected criticism and opposition from the pro-Western portion of Moldova's population. Tkachuk places Kozak's actions in the broader context of the Russia-Moldova strategic partnership, in which he alleges that Russia has consistently failed to deliver on major promises to Moldova. For example, he claims that in 2001 the Putin administration promised to assist Voronin in seeking a settlement by defeating Smirnov in the December 2001 Transdniestrian elections, a commitment that failed to materialize. He ends the article with a rhetorical query: Would not Moldova be better off, like Georgia, seeking NATO membership and paying (in November 2005) $50 less per 1,000 cubic meters for Russian natural gas? With "strategic partners" like this, Tkachuk adds, who needs enemies?

Why did President Voronin reject the Kozak *Memorandum* on the night of November 24–25? Only he can answer definitively. My own guess is that advice and pressure from the United States, the European Union, the OSCE Chair, and other Western sources may have contributed to the decision, but were far from decisive. In retrospect, based in particular on later conversations with the president, I personally believe that he may well have been prepared to face down both domestic and foreign criticisms of the structural deficiencies of the *Memorandum*. In the end, even if the federal system based on the *Memorandum* did not work, Voronin and his party would have remained physically in control of Moldova's right bank—thus, he would be no worse off than he was before the negotiations started. I believe the key elements behind his decision were the chance combination of (1) the introduction of a treaty providing for a long-term Russian troop presence, (2) the simultaneous example of the Rose Revolution in Georgia, and (3) the growing angry crowd on the streets of Chisinau outside his office. Acceptance of the *Memorandum* with the provisions on the Russian troop presence was clearly becoming a real threat to his own political survival. Politicians will sometimes gamble their own careers to do what they believe is right, but they will almost never throw away their careers for an obviously losing proposition. As painful as it was, President Voronin clearly chose to survive and fight another day.

The Immediate Lessons of the Kozak *Memorandum*

A number of other observations arise from examining the history of the Kozak negotiations. First, as far as I was able to determine, the original draft of the *Memorandum* was the product largely of President Voronin's closest advisers, in particular Mark Tkachuk, Artur Reşetnikov, and Vadim Mişin. Kozak himself may have contributed to the original draft, but neither he nor his closest Moldovan collaborators made such a claim to me. The draft then evolved as Kozak shuttled between Tiraspol and

Chisinau, making additions or deletions at the demand of one side or the other. At no point during this process, even after its completion, did President Voronin or his administration publicly acknowledge their contributions to the writing of the document, nor—more important—did they seek to develop domestic political support for the effort. Thus, much like the 2002 Kiev Document, the Kozak *Memorandum* was presented to the Moldovan public as something foisted on Chisinau by outsiders. The fact that, in the case of Kozak, the outsider was a Russian only served to increase the outrage and opposition of Moldovan civil society, in particular nationalist and right-wing political forces.

Second, both the Moldovans and the Russians, both President Voronin and Kozak, attempted to restrict participation in the process of negotiation to a very limited circle. They then asked both Moldovan society and the international community to accept and support a fait accompli, take it or leave it. This circumscribed process was fundamentally flawed because Moscow, Chisinau, and Tiraspol—perhaps not all for the same reasons—sought to exclude from the process domestic and international actors that clearly had a stake in at least some of the issues to be resolved by the provisions of the comprehensive political settlement represented in the *Memorandum.* Such an approach almost guaranteed that at some point fierce opposition would erupt from some quarter. Perhaps Kozak and his superiors reasoned that after the conflict had been "frozen" for so long a time, if and when a Transdniestrian settlement was reached, no one would complain about what kind of a settlement it was. Events nearly proved them right.

Third, the idea of reaching a settlement via the establishment of a federal system in Moldova received excessive and undeserved calumny because of the Kozak experience. It is simply nonsense to assert, as do some of the most vituperative critics of a proposed federal solution in Moldova, that this is contrary to European democratic values and norms. To be sure, the federal arrangement proposed in the Kozak *Memorandum* ensures an unviable state, and in this respect it is unacceptable, and even abhorrent. The Kozak experience in theory should not preclude, but in reality has precluded, the idea of federalization in Moldova as a possible resolution of the Transdniestrian question.

Some of the critics of proposed federal solutions in Moldova may truly believe that a unitary, centralized state is a better system in both theory and in practice. Other opponents of federalization continue to argue that any federal entity on the left bank will be dominated in reality

by Moscow, and therefore will allow Russia to exercise disproportion-
ate, unwanted, and illegal influence in domestic Moldovan politics—in
effect, would be a Trojan horse in the Moldovan body politic and an
infringement on Moldova's sovereignty. Moscow's behavior during
the Kozak mediation process did much to bolster the arguments of
Moldovans who were critics of federalization because they were suspicious of Russia. I personally remain convinced that a federal model
could be constructed for Moldova that would avoid this danger. But if
the majority of Moldovan voters believe otherwise, it is their collective
voice that will prevail.

The most counterproductive criticism of a proposed federal solution
in Moldova in my estimation was that such a course in effect recognized
the illegal Tiraspol regime by negotiating with its representatives over
status. Whatever questions there may be about the legitimacy of its origins, the Transdniestrian regime has been in place now for two decades;
political settlement negotiations with it have been ongoing since 1993.
Any question of de facto acceptance (not de jure recognition) has long
since become moot. Negotiating with the Transdniestrians over a federal
arrangement is in this sense no different from negotiating over broad
autonomy within a unitary state. Little is gained in such negotiations, at
least in my view, by seeking to demonize the Transdniestrian representatives. What I sense is an unspoken desire of many critics not to negotiate
at all, but to find external actors to help apply pressure on Tiraspol to
accede to Chisinau's proposals—in effect to win at the negotiating table
what could not be won in 1992 on the field of battle.

Some two months after the Kozak fiasco, in February 2004 I explained the affair to the OSCE Permanent Council:

> From my vantage point there were two parallel negotiating processes
> at work most of last fall. Representatives of the three mediators met
> during September and October in Zagreb, Chisinau, and Kiev, and
> agreed on a document, "Proposals and Recommendations of the
> Mediators from the OSCE, Russian Federation, and Ukraine on Set-
> tlement of the Transdniestrian Question." At the same time Deputy
> Head of the Presidential Administration of the Russian Federation
> Dmitri Kozak was engaged in developing the text of the "Memoran-
> dum on the Basic Principles of the State Structure of a Unified State,"
> which was completed in the second half of November. From my per-
> spective it was unfortunate that agreement could not be reached to

coordinate or merge the two processes. This is my first lesson from last fall. Although others may dispute this conclusion, it is my belief that this failure to coordinate in the end worked to the detriment of achieving a settlement.[18]

More than seven years later, I find little to change in this general assessment.

Chapter 12

Conflict Resolution in Moldova and East-West Relations after Kozak

The events of November 2003 were as close as Chisinau and Tiraspol have ever been to reaching a comprehensive political settlement. Both sides were in agreement on uniting the territories under their control in an asymmetric federation. Further, they both agreed on many of the most basic elements of the nature, structure, and division of powers within that federation. Yet a final agreement eluded the representatives of the two sides and the mediators in the conflict, with devastating consequences not only for Chisinau and Tiraspol but eventually also for relations between Moscow and its major Western interlocutors.

The Kozak *Memorandum* represented the high-water mark of Russia's influence in the Transdniestrian political settlement process. With a clarity available especially in retrospect, one might also assert that the failed agreement marked a turning point in both the nature of Russia's involvement in Moldova and the character of Moscow's relations with the major European and North Atlantic powers in the processes of addressing the conflicts of the post-Soviet perimeter. Before 2003, Russia served as a virtual "older brother" (*starshii brat*) to the government of Moldova in its efforts to return its wayward Transdniestrian territories to Chisinau's effective control. Although Moscow had partners in the Transdniestrian settlement process throughout the 1990s, there was no question as to its de facto dominance of the effort, illustrated by then–foreign minister Primakov's role in negotiating the 1997 *Moscow Memorandum*. It was Voronin's belief in Moscow's dominant and decisive role that in early 2003 first led him to ask Russian president Putin to appoint an envoy such as Kozak, who could presumably dictate terms to Smirnov and his associates on the left bank.

The contents of the Kozak *Memorandum* and the manner in which the process played out did near-irreparable damage to the fraternal relationship between Moscow and Chisinau. Since 2003, Russia has remained an overwhelmingly important country (if not the single most important country) for Moldova, but the relationship has increasingly been as much adversarial as cooperative and brotherly. In fact, the disruption of Chisinau's relations with Moscow in late 2003 can be seen as an early but important engagement in Russia's campaign throughout the decade to retain its waning influence and to resist growing Western involvement in the heart of the former Soviet empire—that is, the countries of the "near abroad" that have been gradually asserting their sovereignty and freedom of direction from Moscow. After the failure of the Kozak *Memorandum,* a host of events all appeared to Moscow to be part of a Western plan to weaken Russia and eventually drive it from what it saw as its historic patrimony—the 2003 Rose Revolution in Georgia; the 2004–5 Orange Revolution in Ukraine; the 2005 prodemocracy revitalization of the regional organization of four post-Soviet states, Georgia, Ukraine, Azerbaijan, and Moldova (known as GUAM, from the first letters of the countries' names); increasing contacts by Moldova, Georgia, and Ukraine with NATO; Western criticism of Putin's 2004 reelection; and Western support for Georgia, Moldova, Ukraine, and even Belarus in the face of Russian wine embargos and gas cutoffs. Although the Kozak effort did not cause these subsequent events, the Russians nonetheless saw them all as part of a historical pattern. In this case, perception was arguably far more powerful and important than reality.

The Deterioration of the Political Settlement Process

During 2004, the five-sided negotiating process gradually fell apart. Under the new 2004 Bulgarian Chairmanship of the Organization for Security and Cooperation in Europe (OSCE), Russian, Ukrainian, and OSCE representatives met in Sofia in late January 2004 to attempt to pick up the pieces and get the political settlement negotiation process going again. The Russian negotiators at long last formally presented their colleagues from Ukraine and the OSCE with the complete draft of the Kozak *Memorandum,* including the articles on a Russian military presence. Formal negotiation meetings indeed did resume in late winter, and several sessions were held over the next few months.[1] However, the negotiations were largely an exercise in frustration, heavy on recriminations but short on substance. The OSCE Bulgarian chair and Mission to Moldova, along with our Russian and Ukrainian colleagues, attempted to salvage portions of the Mediators' Document and the Kozak *Memorandum.* The Moldovan side redrafted its own variant of the Kozak *Memorandum* and for a time pursued its own version of a federal solution in the talks. However, though not explicitly rejecting the idea of an asymmetric federation, the Transdniestrian leaders went back to earlier proposals for, in effect, a loose confederation of the sort that they had advanced before the Voronin constitutional initiative and Kozak's involvement in the political settlement process. The result was deadlock.[2]

Even though President Voronin and his closest advisers maintained their ostensible support for a federal solution to the Transdniestrian question well into 2004, they were already looking for other solutions that would bring additional outside support to Chisinau and additional external pressure on Tiraspol. By early 2004, President Voronin had come up with the idea of a "Stability Pact for Moldova," in effect a system of formal guarantees from major world powers—in particular, the United States, Russia, Ukraine, the European Union, and the OSCE— for the independence, territorial integrity, and security of a reunited, neutral, federal Moldova.[3] Although the proposed pact contained many provisions designed to make it attractive or at least acceptable to Tiraspol and Moscow, discussions with Voronin and his advisers made clear to me that the main purpose was to involve the United States and EU more deeply in the Transdniestrian settlement process. For this very reason, the initiative received only a lukewarm response from Moscow.[4] Furthermore, neither the EU nor the United States was eager to provide the kind of binding, treatylike guarantee that Voronin desired. Although the proposal ended up going nowhere, the initiative was a clear example of President Voronin's relentless search for support from powerful external actors to bring pressure on his interlocutors in Tiraspol to produce a Transdniestrian settlement along the lines favored by Chisinau.

As a presumed sign of their displeasure at the Western role and Moldova's rejection of the *Memorandum,* the Transdniestrians engaged in obstructionist behavior on a number of important issues, most notably the withdrawal of Russian arms and ammunition from the region. Despite stops and starts, during 2003 the Operative Group of Russian Forces withdrew more than 16,000 metric tons of ammunition from the munitions depot in Colbasna (about 40 percent of the total stored there), and received about €5 million in donor support for these operations through the OSCE Mission to Moldova.[5] As Russian troops loaded the first train of 2004, Transdniestrian security forces unexpectedly blocked access to Colbasna by OSCE Mission military inspectors, knowing that failure to verify contents of the train at loading would prevent receiving compensation for expenses from the OSCE Voluntary Fund.[6] The Russian Ministry of Defense dispatched the train anyway, offering the possibility of inspection upon arrival in the Russian Federation. I was unable to authorize payment to the Russian Federation from the Voluntary Fund. As things worked out, that was the last withdrawal of ammunition from Colbasna to this day.

The OSCE Bulgarian Chair and Mission to Moldova looked for something new to spark movement in the negotiations. We decided to use Chairman in Office (CiO) Solomon Passy's June visit to Moldova to inject into the process a detailed package of proposed confidence- and security-building measures (CSBM) between Chisinau and Tiraspol on which the OSCE Mission had been working for more than a year, an initiative modeled on the OSCE's broader CSBM agreements, including the 1999 and earlier Vienna documents.[7] The general idea was to foster contacts, transparency, and confidence between Moldovan and Transdniestrian political, security, and military officials, and thus lower the level of mutual suspicion and hostility between the sides that constituted a constant hindrance to the achievement of significant political agreements.

Alas, in our desire for a deliverable from the Passy visit, both the Mission to Moldova and the Bulgarians proceeded with undue haste. After the CiO gave the package to Moldovan president Voronin and Transdniestrian leader Smirnov, and the Moldovans commented favorably (if hesitantly), the Transdniestrians used the existence of a new, long document as an excuse to cancel their participation in the next round of political settlement talks.[8] In addition, we failed to coordinate fully both the final document and (more important in my estimation) the CiO's presentation with our Russian and Ukrainian colleagues, who were understandably miffed by what they saw as our unilateral introduction of the package. The CSBM proposal went nowhere for the rest of 2004. Ultimately, during the first months of 2005, Russian, Ukrainian, and OSCE military experts met regularly in Vienna to refine the package, and they jointly presented a revised, improved version to the Moldovan and Transdniestrian leaders in the late summer of 2005.[9] Unfortunately, the improvements in the package had no effect on its appeal to the parties to the conflict. Nonetheless it remained on the table, a testament to the efforts and expertise of international mediators and their lamentable irrelevance in the face of strongly held local suspicions and interests.

During 2004, the Transdniestrian authorities also took practical steps to retaliate for Chisinau's rejection of the *Memorandum,* in particular by bringing increased pressure on the seven Romanian-language, Latin-script schools in Transdniestrian territory administered by the Moldovan Ministry of Education. The presence of these schools, which used the Chisinau-sponsored curriculum and were seen by Tiraspol as agents of Moldovan state power on their territory, had been a constant irritant between right- and left-bank authorities since the initial cease-fire in 1992. Tiraspol threatened or tried several times during the 1990s and early 2000s to physically close the schools, and launched another effort in the summer of 2004. Against a background of mounting threats, during a July 14 visit to Tiraspol, OSCE high commissioner for national minorities Rolf Ekeus wrested from Transdniestrian authorities a seeming commitment not to take action against the schools.

The very next day, the Transdniestrian authorities commenced seizing and closing several of the schools in question.[10] These actions caused an international uproar. Believing that he had been intentionally deceived, Ekeus issued a statement on July 15 calling the Transdniestrian actions against the Moldovan schools "linguistic cleansing."[11] The three mediators—Russia, Ukraine, and the OSCE—all sent high-level special representatives to try to broker a compromise between Chisinau and Tiraspol. As the Transdniestrian authorities ignored the international outcry and continued their moves against the schools, the government in Chisinau formally withdrew from the negotiating process for a political settlement and promised economic retaliation against Transdniestria.[12] Finally, some two months after the initial Transdniestrian action, and three weeks after the beginning of the school year, Transdniestrian negotiator Valerii Litskai and I reached an agreement for the registration and reopening of the Moldovan schools.[13] However, it was too late to restart the political settlement negotiations.

Meanwhile, Smirnov and his cronies threw more gasoline on the fire by seizing all physical assets on Transdniestrian-controlled territory of the hitherto jointly operated Moldovan State Railway enterprise.[14] In addition, the Transdniestrians stopped the delivery of electricity to the Moldovan power provider, Union Fenosa, and cut off power to Moldovan communities on the left bank supplied directly by the Transdniestrian state power authority. Both the Moldovan and Transdniestrian authorities stepped up police, customs, and border checks of road and rail traffic of all sorts through the region.[15] Finally, in the early autumn of 2004, as tensions over the school and railroad issues were barely abating, Transdniestrian troops produced a tense confrontation with armed Moldovan police by preventing access by Moldovan farmers living on the left bank to their lands across a highway, which were under de facto Transdniestrian control.

The Transdniestrian actions and provocations of 2004 marked an egregious but, from my point of view, unsurprising return to their normal patterns of behavior. The acceptance by Smirnov and his cronies of the Kozak *Memorandum* had been the real deviation from the norm. Implementation of the *Memorandum* would have meant the integration of the left bank into the larger Moldovan entity, albeit on terms extremely favorable to the separatist authorities. Nonetheless, Smirnov's unchanging aim since 1992, at least as I perceived it, had been to preserve the de facto independence of his "republic," while participating sufficiently in the political settlement negotiation process to avoid unduly offending those same Russian Federation authorities upon whose largesse the economic well-being of his fiefdom depended. Given Russian dissatisfaction with Chisinau and President Voronin in the aftermath of the Kozak *Memorandum's* failure, I believe Smirnov saw an opportunity to rid his territory of a number of vestiges of Chisinau's administrative and political presence that had been constant irritants since the 1992 cease-fire. The Transdniestrian actions against the Moldovan schools, railroads, and farmers during 2004 were in essence exercises in pushing the envelope until external disapproval, particularly from Moscow, became too great, followed by tactical retreats that preserved the gains won by Tiraspol during the furor over the provocations. This pattern of behavior has been typical of Tiraspol from 2004 to the present day.

Moldova's Turn toward Europe

As far as Chisinau and President Voronin were concerned, the school crisis of August 2004, along with the other clashes and provocations in relations between Chisinau and Tiraspol, accelerated and completed a basic reorientation of President Voronin and his administration from

East to West. The failure of Kozak and Putin to place greater pressure on Smirnov in late 2003 to adopt positions more favorable to Chisinau was a severe disappointment to Voronin. However, Moscow's ongoing reluctance to prevent provocations or restrain Transdniestrian behavior during 2004 both frustrated and outraged the Moldovan leader. With increasingly strident criticism from most of Moldova's Romanophone intellectual community of the proposed federal arrangement with the Transdniestrian leadership and a national election impending sometime in early 2005, by late 2004 Voronin abandoned his reliance on Moscow and turned to the European Union and a policy of European integration as the primary path toward the reintegration of his country.

Although my mission members and I often met with domestic opponents of federalization, we usually received the guidance that Chisinau should not negotiate with the "criminals" who were in charge on the left bank, but should simply order the Russian troops to leave and extend its legitimate constitutional authority to Transdniestria. But we rarely received any specific suggestions on how to actually bring this about. However, during 2003 Oazu Nantoi, an independent, former government analyst, together with colleagues from Chisinau's Institute for Public Policy and a few other independent think tanks, formulated an approach to the Transdniestrian settlement process—widely publicized in 2004 as the "Three D" Strategy, calling for demilitarization, decriminalization, and democratization—which provided comprehensive and specific alternatives to federalizing Moldova. The Three D Strategy argued that a durable settlement of the Transdniestrian question could not be achieved without fundamental reforms and changes on the left bank and in the country as a whole.[16] These involved (1) demilitarization, in particular withdrawal of Russian troops and demobilization of "illegal" military formations (in other words, the Transdniestrian army and security forces); (2) decriminalization, or elimination of the influence of organized crime in the political and economic life of the country, including Igor Smirnov's clan; and (3) democratization, through the adoption and implementation of broad democratic principles of governance throughout the country, in particular on the left bank.[17] Given the bad behavior by the authorities on the left bank, and particularly the August school crisis, Nantoi's approach struck a chord in Moldovan intellectual and political circles. By the late summer of 2004, there was practically no one left in Chisinau but foreigners who believed that federalism was a desirable or feasible approach to resolving the Transdniestrian issue.

By the autumn of 2004, President Voronin was clearly more inter-ested in winning a second term than in pursuing his discredited 2003 initiative to reunite the country through a new federal Constitution. In contrast with the 2001 elections, Voronin's Party of Communists (Partidul Comuniştilor din Republica Moldova, PCRM) in late 2004 faced a more united and seemingly significant opposition. Most important was the Bloc for Democratic Moldova (Blocul Electoral Moldova Democratică), a center–center-left alliance that coalesced around the popular mayor of Chisinau, Serafim Urechean. As the election campaign geared up, Voronin simply stole the European integration platform from the op-position. By mid-February 2005, a couple of weeks before the vote, the Voronin administration signed a three-year Moldova-EU Action Plan designed to bring Chisinau into closer association with Brussels.[18] The approach was highly popular, and the PCRM won more than 45 percent of the popular vote and 56 of the 101 seats in Parliament.[19]

Developments in the region and across broader Europe during 2004 also combined to pull Voronin and his compatriots away from Moscow and toward Western Europe. The extensive enlargement of the spring of 2004 brought the borders of the European Union much closer to Moldova. In addition, by May 2004 it was clear that Romania and Bulgaria would also obtain EU membership within a few years, making Moldova a direct neighbor of the EU. Furthermore, of the new EU members, the Baltic states and the former Soviet satellites Poland, Hungary, Slovakia, and the Czech Republic were much more aware of and concerned about conditions in Moldova and about Chisinau's rela-tions with Moscow than were most of the older EU member states. The result was both a much greater interest from the EU in developing a re-lationship with Moldova, and because of the proximity of the EU after enlargement, a much greater sense in Moldova that association with or membership in the EU could be a realistic dream.

With the post–May 2004 EU wondering how to handle relations with its new eastern neighborhood, an orange wave inundated Southeast and Eastern Europe. In Romania, the right-center mayor of Bucharest, Traian Băsescu, unexpectedly defeated Prime Minister Adrian Năstase, the candidate of the ruling Social Democratic Party (Partidul Social Democrat, PSD) for the presidency, and the right-center parties also rolled up impressive results in the concurrent national parliamentary elections. The result was a surprise for much of Europe, and gave a boost to Romania's EU candidacy. The result in Moldova was electric. Romania's PSD was widely seen in the region—one might debate whether justly or not—as the heir to Ceauşescu's Romanian Communist Party. The main opposition parties in Moldova hoped that Băsescu's victory over the PSD might augur a victory over the PCRM in the upcoming Moldovan parliamentary elections. President Voronin wasted no time in reaching out to establish good relations with Băsescu and the new government in Bucharest, in the hope of blunting any electoral advantage for the opposition. At the same time, Băsescu and his new government adopted a far more proactive policy than former president Ion Iliescu and the PSD in cultivating ties with Chisinau, promoting Moldova's European orientation, and seeking to facilitate the reintegration of the left bank into Moldova.[20]

The Orange Revolution in Ukraine had arguably an even greater effect on Moldova's politics and orientation. Putin's intervention on behalf of Yanukovych in the first round of Ukraine's presidential elections, the mass popular uprising against the alleged theft of the election by the Party of Regions, and the eventual election of Viktor Yushchenko persuaded many Moldovans that they might follow a similar path to rid their country of Russian influence, post-Soviet Communist politicians, and the Transdniestrian regime, the alleged Russian fifth column in their country. Right-wing Moldovan leaders, such as Iurie Roşca and his Christian Democratic Popular Party (Partidul Popular Creştin Democrat, PPCD), immediately donned orange ties, scarves, and other bits of orange clothing to show their solidarity with and similarity to the Ukrainian "revolutionaries." However, sympathy for and identification with Ukraine's Orange parties was widespread among all segments and levels of Moldovan society, including many in the PCRM.[21] The combined effect of EU expansion, the Romanian elections, and Ukraine's Orange upheaval by early 2005 produced a widespread hope and conviction in Moldovan society that a fundamental reorientation of the country's politics was possible, to eliminate lingering, unwelcome vestiges of Russian influence and neo-Soviet practice.

At the same time, the Transdniestrian political settlement process was effectively dead, at least in the form it had taken during the past three years. Former Bulgarian president Petar Stoianov brought the Moldovan and Transdniestrian negotiators and the three mediators together in Varna in November 2004 in a vain attempt to get negotiations going again. But the two sides were already too far apart. Bitterness spread even further when Moldovan foreign minister Andrei Stratan called the

Russian troops on the left bank "occupiers" in his intervention at the OSCE Ministerial Meeting in Sofia in December 2004.[22]

During the campaign for the March 6, 2005, elections, Voronin and the PCRM took an increasingly strident anti-Russian line, while Moscow offered clear support to a number of opposition candidates and parties. The Moldovan authorities trumpeted the arrest of alleged Russian "political technologists" in the country providing illegal technical and financial assistance to the opposition. On one occasion, the Moldovan security uthorities stopped the regularly scheduled Saint Petersburg–Chisinau passenger train at Bulboaca, a small station about 30 kilometers east of the capital, and turned it back to Russia without allowing passengers to disembark, citing the presence of Russian workers coming to engage in illegal activities to influence the election.[23] The Russian authorities also staged anti-PCRM rallies of the Moldovan diaspora in Moscow and other cities, and it broadcast reports about them on Russian television stations carried on cable channels in Moldova.[24] By the time Voronin was elected to his second term in April 2005, Moldova-Russia relations were on a general downhill slide that continued well into 2007, and perhaps even longer.

The Transformation of the Transdniestrian Settlement Process

Following the 2005 elections and President Voronin's reelection, the second Voronin term took an entirely different approach to settling the Transdniestrian question and reunifying the country. To obtain reelection in the vote in Parliament for head of state, Voronin forged an alliance with his hitherto most vocal critics, Roşca and the right-wing PPCD. Voronin and his PCRM professed their dedication to Moldova's European integration (the same party that won its first term promising to join the Russia-Belarus Union!), and agreed to a ten-point program of democratic reforms demanded by Roşca and his supporters. In June 2005, the Moldovan Parliament unanimously adopted a resolution dedicated to democratic principles and pro-Western policies in the pursuit of a political settlement of the Transdniestrian question.[25]

Voronin had two committed foreign allies in his new approach to the Transdniestrian conflict—Georgian president Mikheil Saakashvili and Ukrainian president Viktor Yushchenko. Both offered support for

Voronin's new, pro-European course during his reelection campaign. At a GUAM Summit in Chisinau on April 22, 2005 (the 135th anniversary of Lenin's birth), Yushchenko presented the outline of a new Ukrainian plan to resolve the Transdniestrian deadlock, which offered a number of provisions that had long been extremely attractive to Moldova: participation of the EU and the United States in the settlement process, international inspection of Transdniestrian military industrial facilities, replacement of the current peacekeepers with an international mission, and international inspection of the Transdniestrian segment of the Ukraine-Moldova border. The heart of the Yushchenko Plan was a proposal for internationally supervised free elections in Transdniestria, in order to provide a legitimate negotiating partner for Chisinau, a seeming adoption of one key element of the Three D Strategy.[26] Although the Yushchenko Plan did not succeed, in the sense of producing a political settlement, the initiative fundamentally changed the composition and dynamics of the Transdniestrian settlement process, bringing both the United States and the EU into the mix as distinct actors, and establishing the rough East-West standoff that has characterized the process since that time.

Wary of any steps that might offer legitimacy to the existing left-bank regime, the Moldovan negotiators bargained stubbornly with their Ukrainian counterparts from late April into May before they finally endorsed the Ukrainian initiative. The final version of the Yushchenko Plan called in essence for the process of democratization, elections, and determination of status for Transdniestria to be conducted according to Moldovan legislation.[27] In July, the Voronin administration then pushed through the Parliament an organic law on a Transdniestrian settlement, which unilaterally legislated many of the crucial details that had long been under negotiation in the settlement talks.[28] In particular, the law returned to the Moldovan position during most of the 1990s, offering Tiraspol broad autonomy within a unitary state. Any talk of federalization was dead. All of Moldova's international interlocutors expressed reservations about the law, especially with respect to its potential effect on Tiraspol's willingness to engage in negotiations.[29] Confident of what they perceived as widespread international support, the Moldovans were not inclined to heed unwelcome calls for moderation.

Although the Voronin administration was able to convince its own Parliament and those segments of Moldovan society that had never been very interested in negotiating with the Transdniestrians, Smirnov and the Russians proved an entirely different story. Because Smirnov was interested in maintaining decent working relations with Kiev, he met Yushchenko in early July 2005, endorsed his plan, and grudgingly consented to the EU and United States joining the settlement negotiations as observers. The Transdniestrian negotiator Litskai and I worked out the details, which allowed the United States and EU all the rights enjoyed in the negotiating process by the three mediators except chairing negotiating sessions and voting on decisions (a meaningless restriction, because all decisions were made by consensus).[30] Formal negotiations resumed in the new five-plus-two format (it was not clear whether the "two" were Moldova and Transdniestria, or the United States and EU) in October 2005 but went nowhere, because Chisinau insisted on negotiating on the basis of its July 22 law, whereas Tiraspol insisted that Moldovan legislation was neither relevant nor binding for it.[31]

Meanwhile, Smirnov and his colleagues set out to be as uncooperative with Chisinau as possible, and to create as much inconvenience as they could in areas where the Moldovan and Transdniestrian authorities were forced to deal with one another. In particular, throughout 2005 Tiraspol made it impossible for Moldovan farmers from Moldovan-controlled settlements on the left bank to cultivate their fields, which were across the main highway in territory under Tiraspol's control. Schools, railroads, the police in Bendery, and other traditional areas of controversy were also tense, but the Moldovan police and Transdniestrian security forces several times almost came to blows over the so-called Dorotskaia issue, the name of one of the settlements inhabited by farmers affected by the Transdniestrian restrictions. Several times during 2005, both Chisinau and Tiraspol claimed frantically that the other side was preparing a surprise military attack.[32] I sent mission members out through the Security Zone on daily patrols; these charges all turned out to be false alarms. Luckily, neither side really wanted to fight so much as to blame the other for the deterioration in relations and impasse in the settlement talks.

There was no progress in the formal negotiations in 2005 and no statement at the Ljubljana OSCE Ministerial Meeting—nothing new, but still a disappointment on the local and European levels. However, the OSCE and EU remained busy on two other aspects of the Yushchenko Plan, and finally broke through on one. In November 2005, Ukraine and Moldova finally agreed to accept international monitoring by EU personnel on the Ukraine-Moldova border, including on

Ukrainian territory along the Transdniestrian segment. The EU Border Assistance Mission established a presence at a number of major crossing points into Ukraine out of Transdniestria, after a high-level signing ceremony on November 30, 2005.[33]

With a European presence between Ukraine and Transdniestria, the Moldovans believed they were only one step away from realizing their dream of shutting down "illegal" Transdniestrian trade with the outside world and essentially starving the rebel region into submission. Indeed, on March 3, 2006, Ukrainian prime minister Yuri Yekhanurov, shortly before leaving office, gave Ukrainian agreement to enforce Moldovan documentation requirements for Transdniestrian goods—in effect, halting exports and imports for all enterprises from the left bank that were not registered and paying taxes to Chisinau.[34] Tiraspol responded immediately with howls of protest over this "economic blockade." Moscow offered quick material and financial support to Transdniestria, while the United States, EU, and other Western states supported Moldova's legal right to the steps it had taken. Moscow also brought quiet economic pressure on Kiev, which resulted in a gradual, de facto relaxation of the border regime with the passage of weeks and months. Chisinau reduced to almost nothing the taxes and fees for left-bank enterprises that registered with the Moldovan authorities, and subsequently a significant number did.[35]

There were other important negative effects in the overall fallout from the Moldovan-Ukrainian attempt to use economic pressure on Transdniestria. Fresh from its January shut-off of natural gas to and through Ukraine, Moscow responded to the Moldovan economic actions by banning the importing of Moldovan wines, vegetables, and fruits into the Russian Federation.[36] Although the Russians used environmental and sanitary concerns as pretexts for their actions (as they did in a similar dispute with Georgia at roughly the same time), the message was clear: Chisinau needed to play ball with Moscow or lose its most important market for the bulk of its agricultural produce.

Second, Moldovan negotiators walked out of the political settlement talks in February 2006 in protest over continued Transdniestrian provocations on the Dorotskaia issue. To their dismay, not one of the mediators or observers supported them in this action. The OSCE Mission subsequently successfully brokered an interim solution to the Dorotskaia issue that permitted the Moldovan farmers in question to plant and harvest their fields for the first time in more than two years. However, the leadership in Tiraspol welcomed the Moldovan walkout, and for almost six years refused to return to formal settlement negotiations, citing one or another pretext. Instead, Smirnov organized a popular referendum in September 2006 in which he engineered an overwhelming vote for independence from Moldova and association with or joining the Russian Federation.[37]

Transdniestria as a European, East-West Issue

The divisions in the Transdniestrian political settlement negotiations since 2005 have increasingly mirrored the political divisions in wider Europe, as Russia has reflexively stood with the regime in Tiraspol, and the United States and EU have almost without fail supported Chisinau. Attempts during 2006 and 2007 to find agreement among the mediators and observers on a joint position for a political status for Transdniestria within a united Moldova, and on the transformation of the peacekeeping operation into a multinational body with a recognized international mandate, absorbed much time and effort but came nowhere near achieving agreement. Efforts to resume the withdrawal of Russian arms and ammunition from the Transdniestrian region, let alone troops, also were without result. Indeed, regular OSCE access to Russian military facilities on the left bank, once taken for granted by both the OSCE Mission and our Russian counterparts, became so restricted that a late 2006 OSCE visit to the ammunition depot in Colbasna was deemed a major event.[38]

Although the impasse over the Russian troops in Moldova was not the sole, or even the main, cause of East/West disagreement over the Adapted Conventional Armed Forces in Europe (CFE) Treaty, the inability of negotiators to resolve the Moldova issue increasingly put the CFE regime in limbo. Fulfillment by Russia of its 1999 Istanbul commitments before ratification and entry into force of the Adapted CFE Treaty had become by 2005 a theological tenet for the United States and EU. Moscow maintained that it had met its obligations by removing all CFE Treaty-Limited Equipment before the end of 2003. Moldovan society on the right bank was vehemently opposed to allowing any Russian troops to remain in Transdniestria. Moldova's Western supporters were highly reluctant to be seen to betray Chisinau by cutting a deal with Moscow on the CFE Treaty at Moldova's expense. Russian diplomats charged that the Western reference to the Moldova Istanbul issue was a ploy to avoid ratification of the Adapted CFE Treaty and the imposition of treaty-based limits on NATO forces in the Baltic states, by 2004 full-fledged members of the Alliance.

After several years of increasingly fruitless negotiations and the unsuccessful 2006 review conference of the CFE Treaty, in 2007 Putin announced Russia's "suspension" of its observance of the CFE regime (an act not foreseen or allowed by the original treaty). A 2008 offer by U.S. negotiators for a step-by-step compromise resolution of the impasse over the Russian troops in Moldova did not produce a response, and the 2008 summer war in Georgia ended any prospects of restoring conventional arms control in Europe during the George W. Bush administration. President Voronin did not help matters when he visited Moscow in March 2009, seeking Russian support in the upcoming April national election, and in a tripartite statement with Russian president Dmitry Medvedev and Smirnov agreed to language from the 1994 bilateral treaty with Russia (never ratified by Moscow and later disavowed by Chisinau) on the "synchronization" of the Russian withdrawal with achievement of a political settlement in Transdniestria.[39] The Barack Obama administration has undertaken an effort to revive the CFE Treaty regime; as of this writing, it is hard to evaluate its prospects beyond the usual unhelpful caveat that the process will be long and difficult.

One important result of the Russian wine ban and other economic pressures put on Moldova was to bring Voronin back to bilateral dealings with Moscow to seek a Transdniestrian settlement. For its part, Moscow was quite pleased to try to restore the leading, almost unilateral role it had enjoyed in Moldova and the Transdniestrian settlement process a decade before. In late 2006, Voronin's chief advisers on the issue, in particular political adviser Mark Tkachuk and chief negotiator Vasile Şova, put together a comprehensive "package," which they then spent some two years trying to sell to the Kremlin.[40] The main elements of the Moldovan package included a proposal that Russia bring pressure on or otherwise convince the Transdniestrian authorities to accept a status of broad autonomy within a united Moldova. In return, Chisinau would guarantee all Russian property in the Transdniestrian region, and ensure unfettered operation of Transdniestrian and Russian economic agents. As part of the settlement, the peacekeeping force would be transformed into an international mission of civilian observers, with significant Russian participation.

Moscow remained in a listening mode but was noncommittal on the Moldovan package. However, the Russians gradually relaxed their economic measures against Moldova. In the spring of 2008, the Russian Duma declined to call for Transdniestria's independence while adopting a declaration in support of Abkhazia's and South Ossetia's separation from Georgia.[41] Nonetheless, Moscow continued to provide significant economic assistance to Transdniestria, and it upped the level of its diplomatic and governmental contacts with Transdniestrian officials. In August 2008 and March 2009, President Medvedev forced Smirnov to meet with Voronin, but the substance and results of these meetings suggested that their main purpose was to burnish Moscow's image in the West as a peacemaker, rather than to make substantive progress toward a political settlement. In the end, even with all this activity the Russians were either unable or unwilling to produce substantive results, thus satisfying neither the Moldovans they were trying to pressure nor the Westerners they were attempting to impress.

The example of Moldova in this case is instructive. Moscow's behavior vis-à-vis Moldova after 2003—with its efforts to retain special influence; exclude other, particularly Western, actors; and compel action through economic pressure—reflects a general pattern seen in its relations and actions toward other neighbors from the former Soviet Union, such as Georgia, Ukraine, and Belarus. Just as Russia's failure after 2003 to produce results and subsequent economic pressure essentially drove Voronin into the arms of his former domestic opponents and toward closer ties with the West, Moscow's actions toward many of its neighbors and erstwhile allies in the near abroad have shown many of the same self-defeating tendencies. Indeed, an uninvolved observer might well discern three key paradoxes in the overall mode of Russian conduct in the near abroad. First, all the unrecognized entities—Nagorno-Karabakh, Abkhazia, South Ossetia, and Transdniestria—depend heavily on Russia, if not owe their continued existence to it. This fact leads Armenian, Azerbaijani, Georgian, and Moldovan interlocutors to wonder why Moscow has not simply dictated a solution to one or more of these conflicts, and to speculate that the failure to do so must be explained by Russian territorial designs or neo-imperial ambitions. Many Russian colleagues respond that these entities, though heavily dependent on Russia, have a degree of independence; in supporting these breakaway enclaves, Russia has been defending minorities against the majority ethnic populations of the recognized states. Whatever the real explanation, it is difficult to comprehend why Moscow spends so much in material resources and political capital in support of these unrecognized entities to the detriment of its standing and ties vis-à-vis its larger, recognized neighbors, of which these entities were once a part. For more than a decade, Russia overwhelmingly dominated the settlement processes in Moldova and Georgia, but it clearly failed to employ in sufficient measure either sticks or carrots in conflict resolution efforts that might arguably have cemented its influence with both sides in each conflict.

Second, though it appears to avoid strong-arming the unrecognized entities, Russia has not hesitated to use economic pressure against the recognized states in the near abroad. The gas weapon is one of Moscow's favorites, and it seems to be applied with relatively little discrimination with respect to political leanings. The cutoffs of Ukraine in 2006 and 2009 and the cutoff of Belarus in 2007 are only the most recent of a large number applied to former Soviet republics since 1991. Moldova has been cut off a number of times, most notably in February 2000, in the popular perception for political ends. Georgia has also suffered multiple cutoffs. When the main pipeline from Russia to Georgia was blown up by unknown actors in 2006, many Georgians almost automatically blamed the Russians. In addition, Moscow has imposed embargoes on key imports from both Moldova and Georgia to the Russian market, including wine, mineral water, meat, fruits, and vegetables. The Russians, in turn, assert that considerations of price, nonpayment, theft, environmental protection, and public health were behind these actions. But almost no one in the affected states believes them. This fact alone suggests the counterproductive nature of Russia's use of the economic instrument against the neighbors and states in the near abroad with which it presumably desires to build good relations. It is a fact of life that the newly independent former Soviet states on Russia's periphery simply will not always act or behave precisely as Moscow wishes. However, this does not mean that these states will always act against or oppose Russia. There are enough Moldovans and Georgians, for example, who still perceive positively many elements of their common heritage of language, culture, and history with the Russians that it should be possible to build an overall positive relationship between their countries. However, Moscow's use of economic pressure on Chisinau and Tbilisi (or even Minsk, in the case of natural gas) appears to be having precisely the opposite effect from that intended—instead of making them more cooperative, it creates resentment and drives the Moldovans and Georgians farther away from Russia.

Third, as Voronin's turnabout through the middle of the past decade demonstrates, near abroad leaders and states resentful of Russian diplomatic, economic, or military pressure do not simply go off in a corner and sulk—in the twenty-first century, in particular after EU and NATO expansion, they have alternatives to which they can turn. For years following the 1991 Soviet collapse, Moscow attempted to keep the near abroad as much as possible its own private preserve. In the early years, with the West busy in the Persian Gulf, Somalia, and the former Yugoslavia, there was relatively little argument about Russia assuming a leading role in addressing the conflicts in Nagorno-Karabakh, Abkhazia, South Ossetia, and Transdniestria. When the processes of enlargement began in the early 1990s, it was arguably not inevitable that NATO and the EU would absorb almost all the countries on the continent, while the Russian Federation remained outside. However, even if one contends that Russia ended up with little choice about the security and economic arrangements on the territory of the former non-Soviet Warsaw Pact, it certainly had far more control over its influence and fate in the near abroad. But here Moscow chose to emphasize exclusivity and unilateralism, which in the end worked against its long-term standing and interests. Russia's failure to provide security solutions to the recognized states with separatist problems eventually motivated these states to seek alternatives, while the growing wealth and attractiveness of the EU project beckoned Russia's neighbors away from the moribund structures of the Commonwealth of Independent States. Moscow's apparent insistence on an either/or choice between Russia and the Commonwealth on the one hand, and NATO, the EU, and the United States, on the other hand, in the end pushed substantial portions of the populations in the near abroad toward the West.

This process remains neither inevitable nor complete. For example, there are still large portions of the population in Moldova that are quite well disposed toward Russia and Russians. Recent polls in Moldova have reported that 60 to 70 percent of the population considers Russia the country's most important partner, and that Putin is more popular in the country than any local politician. At the same time, the same polls indicate that 60 to 70 percent of the Moldovans favor a policy of European integration. Clearly, many Moldovans do not see an insuperable contradiction between these two policies; unfortunately, Russia apparently still does.

Moscow's encomiums to and engagement in the "two-plus-one" process (Moscow-Chisinau-Tiraspol, or Medvedev-Voronin-Smirnov) sug-

gest a continuing unilateral, zero-sum Russian approach to conflict resolution in Moldova, and indeed in the entire near abroad. Medvedev's
reference to a Russian zone of "privileged interests" in the wake of the
war with Georgia certainly applies also to Moldova.[42] Despite episodic
cooperation with the West in Moldova, whether bilaterally or via the
OSCE, Moscow still apparently regards all of Moldova—not just the left
bank—as its turf and prefers to maximize its influence by excluding or
reducing the role of other major external actors. The Moldovan elections
of 2009, in particular the coalescence of the opposition against the
Communists, can in this light be explained in part by a widespread sense
in Moldovan society that increased Russian influence comes generally at
the expense of European integration. Yet the new Moldovan government clearly recognized that—given geography and history—good relations with Russia are a sine qua non for any successful Moldovan regime, irrespective of how it develops its relations with the rest of Europe.
It remains to be seen how well Moscow can and will tolerate a Moldovan
administration that tries to look simultaneously East and West.

Russia, the Near Abroad, and East-West Cooperation in Europe

The Obama administration has been engaged for more than two years
(at this writing) in an effort to restore relations with Russia after the
rupture and deep freeze following the war with Georgia. This policy has
seen some success already. The New START agreement was signed in
Prague in April 2010, and was ratified by both parties by early 2011.
NATO-Russia relations have been significantly restored, and cooperation in fighting the insurgency in Afghanistan and some of its fallout is
gradually growing. Bitter disagreement over planned U.S. anti–ballistic
missile facilities in Eastern Europe abated somewhat after President
Obama canceled proposed deployments in Poland and the Czech Republic, but cooperation in the field of missile defense is far from becoming
a reality and may yet act as a showstopper in U.S.-Russia and NATO-
Russia relations.

Against this moderately encouraging background, Moldova and the
Transdniestrian question remain one of the pieces in the puzzle of Russia
and the near abroad that will be the most difficult for any U.S. administration to solve. Moldova-Transdniestria is not the most dangerous right

now of the long-term post-Soviet conflicts. Nagorno-Karabakh (or perhaps Abkhazia and South Ossetia) likely get the nod in this respect. However, as events during the past decade demonstrate, the conflict in Moldova can flare up quickly and pose real threats to peace and stability in the region as well as political comity between the major Euro-Atlantic powers. The presence of Russian troops in Transdniestria, contrary to Chisinau's wishes, remains an apparently insuperable barrier to a revival of the CFE Treaty or some other form of conventional arms control and transparency in Europe. Right now, as the political crisis that began with the 2009 national elections remains basically unresolved, Moldova is once again wavering between East and West, Russia and Europe. If one reads the Russian press, it is not hard to find articles that portray Western activities and attempts to influence events in Moldova as part of a broader effort to reduce or eliminate the Russian presence and influence in the country and the region.[43] It remains an open question to what extent such a view informs and influences current Russian policy in Moldova, in the region, and in broader Europe.

Moscow in fact continues at times to pursue the chimera of unilateral Russian influence in managing and resolving the conflicts around the periphery of the former Soviet Union, while at other times seeking coordination and cooperation within established international forums and institutions. Since the 2008 war with Georgia and Russia's recognition of South Ossetia and Abkhazia, the processes of conflict resolution in Georgia are dead in the water. In his meetings with French president Nicolas Sarkozy during and after the war, President Medvedev emerged with a relatively favorable cease-fire, but he obtained no resulting traction with the European Union on his proposal for a formal European security treaty. Moscow's subsequent failure (as perceived by a number of EU states and many in the United States) to completely live up to the terms of the cease-fire and its uncompromising stance in the Geneva negotiations on Georgia, have probably cost the Russians any advantage they might have gained from the findings of a 2009 report by the Swiss diplomat Heidi Tagliavini, commissioned by the EU, which moderated some of the more strident accusations against Moscow for responsibility for the war with Tbilisi. Russia remains internationally isolated in its formal ties with Sukhumi and Tskhinvali, and disadvantaged in improving its relations both with its neighbors and its putative EU partners by the continuing instability arising from its unremittingly hostile relationship with Georgia.

With respect to Nagorno-Karabakh, President Medvedev has met several times with presidents Ilham Aliyev and Serge Sarkisian without the company of his co-mediators from the OSCE Minsk Group. However, the substantive chasm between Armenia and Azerbaijan has not lent itself to bridging at either the working or highest levels. Yerevan and Baku each seem more intent on finding supporters who will add to international pressure for their desired solutions, rather than impartial mediators. Because Moscow desires good relations with both parties to the conflict, it is particularly ill positioned to negotiate a solution unilaterally between two sides that are mutually uninterested in compromise. Russia has generally worked well with its U.S. and French cochairs in the Minsk Group, but Azerbaijan and Armenia both show signs of having grown tired and frustrated with that OSCE-based forum. Meanwhile, Turkey and Iran, among others, have been showing increased interest and activity with respect to the Karabakh question. Just as the growing role of China in central Asia challenges Russia's historic primacy in that part of the former Soviet empire, the rise of regional powers around the south Caucasus may well be an unsettling development for Russian pretensions to "privileged interests." Russia may remain primus inter pares, but the cards do not seem stacked in Moscow's favor.

In Moldova, Moscow's efforts to preserve exclusivity also appear to be a losing proposition. Medvedev's achievement of a joint statement in his 2009 "two-plus-one" meeting with Voronin and Smirnov was so self-serving with respect to the Russian troop presence in Moldova that any short-term political advantage was probably far outweighed by the widespread hostility the action prompted in Moldovan society and political elites (see above). And since the installation of the Alliance for European Integration government in autumn of 2009, Moscow has tried without particular success to establish good working relations with the leaders of at least two of the parties in the Alliance, the Partidul Liberal Democrat din Moldova (Liberal Democrats) and Partidul Democrat (Democrats). However, the Russians have been unable to produce the one thing that might win them credibility with the new Moldovan administration—tangible, visible progress on the Transdniestrian question. For almost two years (as of this writing), Moscow has echoed and supported Chisinau's calls for resumption of the formal political settlement negotiations, but for most of this period it seemed unable to get Tiraspol to the table. Russian freelancing with the EU has been no more productive. President Medvedev's meeting with German chancellor

Merkel in Meseburg in the summer of 2010 produced great speculation and agitation over the prospect that Moscow would obtain a new European security forum with the EU—seen by many as a way to split Europe from the United States—in return for minimal progress on the Transdniestrian issue. So far, worries on this score have proved groundless; Moscow has been unable (or unwilling) to produce any significant movement from Tiraspol. Meanwhile, public commentary in Russia continues to proclaim zero-sum fears that Moscow is losing its position and influence in Moldova to foreign competitors, in particular Romania and NATO.[44]

Moscow's current position in Moldova and Transdniestria reflects the broader dilemma Russia faces in how to balance its seemingly instinctive need to preserve its formerly dominant position and influence in the new states and unrecognized entities from the former USSR with its desire to build new relations as a major world power with Europe and the United States. Moscow's claims to exclusive influence are increasingly counterproductive, as they anger the new states that are attempting to consolidate their sovereignty and to assert their independence, while they preserve the impression in many European and American circles that Russia is essentially a neo-Soviet or neo-imperial power bent on restoring territory and influence from a lost empire. Moscow has yet to adapt to a world in which Russian participation in collective, collaborative conflict resolution in states and areas once part of the Soviet Union is a necessary, but not exclusive or sufficient, condition for success.

Conversely, the 2008 war with Georgia showed the power of unilateral Russian policy and actions in the near abroad in and of themselves to make or break Russia's relations with Europe and the United States. Improved relations notwithstanding—despite progress in other areas in the "reset," and despite Nordstream, Meseburg, and countless EU-Russia summits—this truism still holds. Unless and until the Russians can overcome their deeply ingrained suspicions, insecurities, and us-against-them mentality, their efforts to exercise unilateral influence and resolve long-standing problems in the near abroad will likely continue to frustrate their broader aspirations to a real voice and broader role in Euro-Atlantic security affairs.

Chapter 13

Russia and the West: An Endless Dilemma?

Until the events that led to the failure of the Kozak *Memorandum,* working relations between Russia, Western Europe, and the United States in the Organization for Security and Cooperation in Europe (OSCE)—and, I would also assert, in the field of European security in general—vacillated between sporadic cooperation and recurrent disagreements over difficult questions. In retrospect, the OSCE Maastricht Ministerial Meeting marked the end of an era of cooperation and the start of a period—which may not yet have reached its conclusion—of steady drift of Russia and the West ever further from one another. Since Maastricht, within the context of the OSCE, participating states have been unable to reach an agreed-on, comprehensive ministerial statement or to set an agreed-on agenda serious enough to produce a summit with truly substantive achievements. On the operational level, OSCE field and election observation activities are increasingly being hampered and limited by this recurrent, growing gulf between East and West. On more general European and global levels, relations with Russia have become more difficult and acrimonious, and cooperation more restricted and grudging.

Russia's pretensions to serve as a mediator in the Moldova/Transdniestria and other conflicts were not advanced by the Kozak experience. President Voronin recognized Moscow's great influence over the authorities on the left bank of the Dniestr and sought President Putin's assistance in reaching a settlement. He was repaid with a proposed solution that—in the words of one Moldovan former prime minister—"would have left us not even masters in our own house." In addition, Russian leaders failed to recognize—and in my personal experience still fail to understand—the visceral nature of the Moldovan public's opposition to any foreign military

182

presence, particularly a Russian one. This does not mean that Russian forces could not participate at all in security guarantees of a settlement in Moldova. However, insistence on perpetuating the unilateral Russian military presence in its present form is a political red flag in Moldova, and provokes precisely the emotional, nationalistic reaction that Moscow professes to deplore. Nonetheless the Putin administration, including apparently the president himself, throughout 2003 pursued the goal of maintaining a unilateral Russian troop presence in Moldova, and refused all efforts of Western partners to discuss any other possible collaborative alternative. Unless and until this Russian attitude changes, the prospects for a real political settlement in Moldova and the country's reunification will be significantly less likely than they otherwise should be.

What does the history of the Kozak *Memorandum* show about Russia's broader approach to international cooperation and European security? First of all, Moscow clearly prefers a unilateral approach to resolving key political and security questions in what it considers its legitimate sphere of influence. Although I personally found Kozak a talented, engaging interlocutor, the Russian approach throughout the year was heavy-handed and clumsy, and thus almost bound to fail. More than seven years later, I still do not understand in particular how otherwise intelligent Russian colleagues could expect to get away with introducing the last-minute fait accompli of a long-term troop presence without provoking serious Western objections. One might speculate that they thought the prize in Moldova was more important than hurt feelings on the part of Western governments, a situation that they presumably surmised would not be serious or long-lasting. Or perhaps they truly believed, as one Russian deputy foreign minister told me some nine months later, that "there was enormous room for Western participation in the security guarantees envisioned by the *Memorandum*—enormous room!"

Whatever Moscow's motives and calculations throughout the experience, the result of the *Memorandum*'s failure was to further entrench and strengthen Russia's already-existing view of European international political and security affairs as zero-sum, us-versus-them exercises. Russian relations with the United States and its Western European Allies, which had been deteriorating since the first round of NATO's expansion in 1997 and particularly the start of NATO's operations in Kosovo in 1999, continued to worsen throughout the next decade. To be sure, hopes were raised in some quarters by the brief period of warming and cooperation that ensued after the first Bush-Putin meeting in Slovenia and the

September 11, 2001, terrorist attacks on the United States. And hopes were raised again by the celebrated "reset" in 2009.

Notwithstanding occasional periods of warming relations and easings of tensions, the overall direction of Russia's relations with the West since the turn of the century has been mostly downward. There have been many reasons for this. The U.S. invasion of Iraq obviously did not help overall relations, and Western support for Saakashvili's Rose Revolution in Georgia also provoked Russian suspicion and hostility. The latter action— along with the Western reaction to the Kozak *Memorandum* and Voronin's last-minute rejection of the document at the behest of Western leaders— offended Moscow in a particularly deep, fundamental manner. Russia saw these Western actions as a challenge to its right to an important, independent role in European security affairs, and as a repudiation of its interests and influence in an area where it had predominated for decades, if not centuries. Moscow would later fit the Western response to its Kozak effort into what it saw as a pattern of the West's denying Russia's standing as an equal partner in European regional security affairs. The Russian perception of this pattern, which led to Putin's February 2007 diatribe in Munich, really took form with these seminal events in Moldova in 2003.

Despite improvements in the transatlantic relationship since the Obama administration entered office, Russia's suspicious, hostile manner of perceiving and responding to Western involvement in its near abroad is fully developed and deeply entrenched seven years later, and will likely remain exceptionally difficult to challenge or to change. Moscow also remains jealous of the Western powers, in particular Washington, for their authority and embittered by Russia's relative lack of influence in global political and economic institutions—a fact demonstrated by numerous aggrieved comments from both Putin and Medvedev during and since the 2008 global financial and economic crisis. Even if sore points such as NATO's expansion and missile defense deployment in Europe are successfully resolved, Moscow's extreme sensitivity to perceived geopolitical challenges in its immediate neighborhood will continue to be a formidable obstacle to real partnership and cooperation between Russia and its former Cold War adversaries. For improvement on this score depends not so much on changes in the West's understanding and behavior—no matter how necessary and desirable these may be—as on a fundamental change in how Russia's political elite perceives and acts in relation to the world around it, a far less predictable and lengthier historical process.

Appendix A

The Mediators' Document

PROPOSALS AND RECOMMENDATIONS
Of the mediators from the OSCE, the Russian Federation, Ukraine with regards to the Transdniestrian settlement

The Republic of Moldova and Transdniestria,

Striving for a rapid and final settlement between the Republic of Moldova and Transdniestria exclusively through peaceful political means,

Recognizing the principles and norms of international law,

Recognizing their responsibility for the unification of the country, upholding civil peace, trust, mutual understanding and harmony in society,

Taking as a basis the provisions of prior agreements,

Manifesting their goodwill in the name of peace and stability in the given region of Europe,

Have agreed upon the following:

The reunited Republic of Moldova is a federal, democratic state with an integral territory and based on the democratic rule of law (hereafter "the Federal State").

The Federal State is a subject of international law.

The form of state government is a republic.

The policies of the Federal State are aimed at creating conditions ensuring a decent life and free development of the individual.

The composition of the Federal State includes subjects—special territorial federal units (hereafter "federal subjects").

Transdniestria is a subject of the Federal State.

A federal subject has the right to its own constitution and legislation consistent with the Constitution of the Federal State.

National sovereignty is vested in the people of Moldova, who are the only source of state authority in the Federal State.

The people shall exercise their authority directly and through bodies of state authority and of local government.

The Constitution and laws of the Federal State have supremacy on its entire territory.

The Constitution of the Federal State and federal laws on competences of the Federal State adopted consistent with it apply directly to its entire territory.

Ratified international treaties and agreements of the Federal State and generally accepted principles of international law shall have precedence over the legislation of the Federal State.

The individual, his or her rights and freedoms are the highest value in the Federal State.

Recognition, observance and protection of human rights and freedoms and rights and freedoms of the citizen are the responsibility of the Federal State.

Every person is guaranteed legal protection of his or her rights and freedoms.

Decisions and actions (or failure to act) of the organs of the entire system of authority in the Federal State, of public associations and officials can be contested in court.

Every person has a right, pursuant to the international treaties to which the Federal State is a party, to appeal to the international instances on human rights protection in case all instruments of legal protection existing within the state have been exhausted.

Free movement of people, goods, services and financial resources is effected within the economic sphere of the Federal State, and freedom of economic activity is upheld.

The establishment of internal customs borders, duties, dues or any other barriers obstructing free movement of people, goods, services and financial resources shall not be permitted on the territory of the Federal State. Restrictions on movement of goods and services can be introduced pursuant to the laws of the Federal State provided this is necessary for ensuring the safety, protection of life and health of people, protection of the environment and cultural values.

All forms of property—private, state and other—are equally recognized and protected on the territory of the Federal State.

In the Federal State shall be observed the principles of separation, independence and interaction of the legislative, executive and judicial branches of authority during their exercise of power in accordance with the provisions of the Constitution of the Federal State.

In the Federal State as well as in all its federal subjects political diversity and political freedoms are ensured, including the right to establish political parties.

The status of each of the federal subjects is determined by the Constitution and laws of the Federal State. This status cannot be changed without clearly expressed consent of the federal subject in question.

The list of competencies reserved exclusively for the Federal State includes the following:

- Adoption and amendment of the constitution and laws of the Federal State, and control over their observance;
- Ratification of international treaties and agreements pertaining to competencies of the Federal State;
- State structure and administrative and territorial division of the Federal State;
- Setting national standards in the sphere of protection of human rights and freedoms, protection of the rights of national minorities, maintaining and upholding law and order, the rule of law and implementation of measures for their application on federal level;
- Citizenship of the Federal State;
- Establishing the legislative, executive, and judicial; systems of the Federal State and the procedures of their organization and functioning;
- Forming bodies of Federal State authority;

- Defense of the Federal State, including the creation and maintenance of armed forces, establishing legal basis of and regulations for the manufacture, sale and purchase of weapons, munitions, military equipment, and military property;
- Foreign policy and international relations; participation in international organizations for which a condition of membership is to be a subject of international law, and also in those international organizations in which the above is not required; establishing diplomatic relations with other states; establishing relations with international organizations; concluding international treaties and agreements;
- When international treaties and agreements involving competences of federal subjects are concluded, preliminary consultations with the authorities of the subject in question are held pursuant to the regulations stipulated by the laws of the Federal State;
- Foreign economic relations and foreign economic obligations of the Federal State; regulation of common principles of foreign economic activity of federal subjects;
- Determining and implementing policy pertaining to immigration and migration issues;
- Setting common legal bases of a market economy; financial, monetary, credit, customs regulation, currency emission; determining the foundations of price policy; the functioning of economic agencies, including the National Bank, on the entire territory of the Federal State;
- Matters pertaining to the budget, taxes and duties of the Federal State as well as common principles of taxation in federal subjects;
- Determining the status and regime, protection of the state border and airspace of the Federal State; border zones regime;
- Criminal procedure and civil procedure legislation; regulation of intellectual property by law;
- Establishing common principles of structure of the system of public authority and local self-government;
- Setting minimum standards in the sphere of public health, education, labor relations, pensions and social welfare;
- Establishing general federal rules and regulations on matters pertaining to ownership, use and disposal of land, mineral resources, water and other natural resources;
- Setting general federal minimum standards acceptable in management of nature, environment protection and ensuring environmen-

tal safety; protection of nature reserves, monuments of history and culture;

- Establishing general regulations for and coordination of activities related to catastrophes, natural calamities, epidemics and their management;
- Establishing general rules of selection and appointment of personnel of the judiciary, the Bar, the State's Notary Office;
- Meteorological service, weights and measures system, time measurement, geodesy and cartography, official statistics and accounting;
- State awards and honorary titles of the Federal State.

Every federal subject has exclusively within its competence powers stipulated in its constitution or its act of formation, within the framework of and pursuant to the provisions of the Constitution of the Federal State. Powers reserved exclusively to the competencies of each federal subject can be augmented or altered only with the consent of the legislative bodies of the Federal State and federal subject. Disagreements arising with regard to the exercise of powers by a federal subject which cannot be resolved by other means should be arbitrated by the Federal Constitutional Court.

The list of competencies reserved exclusively to the federal subject of Transdniestria (hereafter Transdniestria) includes the following:

- Establishing its own organs of authority and of government of the federal subject within the framework of the Constitution of the Federal State;
- Formation of organs of authority of the federal subject, appointment of office-holders to offices in government and institutions of Transdniestria;
- Exercising executive and administrative functions aimed at protection of human rights and freedoms, protection of rights of national minorities, observance of and upholding law and order and the rule of law within its territory;
- Establishing the system of direct taxation, crediting of revenues to the Transdniestrian budget and regulations for expenditure of revenues, consistent with the Constitution, laws and general principles of the Federal State;
- Adoption and application of Transdniestria's own legislation within the framework of the Constitution and the laws of the Federal State;

- Matters pertaining to property and economic activity within Transdniestria, consistent with the Constitution of the Federal State;
- Establishing Trade-Commerce and Registration Chambers, legislative regulation of their activities;
- Maintaining international ties, foreign economic and trade relations consistent with the Constitution and legislation of the Federal State; concluding international agreements pertaining to competencies of Transdniestria; establishing representations, which do not have status of diplomatic missions and consulates, in other states;
- International agreements on subjects within Transdniestria's competencies enter into force subject to being approved by the relevant Transdniestrian authorities;
- Participation in international organizations for which the status of subject of international law is not a condition of membership;
- Establishing a system of organs of municipal and local self-government within Transdniestria consistent with the Constitution and legislation of the Federal State;
- Matters pertaining to healthcare, education, labor relations, pensions and social welfare in Transdniestria taking into consideration standards set at the federal level;
- Matters pertaining to ownership, use and disposal of land, mineral resources, water and other natural resources on the territory of Transdniestria taking into account general federal rules and regulations;
- Matters pertaining to legal proceedings on the territory of Transdniestria, including establishing courts and their activity, consistent with the Constitution and legislation of the Federal State;
- Personnel of the judiciary and law-enforcement agencies, the Bar, the State's Notary Office in Transdniestria consistent with the Constitution and laws of the Federal State;
- Cultural and historical heritage, art, monuments, architecture, archaeology and scientific patrimony of local significance;
- Regulation by law of the organization and activities of associations engaged in educational, cultural, artistic, charitable activities and activities pertaining to social assistance, et al. within Transdniestria;
- Regulation by law of organization and activities in the sphere of sports, leisure and entertainment on the territory of Transdniestria;
- Other matters clearly designated in the legislation and Constitution of the Federal State or transferred to Transdniestria by the Federal State.

Within the limits of the competencies of the Federal State, delegation to Transdniestria of powers pertaining to the adoption of its own legislative norms within the framework of the principles designated by the law of the Federal State is permitted.

Mechanisms controlling Transdniestrian legislative norms within Transdniestria should be set up, without violating judicial authority of the Federal State.

The Federal State can transfer to Transdniestria those powers of the Federal State which are inherently subject to transfer. In each specific case, control by the Federal State and transfer of the appropriate financial resources should be provided for.

Outside the competencies of the Federal State and its powers pertaining to competencies reserved exclusively for the Federal State, Transdniestria enjoys the full plentitude of state power.

A single currency exists in the Federal State. Currency emission is effected exclusively by the National Bank of the Federal State. With the agreement of the National Bank and the Federal State, banknotes and coins with a special design may be emitted by a subsidiary branch of the bank of Transdniestria.

Constitutional laws are adopted pertaining to the competencies of the Federal State, having direct effect on the entire territory of the Federal State.

Outside the competences of the Federal State, Transdniestria enacts its own legal regulations, including the adoption of laws and other normative legal acts.

Laws and other normative legal acts of Transdniestria must not contradict the laws of the Federal State. In case of such contradictions the law of the Federal State applies.

The system of public authorities of Transdniestria is established by Transdniestria independently, consistent with the fundamental principles of the constitutional order of the Federal State and the general principles of the organization of the legislative and executive bodies of the state authority.

For the purposes of exercising their powers, the executive authorities of the Federal State can appoint appropriate officials to respective local territorial and municipal bodies.

Executive bodies of the Federal State can delegate the exercise of some of their powers to the executive bodies of Transdniestria by agreement with the executive bodies of Transdniestria, provided this does not contravene the Constitution and laws of the Federal State.

Executive bodies of Transdniestria can delegate the exercise of some of their powers to the executive bodies of the Federal State under agreement with the executive bodies of the Federal State.

On the territory of the Federal State legislative, executive and judicial powers are exercised directly by the Federal Parliament, Federal President, Federal Government and federal courts respectively, and in cases stipulated by federal law these powers are exercised by relevant authorities of the federal subject.

In the Federal State, only those federal state institutions are created which are necessary for effective exercise of those powers within its competencies and for effecting coordinating procedures between the bodies of the Federal State and Transdniestria.

The Parliament of the Federal State consists of two Chambers: Upper and Lower (the names of these chambers are designated by the Constitution of the Federal State).

Election of members of the Upper and Lower Chambers is carried out in conformance with the law on the basis of equal and direct suffrage by free secret ballot.

The number of members of the Upper and Lower Chambers is established by the Constitution and laws of the Federal State.

The Upper Chamber is constituted on the basis of administrative and territorial criteria.

The Lower Chamber is composed of the members elected in single member constituencies and/or single constituency in conformance with the proportional electoral system of the Federal State in conformance with the laws of the Federal State.

The election of the Parliament, organization of its activity, as well as its powers are established by the Constitution and laws of the Federal State.

The power to initiate laws belongs to the President of the Federal State, Members of Parliament, the government of the Federal State and the legislative organ of Transdniestria.

Bills are introduced in the Lower Chamber.

Laws of the Federal State are passed by the Parliament by majority vote in each Chamber of the Parliament, unless otherwise provided in the Constitution of the Federal State. Laws passed in the Lower Chamber are submitted to the Upper Chamber for consideration within fourteen (14) days.

Should a law adopted by both Chambers be rejected by the President within fourteen (14) days from the moment of its submission to him, the Parliament debates the given law again in accordance with established procedures. If during the second reading the law is approved in its redaction approved earlier by three-fifths of the votes in each Chamber of the Parliament, it is subject to promulgation by the President of the Federal State.

Constitutional laws are adopted on matters stipulated by the Constitution of the Federal State. A constitutional law is considered to be passed if it is approved by a two-thirds vote in each Chamber of the Parliament.

The President of the Federal State is the Head of the State.

The President of the Federal State determines the basic course of domestic and foreign policy of the Federal State in accordance with the Constitution and laws of the Federal State.

The procedure for election of the President of the Federal State is established by the Constitution of the Federal State.

In this respect, the President of the Federal State can be elected either by a nationwide vote or at a joint session of both Chambers of the Parliament.

The President of the Federal State can be dismissed from office on the basis of the Constitution of the Federal State.

The President of the Federal State submits for approval by the Federal Parliament candidates for positions in the organs of state power and administrative agencies of the Federal State, and proposals pertaining to the structure of the Government of the Federal State.

Executive power of the Federal State is exercised by the Government of the Federal State. The formation of the Government, organization of its activities and its powers are established by the Constitution and laws of the Federal State.

Justice in the Federal State is administered solely by the courts. The judicial system of the Federal State is established by the Constitution of the Federal State and its laws.

During the period in which the Federal State is being developed, measures of mutual confidence between the Federal State and Transdniestria function and are strengthened.

It will be necessary to work out and put into effect an integrated system of guarantees for complying with and enforcing agreements which will be reached as a result of the Transdniestrian settlement negotiation process in the five-sided format, with the participation of the Republic of Moldova, Transdniestria, the OSCE, the Russian Federation and Ukraine.

Political guarantees provide for Transdniestria's right to secede from the Federal State should a decision about the Federal State's accession to another state be adopted and/or on the grounds of total forfeiture by the Federal State of its status of a subject of international law. The possible secession of Transdniestria from the Federal State is to be effected on the basis of a decision taken in a general referendum in Transdniestria by a majority of voters registered in Transdniestrian territory.

International legal guarantees provide that all agreements signed as a result of the Transdniestrian settlement negotiation process shall be registered with the OSCE and deposited with the guarantor countries—the Russian Federation and Ukraine.

Legal safeguards provide for legislative enactment of all agreements that will be reached as a result of the Transdniestrian settlement negotiation process.

Economic guarantees include economic and financial support for the outcome of the Transdniestrian settlement. These include measures of economic support and coercive measures involving economic and financial leverage on that party which does not adhere to the agreements achieved.

The formation of the budget of the Federal State will be ensured by means of federal taxes, collections, other mandatory payments and by means of income from privatization and other uses of federal property. The formation of the budget of Transdniestria is ensured by means of regional taxes and collections established by Transdniestrian laws, and by means of income from privatization and other use of Transdniestrian property, as well as by means of transfers deriving from federal taxes, collections and other payments, established by the federal law. Composition and marginal rates of municipal levies, established by the federal law, fall under economic guarantees.

Measures pertaining to guaranteeing implementation of agreed provisions in social, cultural and humanitarian spheres should be stipulated.

Military guarantees include military-guarantee insurance (*voenno- garantiinogo obespecheniia*—hereafter military guarantees) of conditions of compliance with and observance of the final agreements on a Transdniestrian settlement.

In order to implement the military guarantees, an appropriate multinational military contingent and multinational unarmed observers will be required.

The parameters of military guarantees are to be elaborated within the five-sided format that is currently in operation.

The role of the OSCE as an international organization that can take such military guarantees under its aegis should be considered.

The willingness of the Russian Federation and the Ukraine, as acknowledged guarantor countries, to take part in the military guarantees of the results of the Transdniestrian settlement should be considered.

The principles should be ensured of not permitting gaps in the military reinforcement of peace and stability and of the gradual transition from one format of military guarantees to another format.

Military guarantees are implemented with the agreement of the authorities of the Federal State and Transdniestria.

During the period in which the Federal State is establishing itself measures to enhance military transparency and trust are to be implemented, in particular, gradual reduction of military capacity, up to demilitarization.

Military guarantees should be elaborated consistent with the contents of the agreements on the Transdniestrian settlement.

Following adoption of the Constitution of the Federal State, the conclusion of final agreements on the settlement of the Transdniestrian question, a transition period shall be established, during which these agreements are to be implemented. All contested questions that arise shall be resolved with the assistance of the existing negotiating mechanisms and newly created conciliation mechanisms, with the assistance of mediators from the OSCE, the Russian Federation and Ukraine.

Appendix B

The Kozak *Memorandum*— September 11 Draft

(OSCE Mission to Moldova translation)

Classified
Draft
11 September 2003

MEMORANDUM

**on the basic principles of the state structure
for the development of the new Constitution
of the Republic of Moldova**

1. The Republic of Moldova and Transdniestria (hereinafter—the Parties), acknowledging their responsibility for uniting the country, ensuring civil peace and full democratic development have agreed that the final settlement of the Transdniestrian problem should be made through the reintegration of the united, independent and democratic state based on the principles of the federal State, within the borders of the Moldovan SSR as of 1 January 1990.

2. The Parties believe that the implementation of practical mechanisms for the settlement of the Transdniestrian problem is possible on the basis of the joint development and preliminary nationwide discussion and adoption of the new Constitution of the Republic of Moldova.

3. To prepare the draft of the new Constitution, the Parties created the Joint Constitutional Commission consisting of the plenipotentiary representatives from each Party, inviting as observers

the international experts from the guarantor-states, the Organization for Security and Cooperation in Europe, European Union, as well as the European Commission for Democracy through Law (Venice Commission) of the European Council.

4. The Joint Constitutional Commission shall function on the basis of its regulation and review the principles of State structure stipulated by this Declaration, as determining and binding when developing the draft of the new Constitution.

5. The following basic principles of the State structure should be established in the new Constitution of the Republic of Moldova:

5.1. The Republic of Moldova is a democratic, federal state, based on the principle of territorial integrity, united state power, common defense, customs and currency and monetary space.

5.2. Free movement of people, goods, services and capital shall be recognized and guaranteed on the territory of the Republic of Moldova.

5.3. The Constitution of the Republic of Moldova, federal organic laws and other acts of the federal bodies of state power, adopted in accordance with the Constitution, and related to the matters that are within the competences of the Republic of Moldova, shall have direct effect throughout the Republic of Moldova and shall be binding upon all bodies of state power, local public authorities and natural and legal entities.

5.4. The Transdniestrian Moldovan Republic shall be the subject of federation and form its own bodies of legislative, executive and judicial power, shall have its own Constitution and legislation, state property, independent budget and tax system.

5.5. The constitutional and legal status of autonomous territorial unit of Gagauzia established by the existing Constitution of the Republic of Moldova (as amended by Law No. 344-XV of July 26, 2003) shall be fixed in the new Constitution, subject to the provisions of this Memorandum.

5.6. Moldovan language shall be state language in the Republic of Moldova. Russian language shall be the official language throughout the Republic of Moldova. The Constitution of the Transdniestrian Moldovan Republic and laws of autonomous territorial unit of Gagauzia can establish other official languages alongside the Moldovan and Russian languages on the territory of the Transdniestrian Moldovan Republic and autonomous-territorial unit of Gagauzia. Record keeping in all bodies of state power and local authorities shall be done in state and official languages.

5.7. The Republic of Moldova shall be the subject of international law and member of international world and regional organizations, membership of which should be conditioned by being subject to the international law.

5.8. The Republic of Moldova shall establish international relations with other states and international organizations, and conclude international treaties and agreements.

5.9. Ratified international treaties of the Republic of Moldova and generally accepted principles of international law shall prevail over the legislation of the Republic of Moldova.

5.10. International treaties that cover issues under the Republic of Moldova competence shall be subject to ratification by federal ordinary laws.

5.11. International treaties that cover competencies shared between the Republic of Moldova and Transdniestrian Moldovan Republic (hereinafter—shared competencies) shall be subject to ratification by federal organic laws. While negotiating an international treaty touching upon shared competencies, the Federal Government shall conduct preliminary consultations with the bodies of state power of the Transdniestrian Moldovan Republic in accordance with the procedure established by a federal organic law.

5.12. International treaties that cover competencies of the Transdniestrian Moldovan Republic shall enter into force provided that they are ratified by the Transdniestrian Moldovan Republic law.

5.13. The Transdniestrian Moldovan Republic can be a member of international world and regional organizations, membership of which is not conditioned by being subject to international law, enter international treaties covering issues that fall under the jurisdiction of Transdniestrian Moldovan Republic and establish representations in other countries that do not have the status of diplomatic missions and consulates.

5.14. The constitutional and legal status and borders of the Transdniestrian Moldovan Republic, and autonomous-territorial unit of Gagauzia cannot be changed without their consent.

5.15. The Transdniestrian Moldovan Republic and a autonomous-territorial unit of Gagauzia shall have the right to secede from the Republic of Moldova if the Republic of Moldova decides to join another state and (or) in case the Republic of Moldova should completely cease to be subject to the international law.

5.16. The secession of the Transdniestrian Moldovan Republic and autonomous-territorial unit of Gagauzia from the Republic of Moldova shall be made on the basis of decisions adopted in nation-wide referendums of the Transdniestrian Moldovan Republic or autonomous-territorial unit of Gagauzia by the majority of voters registered on the territory of the Transdniestrian Moldovan Republic or autonomous-territorial unit respectively. These referendums should be called by the legislative bodies of state power of the Transdniestrian Moldovan Republic or autonomous-territorial unit of Gagauzia respectively, provided there are grounds for secession.

5.17. The Constitution of the Republic of Moldova shall establish the competencies of the Republic of Moldova, shared competencies and competencies of the Transdniestrian Moldovan Republic.

6. The Republic of Moldova shall have the following competencies:

6.1. Federal state property and management of this property;

6.2. Currency, customs regulation, monetary emission, activity of the National Bank;

6.3. Energy systems, air, railway, water, pipe-line transport, communications;

6.4. Foreign policy, foreign trade and international treaties of the Republic of Moldova, issues of war and peace;

6.5. Citizenship of the Republic of Moldova, emigration and immigration issues;

6.6. Defense and security; defense production; establishing the procedure for sale and purchase of arms, ammunition, military equipment and other military property; production of poisonous substances, drug substances and procedure for their use;

6.7. Determining the status and protecting the State borders and the airspace of the Republic of Moldova, border zone regime;

6.8. Collision law;

6.9. Meteorology, geodesy, cartography, standards, calibration, metric system and time measurement;

6.10. Official statistics and accounting;

6.11. Federal State awards and honorary titles.

7. The shared competencies shall be as follows:

7.1. Regulation and protection of human rights and freedoms, rights of the national minorities;

7.2. Judicial system, organization and operation of law enforcement agencies, criminal, criminal procedure and criminal enforcement legislation, amnesty and pardon;

7.3. Civil, civil procedure and arbitration-procedure legislation, legal regulation of intellectual property;

7.4. Ownership, use and disposal of land, earth, water and other natural resources;

7.5. Dividing public property into the federal property, property of the Transdniestrian Moldovan Republic, property of the autonomous-territorial unit of Gagauzia and municipal property;

7.6. Federal budget, federal taxes, dues and other obligatory payments; state regulation of prices for goods and services;

7.7. Environment protection and ensuring ecological safety, protection of unique nature preserves, historical and cultural monuments;

7.8. Education and science;

7.9. Health care, protection of family, motherhood, fatherhood and childhood, social protection, including social assistance;

7.10. Combating disasters, natural calamities, epidemics and eliminating their consequences;

8. Issues not defined by the Constitution of the Republic of Moldova as competencies of the Republic of Moldova and shared competencies shall fall under the competencies of the Transdniestrian Moldovan Republic.

9. Competencies of the bodies of state power of the autonomous-territorial unit of Gagauzia shall be established by the federal organic law.

10 (a). Regulation of relations that fall under the competencies of the Republic of Moldova, including determining the powers of all levels and branches of the public authorities on indicated competencies, shall be carried out by federal ordinary laws.

(b). Regulation of relationships in the case of shared competencies, including determining the powers of all levels and branches of the public authorities in indicated competencies, shall be carried out by federal organic laws.

(c). Federal ordinary laws and federal organic laws that establish the powers of the bodies of public authorities of the Transdniestrian Moldovan Republic and (or) autonomous territorial unit of Gagauzia in case of the Republic of Moldova competencies and shared competencies, exercising of which result in budget expenses, shall contain provisions on allocation of subsidies earmarked for special purposes from the federal budget to the budgets of the Transdniestrian Moldovan Republic and (or) Gagauzia, and (or) municipal budgets, as well as the mode (method) of calculating these subsidies.

(d). Regulation of relations in case of the competencies of the Transdniestrian Moldovan Republic and competencies of the autonomous-territorial unit of Gagauzia, including establishing the powers of the bodies of state power and local authorities of the Transdniestrian Moldovan Republic and autonomous-territorial unit of Gagauzia shall be carried out by laws of the Transdniestrian Moldovan Republic and laws of the autonomous-territorial unit of Gagauzia accordingly.

11 (a). On the territory of the Republic of Moldova, except for the territory of the Transdniestrian Moldovan Republic and the territory of the autonomous-territorial unit of Gagauzia, all powers of the legislative, executive and judicial branches shall be exercised respectively and directly by the federal President, federal Parliament, federal Government and federal courts, and by local public authorities—the latter in cases established by federal laws.

(b). On the territory of the autonomous-territorial unit of Gagauzia, all the competencies of the bodies of state power shall be exercised by the federal bodies of state power, except for the powers that fall under the competencies of the bodies of state power of the autonomous-territorial unit of Gagauzia.

12 (a). The federal budget of the Republic of Moldova shall be constituted by federal taxes, dues and other obligatory payments, established by federal organic laws, as well as of proceeds from privatization and other uses of federal property.

(b). The budgets of the Transdniestrian Moldovan Republic and autonomous-territorial unit of Gagauzia shall be constituted by regional taxes and dues, proceeds from privatization and other uses of property of the Transdniestrian Moldovan Republic and autonomous-territorial unit of Gagauzia, as established by laws of the Transdniestrian Moldovan Republic and autonomous-territorial unit of Gagauzia, as well as from allocations from the federal taxes, charges, dues and other payments, as established by the federal organic law.

(c). The structure and marginal rates of municipal taxes and dues shall be established by federal organic law.

13 (a). The federal legislative body of the state power of the Republic of Moldova shall be the Federal Parliament consisting of two chambers—Senate and Chamber of Representatives.

(b). The Senate shall consist of 26 senators, 5 of whom shall be elected by the National Assembly of the autonomous-territorial unit of Gagauzia, 8—by the Supreme Soviet of the Transdniestrian Moldovan Republic, 13—by the Chamber of Representatives of the federal Parliament of the Republic of Moldova.

(c). The Chamber of Representatives shall consist of 71 deputies, elected in accordance with the federal organic law based on the general, direct, equal and secret vote in a single election district in accordance with the proportional election system.

14 (a). Federal constitutional laws, federal ordinary laws and federal organic laws shall be adopted by the Chamber of Representatives.

(b). Federal organic laws and federal ordinary laws shall be subject to approval by the Senate.

(c). Senate's veto on federal ordinary laws and the Federal President of the Republic of Moldova veto on federal organic laws and federal ordinary laws is overruled by the Chamber of Representatives through second adoption of respective law by a qualified majority of the two-thirds of the established number of the deputies. Senate's veto on federal organic laws shall be absolute.

15. The Head of the state of Republic of Moldova shall be the Federal President, elected at the joint meeting of the Senate and Chamber of Representatives of the Federal Parliament, by the majority of three-fifths of the established number of both chambers during a secret vote.

16 (a). The executive power in the Republic of Moldova shall be exercised by the Federal Government.

(b). The Chairman of the Government shall be appointed by the Senate upon the proposal from the Federal President. The Chairman of the Federal Government shall have two first deputies that are appointed by the Federal President upon the proposal from the Chairman of the Federal Government and in coordination with the Parliament of the Transdniestrian Moldovan Republic and the National Assembly of the autonomous-territorial unit of Gagauzia respectively.

17. The Supreme Court of the Republic of Moldova, courts of appeal and courts of original jurisdiction shall be set up in accordance with the federal organic law to administer civil, administrative and criminal justice in the Republic of Moldova. To administer the constitutional justice, a Constitutional Court that will directly administer the constitutional justice is set up.

17.1. The Supreme Court of the Republic of Moldova shall be the highest court of appeal for civil, administrative and criminal cases. The Supreme Court shall be formed by the Senate.

17.2. The Constitutional Court shall consist of 9 judges, 5 of whom shall be appointed by the Chamber of Representatives, 1—by the National Assembly of the autonomous-territorial unit of Gagauzia, 3—by the Parliament of the Transdniestrian Moldovan Republic.

17.3. Judges in the courts of original jurisdiction and courts of appeals in the Transdniestrian Moldovan Republic shall be appointed in the manner established by the Transdniestrian Moldovan Republic law.

18. The new Constitution of the Republic of Moldova shall incorporate transitional provisions, stipulating that:

18.1. The Senate shall be formed no later than 1 February 2005. The deputies of the Chamber of Representatives of the first convocation shall be elected no later than 31 April 2005. On the territory of Transdniestria, the elections procedure shall be regulated by Transdniestrian laws.

18.2. The Government of the Republic of Moldova shall lay down its powers before the newly elected Senate, which shall approve the Chairman of the Federal Government in accordance with the new Constitution of the Republic of Moldova.

18.3. Elections of the Federal President shall be held on the basis of federal organic law no later than 31 May 2005.

18.4. Restructuring or dissolution of existing courts in the Republic of Moldova and in Transdniestria, and setting up the Supreme Court and other courts in accordance with the new Constitution shall be carried out in accordance with the procedure and within the time limits established by the federal organic law.

18.5. The procedure and time limits for setting up federal bodies of executive power that exercise on the territory of Transdniestrian Moldovan Republic the powers within the competencies of federal bodies of the state power, as well as the shared competencies, shall be established by the appropriate federal laws and federal organic laws. Prior to the adoption of these laws, the bodies of the state power of Transdniestria shall exercise their powers in accordance with the Transdniestrian laws.

18.6. Federal taxes, dues and other obligatory payments on the territory of the Transdniestrian Moldovan Republic shall be levied as from 1 January 2007. Until 1 January 2007, the Transdniestrian Moldovan Republic shall make an annual contribution to the federal budget equivalent to one-sixth of the revenue of federal budget of the Republic of Moldova.

18.7. Financial obligations of the Republic of Moldova that emerged before the new Constitution enters into force shall be fulfilled by resorting to the federal budget, while the financial obligations of Transdniestria—by resorting to the budget of the Transdniestrian Moldovan Republic.

18.8. The rights of state, municipal and private ownership based on Transdniestrian legislation that emerged before the new Constitution of the Republic of Moldova enters into force shall be recognized and protected on the territory of the Republic of Moldova. The division of the ownership rights into the property under the public ownership of Transdniestria, federal property and property of the Transdniestrian Moldovan Republic shall be effectuated in accordance with the federal organic law, on the basis of separation of powers with regards to the competencies within the Republic of Moldova and shared competencies, established in appropriate federal laws and federal organic laws.

19. Modifications to the new Constitution of the Republic of Moldova shall be introduced by federal constitutional law. The right of the Senate to veto federal constitutional laws shall be absolute.

20. The draft of the new Constitution shall be subject to publication in mass media for nation-wide discussion no later than 31 March 2004. The nation-wide referendum on the matter of the adoption

of the new Constitution of the Republic of Moldova shall be held no later than 31 October 2004.

The leaderships of the Republic of Moldova and Transdniestria undertake the commitments and guarantees to create all the conditions necessary for holding a nation-wide referendum on the entire territory of the Republic of Moldova within its internationally recognized borders, in accordance with the democracy standards of the Organization for Security and Cooperation in Europe and European Council.

For the Republic of Moldova   For Transdniestria

Appendix C

The Kozak *Memorandum*— November 23 Redaction

(OSCE Mission to Moldova translation)

MEMORANDUM

On Basic Principles of State Structure of the Unified State

1. The Republic of Moldova and Transdniestria (hereinafter—the Sides), recognizing their responsibility for the unification of the country, upholding civil peace and fully-fledged democratic development, have agreed that the final settlement of the Transdniestrian problem must be carried out by transforming the state structure of the Republic of Moldova with a view to building a unified, democratic state based on federal principles and delimited within the borders of the territory of the Moldavian SSR as of 1 January 1990.

2. The parties believe that the implementation of practical mechanisms for the settlement of the Transdniestrian problem is possible on basis of joint elaboration, preliminary nationwide discussion and adoption of the Constitution of the Unified State—the Federal Republic of Moldova.

3. The following basic principles of state structure are to be enshrined in the Constitution of the unified state:

3.1. The Federal Republic of Moldova (hereinafter for the purposes of the present Memorandum—the Federation) is a democratic, constitutional sovereign federal state, based on the principle of territorial integrity, common principles of organization of the state authority, single defense (for the duration of the transition period), customs, monetary space.

The policy of the Federation is channeled at the creation of conditions ensuring dignified life and free development of a person. The vehicle of sovereignty and the only source of state authority in the Federation are its people. The people exercise their authority directly and through the agencies of state power and agencies of local self-government.

3.2. The individual, his rights and freedoms are the highest value in the Federation. Recognition, observance and protection of rights and freedoms of the individual and the citizen are a responsibility of the Federation and its subjects.

Every person is guaranteed legal protection of his rights and freedoms. Decisions and actions (or failure to act) of agencies of state power and municipal authorities in the state, of public associations and functionaries can be contested in court instances.

Every person has a right, pursuant to the international treaties to which the Federation is a party, to appeal to international instances of human rights protection in case all domestic instruments of legal protection have been exhausted.

3.3. Political pluralism and political freedoms, including the right to setting up political parties, are guaranteed and upheld on the entire territory of the Federation.

3.4. All the forms of property—private, state and other—are equally recognized and protected on the territory of the Federation.

3.5. The Federation is a neutral demilitarized state. The conditions and procedure of the abolition of the Armed Forces, social and other guarantees to the members of the Armed Forces of the Republic of Moldova and Transdniestria are determined by a federal organic law.

Till complete demilitarization of the Federation the Armed Forces are formed and act on the basis of the territorial principle of the formation of military units and cannot be deployed for the enforcement of law and order and public security on the territory of the Federation. The command of the Armed Forces of the Federation is exercised by an authorized federal executive body. The maximum number of staff of law-enforcement agencies, national and public security agencies is determined by a federal organic law.

3.6. Free circulation of people, goods, services and capital is recognized and guaranteed on the territory of the Federation.

3.7. The Constitution of the Federation, federal ordinary laws enacted pursuant to the Constitution on the competencies of the Federation and federal organic laws enacted pursuant to the Constitution on the joint competencies of the Federation and the Subjects of the Federation, and other acts of federal state power agencies enacted in pursuance of the Constitution and of federal laws, have a direct effect on the entire territory of the Federation and are binding for all the agencies of state power, agencies of local self-government, for juridical persons and natural persons.

3.8. The Transdniestrian Moldovan Republic is a Subject of the Federation, a state entity within the Federation, forming its own legislative (the Supreme Soviet of the Transdniestrian Moldovan Republic), executive (the President of the Transdniestrian Moldovan Republic and the Government of the Transdniestrian Moldovan Republic) and judicial agencies of state power, having its own Constitution and legislation, state property, independent budget and taxation system, and state symbols and other attributes of its state status.

Autonomous-Territorial Unit of Gagauzia is a subject of the Federation, forming its own legislative, executive and judicial agencies, having its own Fundamental law and legislation, state property, independent budget and taxation system, and its own state symbols and other attributes of its autonomous status.

3.9. Outside the territories of the Subjects of the Federation all the legislative, executive and judicial powers on the competencies of the Subjects of the Federation are exercised directly by the federal President, federal Parliament, federal Government and federal courts respectively, and in the cases stipulated by laws—by agencies of local self-government.

3.10. Constitutional and legal status and borders of the territories of the Subjects of the Federation cannot be changed without their consent.

3.11. The Federation is a subject of international law and member of the world and regional organizations the membership of which is subject to having international legal personality.

International commitments of the Republic of Moldova undertaken prior to the entry into force of the Constitution of the Federation are recognized and fully fulfilled by the Federation.

3.12. The Federation establishes international relations with other states and international organizations and concludes international treaties and agreements.

Ratified international treaties and agreements and generally accepted principles of international law prevail over the legislation of the Federation.

3.13. International treaties on the competencies of the Federation are subject to ratification by federal ordinary laws.

3.14. International treaties on the joint competencies of the Federation and the Subjects of the Federation (hereinafter—joint competencies) are subject to ratification by federal organic laws. In cases of negotiations about concluding an international treaty involving joint competencies, the federal Government holds preliminary consultations with agencies of state power of the Subjects of the Federation for the purposes of taking into account the views of the Subjects of the Federation, and guarantees the participation of representatives of authorized agencies of the Subjects of the Federation in the negotiations in accordance with the procedure established by a federal organic law.

3.15. The Subjects of the Federation can be members of international, world and regional organizations for the membership of which international legal subjectivity is not a mandatory requirement, can maintain international relations, conclude international treaties on the competencies of the Subjects of the Federation and set up missions that do not have the status of diplomatic missions or consulates in other states.

3.16. The Subjects of the Federation have a right to secede from the Federation only in the event of a decision about the Federation's annexation to another state being taken and (or) on the grounds of the Federation's complete forfeiture of its sovereignty.

3.17. The secession of a Subject of the Federation from the Federation is carried out on the basis of decisions taken in a nationwide referendum of the Subject of the Federation by a majority of votes of the constituents registered on the territory of the Subject of the Federation. The given referendum is called by the legislative agency of state power of the Subject of the Federation provided grounds for secession exist.

Organizational and logistical support of the referendum is provided by agencies of state power and agencies of local self-government of the Subject of the Federation.

3.18. Competencies of the Federation, joint competencies and competencies of the Subjects of the Federation are determined by the Constitution of the Federation.

4. Competencies of the Federation are as follows:

4.1. Federal state property and its administration;

4.2. Currency regulation, currency issue;

4.3. Air, rail and water transport;

4.4. Foreign policy, foreign trade and international treaties of the Federation, war and peace issues;

4.5. Citizenship of the Federation, emigration and immigration issues;

4.6. Establishing the procedure for the manufacture, sales and purchases of weapons and ammunitions; manufacture of poisonous substances, drug substances and procedure for their use;

4.7. Determining the status of and protecting state border, air space of the Federation, border zones regime;

4.8. Conflicts of law;

4.9. Meteorology, geodesy, cartography, standards and measurement standards, metric system and chronology;

4.10. Federal statistical service and accounting;

4.11. Federal state awards and honorary titles.

5. Joint competences are as follows:

5.1. Monitoring human rights and freedoms, rights of national minorities;

5.2. Custom control, the activity of the Central Federal Bank;

5.3. Power systems, pipeline transportation, communication;

5.4. Judicial system, administration and activity of law-enforcement agencies, penal and penal procedure legislation, amnesty and pardon, legislation on administrative infractions;

5.5. Civil, labor, civil procedure and arbitral procedure legislation, legal regulation of intellectual property, common principles of administration and activity of the notariat;

5.6. Ownership, use and administration of land, subsurface resources, water and other natural resources;

5.7. Division of public property into federal property and property of the Subjects of the Federation;

5.8. Federal budget, federal taxes, dues and other mandatory fees, state regulation of goods and services prices, antimonopoly regulation;

5.9. Environment protection and ensuring environmental safety, protection of unique nature reserves, historical monuments and cultural monuments of federal importance;

5.10. Common education and social protection principles;

5.11. Issues pertaining to combating catastrophes, natural calamities, epidemics and to their management;

5.12. Common principles of foreign economic activity of citizens and juridical persons;

5.13. Electoral law.

6. The competencies of the Subjects of the Federation are as follows:

6.1. Regulation of foreign economic activity on the competencies of the Subjects of the Federation which is carried out by agencies of state power of the Subjects of the Federation from own funds of the Subjects of the Federation, and regulation of foreign economic activity of citizens and organizations within the limits of powers determined by federal organic laws.

6.2. Setting up the system of agencies of state power of the Subjects of the Federation;

6.3. Administrative legislation related to the regulation of activity of agencies of state power of the Subjects of the Federation;

6.4. Issues pertaining to local self-government, establishing and guaranteeing the right of citizens to local self-government;

6.5. Family and housing legislation;

6.6. Public health issues;

6.7. The administration and activity of the Bar;

6.8. State property of the Subjects of the Federation and administration of hereinabove property;

6.9. The approval and implementation of the budgets of the Subjects of the Federation, effecting control of the implementation of the budgets of the Subjects of the Federation;

6.10. Art and culture, protection of historic monuments and culture monuments of regional importance, physical education and sport;

6.11. Town-planning and architecture issues;

6.12. State awards and honorary titles of the Subjects of the Federation;

6.13. Issues pertaining to additional social protection measures accorded to the citizens living on the territory of the Subjects of the Federations from the budgetary funds of the Subjects of the Federation;

6.14. Other issues not attributed to the competencies of the Federation or joint competencies.

7 (a). Regulation of relations on the competencies of the Federation, including determination of powers of all levels and branches of public authority on the given competencies, is effected by federal ordinary laws.

(b). Regulation of relations on joint competencies, including determination of powers of all levels and branches of public authority on the given competencies, is effected by federal organic laws.

(c). Federal ordinary laws, federal organic laws, determining the powers of agencies of public authority of the Subjects of the Federation on the competencies of the Federation and on joint competencies, the enforcement of which involves budgetary expenditure, must contain provisions stipulating allocation of earmarked subsidies from the federal budget to the budgets of the Subjects of the Federation and (or) to municipal budgets, and stipulating the way (method) of calculating such subsidies.

(d). Regulation of relations on the competencies of the Subjects of the Federation, including determination of powers of agencies of state power and agencies of local self-government of the Subjects of the Federation, is effected by the laws of the Subjects of the Federation. Agencies of state power of the Subjects of the Federation enjoy the plentitude of state power on the competencies of the Subjects of the Federation.

(e). Relations on the issues attributed by the Constitution of the Federation to the competencies of the Subjects of the Federation outside the territories of the Subjects of the Federation are regulated by laws enacted by the House of Representatives by a simple majority of votes of the established number of members of the House of Representatives and are subject to promulgation by the federal President. The given laws are not subject to the approval of the Senate.

(f). Legal regulation of relations on the competencies of the Federation and on joint competencies within the limits of legislative powers of the Subjects of the Federation established by the Constitution of the Federation, by federal organic laws, by federal ordinary laws, can be effected by laws of the Subjects of the Federation.

8 (a). The federal budget is formed by federal taxes, dues, other mandatory fees, established by federal organic laws, and by the proceeds from privatization and other use of federal property.

(b). The budgets of the Subjects of the Federation are formed by regional taxes and dues established by the laws of the Subjects of the Federation, by the proceeds from privatization and other use of state property of the Subjects of the Federation, and by allocations from federal taxes, dues, duties and other payments, hereinabove allocations being determined by federal organic laws.

(c). The composition and marginal rates of municipal taxes and dues are determined by federal organic laws.

9 (a). The federal Parliament consisting of two houses: the Senate and the House of Representatives, is the federal legislative body of state power.

(b). The Senate consists of 26 senators elected for five years, 4 of which are elected by the People's Assembly of the Autonomous Territorial Unit of Gagauzia, 9—by the Supreme Soviet of the Transdniestrian Moldovan Republic, 13—by the House of Representatives of the federal Parliament.

(c). The House of Representatives consists of 71 members elected for four years in pursuance of a federal organic law on the basis of universal, direct and equal suffrage by secret ballot throughout single electoral district in accordance with proportional election system.

10 (a). Federal organic laws are passed by the House of Representatives by a simple majority of the established number of members of the House of Representatives, are approved by the Senate by a simple majority of the established number of Senate members and are subject to promulgation by the federal President. In the event of the Senate's failure to approve the federal organic law, this law is deemed rejected.

(b). Federal ordinary laws are passed by the House of Representatives by a simple majority of the established number of members of the House of Representatives, are approved by the Senate by a simple majority of the established number of Senate members and are subject to promulgation by the federal President.

The veto of federal ordinary laws by the Senate and veto of federal organic laws by the federal President is overcome by the House of Representatives by re-enactment of the law in question by a qualified majority of no less than 2/3 of the established number of members of the House of Representatives.

(c). Amendments to the Constitution of the Federation are introduced by Federal constitutional laws which are enacted by the House of Representatives by a majority of no less than 4/5 of the established number of Senate members. In the event of the Senate's failure to approve the federal constitutional law, the law is deemed rejected.

11. The Head of the State is the federal President elected for five years in pursuance of a federal organic law.

12 (a). Executive power in the Federation is exercised by the federal Government.

(b). The appointments of the Chairman and members of the Federal Government are approved by the Senate as advised by the federal President. The Chairman of the federal Government has deputies, two of whom are appointed by the federal President as advised by the Chairman of the federal Government and by approbation of the authorized agencies of state power of the Subjects of the Federation.

(c). Appointments of heads and deputy heads of federal agencies of the executive are made in pursuance of the principle of proportionate representation of the Subjects of the Federation. The procedure for guaranteeing the representation of the Subjects of the Federation in federal agencies of the executive is established by relevant federal ordinary and (or) federal organic laws.

(d). Heads and other members of territorial agencies of federal executive bodies which exercise executive and regulatory powers on the competencies of the Subjects of the Federation and on joint competencies, whose appointments and dismissals are effectuated by federal executive agencies, are appointed to their positions and dismissed from them by approbation of relevant agencies of state power and officials of the Subjects of the Federation.

13. The Federal Supreme Court, courts of appeal and first instance courts are set up for the purposes of administering civil, administrative and criminal justice in the Federation.

The Federal Constitutional Court is set up for administering constitutional justice.

13.1. The Federal Constitutional Court is the highest appeals and (or) cassational instance for civil, administrative and criminal cases. The Supreme Court is formed by the Senate.

13.2. The Federal Constitutional Court consists of 11 judges, 6 of whom are appointed by the House of Representatives, 1—by the People's Assembly of the Autonomous-Territorial Unit of Gagauzia, 4—by the Supreme Soviet of the Transdniestrian Moldovan Republic. The members of the Federal Constitutional Court are approved by the Senate.

13.3. The judges of courts of first and appeals instances in the Subjects of the Federation are appointed in accordance with the procedure determined by the laws of the Subjects of the Federation.

14. Transitional provisions to the following effect are stipulated by the Constitution of the Federation:

14.1. The Senate is formed no later than 1 February 2005.

14.2. Members of the House of Representatives of the first convocation following the adoption of the Constitution of the Federation are elected no later than 30 April 2005 in pursuance of election procedures agreed upon by the Parliament of the Republic of Moldova, the Supreme Soviet of Transdniestria and the People's Assembly of the Autonomous-Territorial Unit of Gagauzia.

14.3. The Government of the Republic of Moldova abnegates its powers before the re-elected Senate, which confirms in office the Chairman of the federal Government in pursuance of the procedure stipulated by the Constitution of the Federation.

14.4. The elections of the federal President are held on the basis of a federal organic law no later than 31 May 2005.

14.5. The re-organization or abolition of courts in operation in the Republic of Moldova, Transdniestria and Autonomous-Territorial Unit of Gagauzia upon setting up the Federal Supreme Court and other courts in pursuance of the Constitution of the Federation are carried out in accordance with procedure and within the timeframe determined by a federal organic law.

14.6. The procedure and timeframe of the organization of federal executive agencies exercising powers on the competencies of the Federation and on joint competencies on the territory of the Subjects of the Federation, is determined by relevant federal ordinary laws and federal organic laws. Till the enactment of the hereinabove laws executive agencies of Transdniestria exercise their powers in accordance with the laws of Transdniestria provided agreements between the federal Government and an authorized agency of state power of the Transdniestrian Moldovan Republic do not stipulate otherwise.

14.7. Federal taxes, dues and other mandatory payments are levied on the territory of the Transdniestrian Moldovan Republic as of 1 January 2007. Prior to 1 January 2007 the Transdniestrian Moldovan Republic makes an annual contribution to the federal budget, the aforesaid contribution being equivalent to 1/6 of the federal budget expenses related to the maintenance of federal agencies of state power, save for the expenses related to the settlement and servicing of government debt of the Republic of Moldova incurred as of the date of entering in force of the Constitution of the Federation, and save for the maintenance cost of federal executive agencies, exercising their powers on the competencies of the Subjects of the Federation outside the territory of the Subjects of the Federation.

14.8. Financial liabilities of the Republic of Moldova incurred prior to entering into force of the Constitution of the Federation are discharged from the revenues of the federal budget levied on federal territory and territory of the Autonomous-Territorial Unit of Gagauzia whereas financial liabilities of Transdniestria are discharged from budgetary funds of the Transdniestrian Moldovan Republic.

14.9. State, municipal and private rights of ownership accrued on the basis of Transdniestrian legislation prior to entering into force of the Constitution of the Federation are not to be reviewed, are recognized and upheld on the territory of the Federation.

14.10. Division of ownership right to state property of Transdniestria and to state property of Autonomous-Territorial Unit of Gagauzia, into federal property and property of the Subjects of the Federation is carried out in pursuance of a federal organic law on the basis of delimitation of powers on the competencies of the Federation and on joint competencies, the aforesaid delimitation being established by federal ordinary laws and federal organic laws.

Transfer of state property of the Subjects of the Federation into municipal ownership, and privatization of hereinabove property is effectuated in accordance with the laws of the Subjects of the Federation.

14.11. Till 2015 federal organic laws are approved by the Senate by a 3/4 majority of the established number of Senate members.

A senator's mandate is imperative for the duration of the first two terms of convocation of the Senate.

14.12. Till 2020 the House of Representatives is elected in pursuance of a federal organic law on the basis of universal, direct, equal suffrage by secret ballot in accordance with proportional electoral system on the basis of federal and regional candidate lists (drawn up proportionately to population numbers of the territories in question).

14.13. Till 2015 decisions of the Federal Constitutional Court are adopted by no fewer than 9 votes.

14.14. Till 1 January 2007 matters of currency regulation and currency issue in the Federation, stipulated by item 4.2 of the present Memorandum shall be regulated by a federal organic law.

15. The status and use of Moldovan and Russian languages on the territory of the Federation is determined by the Constitution of the

Federation and by a federal organic law. Herein the following principles are to be enshrined in the Constitution:

Record-keeping in all agencies of state power and agencies of local self-government is conducted in Moldovan and Russian languages:

Every person has a right to receive official information from agencies of state power and local self-government and from their officials in Moldovan or Russian language according to his choice;

Alongside Moldovan and Russian languages, other official and (or) state languages of the Subjects of the Federation can be established on the territories of the Subjects of the Federation by the Constitutions of the Subjects of the Federation;

The Federation guarantees a right to the preservation of mother tongue and creation of conditions for its study and development to all citizens residing on its territory.

16. To elaborate the draft of the Constitution of the Federation the Sides have set up the Joint Constitutional Commission composed of plenipotentiary representatives of each Side, with international experts from the mediator countries, the Organization for Security and Co-operation in Europe, the European Union and the European Commission for Democracy through Law (Venice Commission) of the Council of Europe, being invited as observers.

The Joint Constitutional Commission acts on the basis of its statute and deems the principles of state structure stipulated by the present Memorandum to be governing and binding for the process of elaboration of the draft of the Constitution of the Federation.

The draft of the Constitution of the Federation is to be published in mass-media for nationwide discussion no later than 31 March 2004. A nationwide referendum on the issue of adoption of the Constitution is held no later than 31 October 2004.

The authorities of the Republic of Moldova and Transdniestria undertake the commitments and guarantees to create all conditions necessary for holding a nationwide referendum on the entire territory of the Republic of Moldova within its internationally recognized borders in pursuance of democratic principles of the Organization for Security and Co-operation in Europe and of the Council of Europe.

As of the day of approval of the present Memorandum no restrictions on the activity of political and public associations, propagation of mass-media registered by authorized agencies of the sides, movement of representatives of agencies of state power and citizens are allowed on the territory of the Sides.

Canvassing on the issues related to participation in the referendum and the issues related to the referendum is carried out without any restrictions in accordance with the legislation of the Sides.

The Constitution of the Federation is deemed to be adopted if it was voted by the majority of constituents that took part in the referendum on the territory of the Sides, with a separate count of votes. A single ballot agreed upon by the Sides is to be used for voting in the referendum.

The failure to adopt the Constitution of the Federation in the referendum does not entail a change in the actual position of the Sides. In such event the Sides undertake the commitments to continue work on the elaboration and putting to a referendum of a new draft of the Constitution of the Federation within a time period not exceeding 6 months.

17. The Sides propose to the Russian Federation, Ukraine, OSCE and European Union that the latter should provide political and economic guarantees ensuring compliance with the conditions for unification and territorial integrity of the Federal Republic of Moldova stipulated by the present Memorandum.

For this purpose observers may be deployed on the territories of the Sides.

The Sides also propose to the Russian Federation, Ukraine and OSCE that the latter provide such guarantees that in the event of violation of the conditions of enactment of the present Memorandum by one of the Sides, the Russian Federation, Ukraine and the OSCE guarantee the enactment of its provisions in regard of the other Side (including before international organizations and foreign states) and take measures to revive its enactment by all the parties to the present Memorandum.

18. The Sides propose to the Russian Federation that the latter should provide security guarantees for conditions of unification and territorial integrity of the Federal Republic of Moldova stipulated by the present Memorandum.

For this purpose subject to consent being granted by the Russian Federation, prior to the referendum on the issue of adoption of the Constitution of the Federation being called, the Republic of Moldova signs and ratifies a Treaty with the Russian Federation on the deployment on the territory of the future Federation for the transition period till full demilitarization of the state, but no later than year 2020, of stabilization peacekeeping forces of the Russian Federation numbering no more than 2,000 persons, without heavy military equipment and weapons.

The Treaty enters into force concurrently with the adoption of the Constitution of the Federation. In the event of non-fulfillment of the conditions stipulated by the present item the present Memorandum becomes inoperative.

19. After the entry into force of the Treaty indicated in item 18 of the present Memorandum the European Union, the OSCE and Ukraine can join it as mediators subject to conditions agreed upon by the Sides that are parties to the Treaty.

Notes

Chapter 1

1. For an English-language text, see "Speech of the President of the Russian Federation Vladimir V. Putin at the Munich Conference on Security Policy, Germany, February 10, 2007," www.mid.ru/brp_4.nsf/0/284B878CA1370C27C325728000336 94A.

2. For good general background on Moldovan history, see Charles King, *The Moldovans* (Stanford, Calif.: Hoover Institution Press, 2000); and Rebecca Haynes, "Historical Introduction," in *Occasional Papers in Romanian Studies. No. 3: Moldova, Bessarabia, Transnistria,* edited by Rebecca Haynes (London: School of Slavonic and East European Studies, University College London, 2003), 1–141.

Chapter 2

1. For comprehensive accounts of the events and hopes of this period, see, e.g., Jack F. Matlock Jr., *Autopsy of an Empire: The American Ambassador's Account of the Collapse of the Soviet Union* (New York: Random House, 1995); and Andrei Grachev, *Gorbachev's Gamble: Soviet Foreign Policy and the End of the Cold War* (Cambridge: Polity Press, 2008).

2. *Document of the Copenhagen Meeting of the Conference on the Human Dimension of the CSCE,* June 29, 1990, available at www.osce.org; *Charter of Paris for a New Europe,* November 19, 1990, www.osce.org/mc/39516.

3. Francis Fukuyama, "The End of History and the Last Man," *The National Interest,* Summer 1989; later published in book form: Francis Fukuyama, *The End of History and the Last Man* (New York: Penguin Books, 1992).

4. For excellent insider accounts of this period and these events, see, e.g., Robert L. Hutchings, *American Diplomacy and the End of the Cold War: An Insider's Account of U.S. Policy in Europe, 1989-1992* (Washington, D.C., and Baltimore: Woodrow Wilson Center Press and Johns Hopkins University Press, 1997); and Philip Ze-

likow and Condoleezza Rice, *Germany Unified and Europe Transformed: A Study in Statecraft* (Cambridge, Mass.: Harvard University Press, 1995).

5. See esp. Hutchings, *American Diplomacy,* 135–37; James A. Baker III, *The Politics of Diplomacy: Revolution, War, and Peace 1989–1992* (New York: G. P. Putnam's Sons, 1995), 250–54, 258–59; and George H. W. Bush and Brent Scowcroft, *A World Transformed* (New York: Alfred A. Knopf, 1998), esp. 292–300.

6. For a good sampling of the main views on the disintegration of Yugoslavia into war, see, e.g., Misha Glenny, *The Fall of Yugoslavia* (New York: Penguin Books, 1992); John R. Lampe, *Yugoslavia as History: Twice There Was a Country* (New York: Cambridge University Press, 1996); Warren Zimmermann, *Origins of a Catastrophe: Yugoslavia and Its Destroyers—America's Last Ambassador Tells What Happened and Why* (New York: Random House, 1996); Susan L. Woodward, *Balkan Tragedy: Chaos and Dissolution after the Cold War* (Washington, D.C.: Brookings Institution Press, 1995); Laura Silber and Allan Little, *Yugoslavia: Death of a Nation* (New York: TV Books / Penguin USA, 1996); Cvijeto Job, *Yugoslavia's Ruin: The Bloody Lessons of Nationalism* (Lanham, Md.: Rowman & Littlefield, 2002); and Lenard J. Cohen, *Broken Bonds: Yugoslavia's Disintegration and Balkan Politics in Transition* (Boulder, Colo.: Westview Press, 1993).

7. Among the many accounts and explanations of this process are Matlock, *Autopsy;* Yegor Gaidar, *Collapse of an Empire: Lessons for Modern Russia* (Washington, D.C.: Brookings Institution Press, 2007); and Stephen Kotkin, *Armageddon Averted: The Soviet Collapse 1970–2000* (Oxford: Oxford University Press, 2001).

8. For the political debates and struggles within the Russian Soviet Federated Socialist Republic, see esp. Matlock, *Autopsy.* Some good general accounts of the conflicts arising from the Soviet disintegration and collapse include Stuart J. Kaufman, *Modern Hatreds: The Symbolic Politics of Ethnic War* (Ithaca, N.Y.: Cornell University Press, 2001); Christoph Zuercher, *The Post-Soviet Wars: Rebellion, Ethnic Conflict, and Nationhood in the Caucasus* (New York: New York University Press, 2007); Thomas de Waal, *Black Garden: Armenia and Azerbaijan through Peace and War* (New York: New York University Press, 2003); Charles King, *The Moldovans: Romania, Russia, and the Politics of Culture* (Stanford, Calif.: Hoover Institution Press, 2000), 120ff. For a broad historical account of Armenia, Azerbaijan, and Georgia, including the post-Soviet wars, see Thomas de Waal, *The Caucasus: An Introduction* (Oxford: Oxford University Press, 2010). For a collection of essays on most of the violent conflicts and near-conflicts arising out of the Soviet collapse, see Alexei Arbatov, Abram Chayes, Antonia Handler Chayes, and Lara Olson, eds., *Managing Conflict in the Former Soviet Union: Russian and American Perspectives* (Cambridge, Mass.: MIT Press, 1997).

9. Matlock, *Autopsy.*

10. Ibid., 564–71.

11. See the *International Herald Tribune,* December 9, 1991. Baker also used the phrase in broadcast media interviews, carried widely that day. For a more detailed explication of his views on the possible nuclear dangers posed by the Soviet collapse, see Baker, *Politics of Diplomacy,* 525–26.

12. Hutchings, *American Diplomacy,* esp. 143–73; Baker, *Politics of Diplomacy,* 250–59; Scowcroft and Bush, *World Transformed,* 259–300; interview with Ambassador Robert Frowick (executive secretary of CSCE New York Ministerial Meeting, which prepared the Paris CSCE Summit), May 15, 2002.

13. "Remarks by Secretary of State James A. Baker, III at the First Restricted Session of the CSCE Ministerial," Reichstag, Berlin, Wednesday, June 19, 1991; *Charter of Paris for a New Europe.* See also Baker, *Politics of Diplomacy,* 254–57; Hutchings, *American Diplomacy,* 146–48, 150–53; and Victor-Yves Ghebali, *L'OSCE dans l'Europe post-communiste, 1990–1996: Vers une identité paneuropéenne de sécurité* (Brussels: Emils Bruylant, 1996), 9–25. Also Ambassador Craig Dunkerly (who was deputy chief of mission of the newly formed U.S. Mission to the CSCE) to the author, May 2002.

14. The CSO originally met in both Prague and Vienna, before eventually settling in Vienna.

15. For a particularly good, detailed account of the formation and development of these institutions, see Ghebali, *L'OSCE dans l'Europe.* For basic background on the various OSCE institutions, also see the OSCE Web site, www.osce.org.

16. OSCE, *Vienna Document 1992 of the Negotiations on Confidence and Security-Building Measures Convened in Accordance with the Relevant Provisions of the Concluding Document of the Vienna Meeting of the Conference on Security and Cooperation in Europe* (Vienna: OSCE, 1992), www.osce.org/documents/fsc/1993/03/4263_ en.pdf.

17. Zimmermann, *Origins,* 133–40. Zimmermann attended and reported to Washington all of Baker's meetings, and is thus the most authoritative source on the secretary's effort to avert war in June 1991. For the events that followed, see the works cited in note 8 above.

18. As deputy head of the U.S. CSCE delegation and CSCE coordinator in the Department of State at the time, I attended and at times participated directly in many of the discussions and meetings devoted to these issues; this summary of events is based upon my notes from that time.

19. The best account in English of the Armenia-Azerbaijan war over Nagorno-Karabakh is given by De Waal, *Black Garden;* an excellent shorter account is the chapter on the conflict by Kaufman, *Modern Hatreds,* 49–83. See also Zuercher, *Post-Soviet Wars,* 152–85.

20. "CSCE Advance Team to Nagorno-Karabakh: Final Report," Moscow, May 13, 1992. This report contains a detailed deployment plan for observer teams to monitor a cease-fire, and it was hoped at the time, eventual implementation of a peace treaty. The OSCE Web site is relatively thin on background for the so-called Minsk Process, but it also contains information in the sections on the personal representative of the chairman in office for the conflict dealt with by the OSCE Minsk Conference, www.osce.org/item/13668.html. See also De Waal, *Black Garden,* 229–31. As CSCE coordinator in the Department of State in 1992, I was deeply involved in the formation of the Minsk Conference, and some of this narrative is drawn from my notes and conversations at the time.

21. See www.osce.org/item/13668.html, passim.

22. Again, as CSCE coordinator in the Department of State, I had the opportunity to attend and at times personally contribute to many of the discussions which formulated proposals for the first CSCE Missions of Long Duration in Kosovo, Vojvodina, and Sandjak; I have drawn on my notes for some of this narrative. Also see the OSCE Web site on the Missions of Long Duration at www.osce.org/ item/15753.html. For an excellent account of the war in Bosnia (in addition to a number of the works cited above in note 8, see Steven L. Burg and Paul S. Shoup,

The War in Bosnia-Herzegovina: Ethnic Conflict and International Intervention (Armonk, N.Y.: M. E. Sharpe, 1999).

23. Then, as now, Greece refused to accept use of the name Macedonia, and insisted that CSCE documents refer to the country as "Skopje" or "FYROM" (Former Yugoslav Republic of Macedonia). See the OSCE Web site, at www.osce.org/skopje/.

24. See www.osce.org/georgia/.

25. Conversation of the author with Minister Adam Rotfeld, November, 2005. See also Journal No. 2 of the Fifteenth Meeting of the Committee of Senior Officials, Prague, August 14, 1992, Agenda Item 5, at www.osce.org/documents/osce/1992/08/15846_en.pdf. On establishing the mission, see www.osce.org/moldova.

26. See www.osce.org/estonia/.

27. See the 1992 CSCE Helsinki Summit document, *CSCE Helsinki Document 1992: The Challenges of Change*, www.osce.org/documents/mcs/1992/07/4048_en.pdf.

28. Ibid. Also see Ghebali, *L'OSCE dans l'Europe*, 522–30. For a particularly good collection from a longtime OSCE and HCNM official, see Walter Kemp, ed., *Quiet Diplomacy in Action: The OSCE High Commissioner on National Minorities* (The Hague, 2001).

29. For a particularly good account of the development of the European Community into the European Union, which also contains an illuminating discussion on the evolution of European thinking about NATO after 1989, see Elizabeth Pond, *The Rebirth of Europe* (Washington, D.C.: Brookings Institution Press, 1999). For some detail on the transformation of Europe in the years immediately following the fall of the Berlin Wall, see Hutchings, *American Diplomacy;* Baker, *Politics of Diplomacy;* and Bush and Scowcroft, *World Transformed.*

30. For discussions of the debate over NATO and the CSCE, and the German attitude, see Baker, *Politics of Diplomacy,* 250–59; and, esp., Hutchings, *American Diplomacy,* 278–300.

31. Hutchings, *American Diplomacy,* 274–78; Bush and Scowcroft, *World Transformed,* 265–68; Baker, *Politics of Diplomacy,* 258–59.

32. According to Hutchings, President Bush first used this explicit term in a September 11, 1991, address to a joint session of Congress immediately after a meeting in Helsinki with Gorbachev, where they discussed in particular a joint plan of action in response to Saddam Hussein's invasion of Kuwait; Hutchings, *American Diplomacy,* 146–47. However, it appears from discussion throughout Hutchings's narrative that President Bush was intensely aware from the beginning of his term of the fundamental changes taking place in the world. Beginning with his five major policy speeches from April to June 1989, Bush actively wrestled with the strategic questions of how to transform the world from the forty-year Cold War order into something different; Hutchings, *American Diplomacy,* 38–47.

33. E.g., see James Goldgeier, *Not Whether but When: The U.S. Decision to Enlarge NATO* (Washington, D.C.: Brookings Institution Press, 1999), 17–19; and Hutchings, *American Diplomacy,* 283–87. Also see J. L. Black, *Russia Faces NATO Expansion: Bearing Gifts or Bearing Arms?* (Lanham, Md.: Rowman & Littlefield, 2000), 6–10. I have heard claims more or less to this effect from a variety of senior Russian diplomats and government officials, including two deputy foreign ministers (interviewed in July 1999 and March 2007) and former prime minister Yevgeniy Primakov (August 2000).

34. See Pond, *Rebirth of Europe;* 45–50ff.; and Desmond Dinan, *Ever Closer Union: An Introduction to European Integration,* 3rd ed. (Boulder, Colo.: Lynne Rienner, 2005), 118–28.

35. See Hutchings, *American Diplomacy,* 273–78.

36. E.g., for a good discussion of the changes in NATO immediately after the end of the Cold War, see David S. Yost, *NATO Transformed: The Alliance's New Roles in International Security* (Washington, D.C.: U.S. Institute of Peace Press, 1998), 72–90; for the views of U.S. participants in the process, see esp. Bush and Scowcroft, *World Transformed,* 279–90; Baker, *Politics of Diplomacy,* 250–55; and Hutchings, *American Diplomacy,* 274–94.

37. NATO, "Declaration on a Transformed North Atlantic Alliance," London, July 6, 1990, www.nato.int/cps/en/natolive/official_texts_23693.htm?.

38. NATO, "Declaration on Peace and Cooperation Issued by the Heads of State and Government Participating in the Meeting of the North Atlantic Council ('The Rome Declaration')," Rome, November 8, 1991, www.nato.int/cps/en/natolive/official_texts_23846.htm?mode=pressrelease. On this debate, see Hutchings, *American Diplomacy,* 275–81.

39. NATO, "The Alliance's New Strategic Concept Agreed by the Heads of State and Government Participating in the Meeting of the North Atlantic Council," Rome, November 8, 1991, www.nato.int/cps/en/natolive/official_texts_23847.htm?.

40. For discussions of the events in the former Yugoslavia and the European response, see Zimmermann, *Origins of a Catastrophe;* Silber and Little, *Yugoslavia;* Woodward, *Balkan Tragedy;* Burg and Shoup, *War in Bosnia-Herzegovina;* and Glenny, *Fall of Yugoslavia.*

41. Zimmermann, *Origins of a Catastrophe,* 172–203.

42. For an insider's account of these events, in addition to the studies of the Yugoslav wars cited above, see David Owen, *Balkan Odyssey* (New York: Harcourt Brace, 1995).

43. Burg and Shoup, *War in Bosnia-Herzegovina,* 145–46; Owen, *Balkan Odyssey,* 274–88.

44. Burg and Shoup, *War in Bosnia-Herzegovina,* 322ff. For the events that led to the Dayton Agreement, see also David Halberstam, *War in a Time of Peace: Bush, Clinton, and the Generals* (New York: Scribner, 2001), 308–51; and Richard Holbrooke, *To End a War* (New York: Random House, 1998), esp. 79–198.

45. For the most authoritative account of involving Russia, see William J. Perry and Ashton B. Carter, *Preventive Defense: A New Security Strategy for America* (Washington, D.C.: Brookings Institution Press, 1999), 33–46. Also see Holbrooke, *To End a War,* 258–59; James M. Goldgeier and Michael McFaul, *Power and Purpose: U.S. Policy toward Russia after the Cold War* (Washington, D.C.: Brookings Institution Press, 2003), 199–200; and the author's interview with a senior U.S. CSCE delegation and State Department official, May 2002.

46. Baker, *Politics of Diplomacy,* 571, 584; Goldgeier, *Not Whether but When,* 17–18; Hutchings, *American Diplomacy,* 290–92.

47. In addition to Goldgeier, *Not Whether but When,* one of the best accounts of NATO's enlargement is by one of its strongest proponents in the U.S. government, Ronald D. Asmus, *Opening NATO's Door: How the Alliance Re-made Itself for a New Era* (New York: Columbia University Press, 2002); for the role of the Eastern European leaders, see in particular chaps. 1 and 2, passim. See also Gerald B. Solo-

mon, *The NATO Enlargement Debate, 1990–1997: The Blessings of Liberty* (Westport, Conn.: Praeger), 1998, 19–25.

48. E.g., see Asmus, *Opening NATO's Door,* 16–17.

49. Nicole J. Jackson, *Russian Foreign Policy and the CIS: Theories, Debates, and Actions* (London: Routledge, 2003), 54–59; Black, *Russia Faces NATO Expansion,* 8.

50. Asmus, *Opening NATO's Door,* 30–32; Solomon, *NATO Enlargement Debate,* 21.

51. In my view, the most comprehensive accounts of the policy process in the U.S. are given by Goldgeier, *Not Whether but When;* Goldgeier and McFaul, *Power and Purpose;* and Asmus, *Opening NATO's Door.*

52. For the Baker quotation, see Bush and Scowcroft, *World Transformed,* 239. On the Russian perception, see Goldgeier and McFaul, *Power and Purpose,* 184–85.

53. Goldgeier, *Not Whether but When,* 53–59.

54. Ibid., 86–95; also see Strobe Talbott, *The Russia Hand: A Memoir of Presidential Diplomacy* (New York: Random House, 2002), chaps. 5–9, passim; and Asmus, *Opening NATO's Door,* 99ff.

55. Asmus, *Opening NATO's Door,* 139–46, 175ff.; Goldgeier and McFaul, *Power and Purpose,* 205–8; Talbott, *Russia Hand,* 243–45. I participated in the collective drafting of the Founding Act and attended some of the meetings in Washington with Primakov. From subsequent personal conversations with Primakov (when he was chairman of the Russian State Commission on a Transdniestrian Settlement), he made clear he felt he was given a promise that NATO would not establish bases or station troops on the territory of the new members.

56. In my opinion, the best comprehensive accounts of Russia–United States relations during the 1990s are Goldgeier and McFaul, *Power and Purpose;* and Talbott, *Russia Hand.*

57. Talbott, *Russia Hand,* 343–48; Goldgeier and McFaul, *Power and Purpose,* 262–65. For a detailed discussion of the Russian dash to Pristina Airport, see Robert Brannon, *Russian Civil-Military Relations* (Burlington, Vt.: Ashgate, 2009), 56–98.

58. Goldgeier and McFaul, *Power and Purpose,* 267–86.

59. Ibid., 305–29.

60. NATO, "NATO-Russia Relations: A New Quality—Declaration by Heads of State and Government of NATO Member States and the Russian Federation," Rome, May 28, 2002, www.nato.int/cps/en/SID-CEE7A0FD-CC59BE3l/natolive/official_texts_19572.htm?.

61. Author's interviews with a senior NATO staff official and a senior U.S. State Department official, September 2004.

62. Goldgeier and McFaul, *Power and Purpose,* 315–28. See also, Bobo Lo, *Vladimir Putin and the Evolution of Russian Foreign Policy,* Chatham House Papers, Royal Institute of International Affairs (London: Blackwell, 2003), esp. 115ff.

63. Goldgeier and McFaul, *Power and Purpose,* 318–20; Lo, *Vladimir Putin,* 23.

64. There are many good accounts of Russia's retreat from democratic governance. Two of the best are Lilia Shevtsova, *Putin's Russia,* revised and expanded edition (Washington, D.C.: Carnegie Endowment for International Peace, 2005); and Peter Reddaway and Dmitri Glinski, *The Tragedy of Russia's Reforms: Market Bolshevism against Democracy* (Washington, D.C.: U.S. Institute of Peace Press, 2001).

65. This tale of Russian grievance against the West is best told by Putin himself. For an English-language version of his speech, see www.mid.ru/brp_4.nsf/e78a4807 0f128a7b43256999005bcbb3/284b878ca1370c27c32572800033694a?OpenDocument.

Chapter 3

1. Jack F. Matlock Jr., *Autopsy of an Empire: The American Ambassador's Account of the Collapse of the Soviet Union* (New York: Random House, 1995), 451–63.

2. On the Tajik conflict, see Nicole J. Jackson, *Russian Foreign Policy and the CIS: Theories, Debates, and Actions* (London: Routledge, 2003), 140–70. Also see Alexei Arbatov, "Russian Security Interests and Dilemmas: An Agenda for the Future," in *Managing Conflict in the Former Soviet Union,* edited by Alexei Arbatov, Abram Chayes, Antonia Handler Chayes, and Lara Olson (Cambridge, Mass.: MIT Press, 1997), 448–50; Viktor A. Kremenyuk, *Conflicts in and around Russia: Nation-Building in Difficult Times* (Westport, Conn.: Greenwood Press, 1994); William E. Odom and Robert Dujarric, *Commonwealth or Empire? Russia, Central Asia, and the Caucasus* (New York: Hudson Institute, 1995); and Roy Allison, "Russia, Regional Conflict, and the Use of Military Power" in *The Russian Military: Power and Policy,* edited by Steven E. Miller and Dmitri Trenin (Cambridge, Mass.: MIT Press, 2004), 132–40.

3. As the conflicts on the periphery of the former USSR remain unresolved, develop in their own fashion, and from time to time—especially in Georgia—heat up, there is a growing literature on these conflicts in general, and on each in particular. Good general works with which to begin include Stuart J. Kaufman, *Modern Hatreds: The Symbolic Politics of Ethnic War* (Ithaca, N.Y.: Cornell University Press, 2001); and Thomas de Waal, *Black Garden: Armenia and Azerbaijan through Peace and War* (New York: New York University Press, 2003). Also on the Caucasus conflicts, see Christoph Zuercher, *The Post-Soviet Wars: Rebellion, Ethnic Conflict, and Nationhood in the Caucasus* (New York: New York University Press, 2007); and Thomas Goltz, *Georgia Diary: A Chronicle of War and Chaos in the Post-Soviet Caucasus* (Armonk, N.Y.: M. E. Sharpe, 2006).

4. De Waal, *Black Garden,* 159–83; Kaufman, *Modern Hatreds,* 70–74.

5. Thomas de Waal, *The Caucasus: An Introduction* (Oxford: Oxford University Press, 2010), 74–75; Kaufman, *Modern Hatreds,* 86–89.

6. De Waal, *The Caucasus;* Kaufman, *Modern Hatreds;* and George Hewitt, "Abkhazia and Georgia: Time for a Reassessment," *Brown Journal of World Affairs* 15 (Spring–Summer 2009): 183–96.

7. Kaufman, *Modern Hatreds,* 104–7.

8. This account is based especially on the more detailed narratives given by De Waal, *Black Garden,* 108ff.; and Kaufman, *Modern Hatreds,* 74–76.

9. Kaufman, *Modern Hatreds,* 112–13; Zuercher, *Post-Soviet Wars,* 123ff.

10. Kaufman, *Modern Hatreds,* 112–13.

11. De Waal, *Black Garden,* 194–216; Kaufman, *Modern Hatreds,* 72–74.

12. Kaufman, *Modern Hatreds,* 110–16; Zuercher, *Post-Soviet Wars,* 129–32.

13. For a good discussion of the dissolution of the Soviet Army and the formation of the national armies of the newly independent states, see Richard A. Falken-

rath, *Shaping Europe's Military Order: The Origins and Consequences of the CFE Treaty* (Cambridge, Mass.: MIT Press, 1995), esp. chap. 5: "Dismemberment of the Soviet Army."

14. On the Yeltsin-Nazarbaev mission, see Kaufman, *Modern Hatreds,* 76. For the CSCE mediation initiative, see the author's conversations with Ambassador Jack Maresca, January–March, 1992; author's working notes while CSCE coordinator, U.S. State Department, January–May 1992; and "CSCE Advance Team to Nagorno-Karabakh: Final Report, Moscow," May 13, 1992.

15. De Waal, *Black Garden,* 251–68.

16. De Waal, *Caucasus,* 143–44; Kaufman, *Modern Hatreds,* 115.

17. For OSCE involvement, see www.osce/org/georgia.

18. For the conflict in Abkhazia, see De Waal, *Caucasus,* 157–64; and Kaufman, *Modern Hatreds,* 115–23.

19. On the UN Mission in Georgia, see www.un.org/en/peacekeeping/missions/past/unomig/background.html; for the mission's mandate, see www.un.org/en/peacekeeping/missions/past/unomig/mandate.html.

20. On the UN Friends of Georgia and the UN Mission in Georgia, see the documents at the UN Web site cited in note 19; on UN-OSCE cooperation, see www.osce.org/georgia.

21. On Russian peacekeeping in the former Soviet Union, see Allison, "Russia," 132–37. Also see Kevin P. O'Prey, "Keeping the Peace in the Borderlands of Russia," in *UN Peacekeeping, American Politics, and the Uncivil Wars of the 1990s,* edited by William J. Durch (New York: St. Martin's Press, 1996), 409–65, esp. 410–12. The Helsinki 1992 document, *The Challenges of Change,* provides for possible OSCE-mandated peacekeeping operations, an aspiration that has never been realized in practice. However, senior Russian officials long kept in mind the possibility of using an OSCE mandate to legitimize Russian peacekeepers' presence in states like Georgia and Moldova—e.g., the author's conversations with former prime minister Primakov, August 2000, and with Russian Federation OSCE delegation heads, 2000–2003.

22. Russian military and senior diplomatic officials consistently took this line with me and emphasized the contribution of Russian forces to ensuring stability when discussing Moldova or Georgia with me during my tenure as OSCE head of mission.

23. William J. Perry and Ashton B. Carter, *Preventive Defense: A New Security Strategy for America* (Washington, D.C.: Brookings Institution Press, 1999); for one example of expert warnings of neo-Soviet imperial ambitions, see Fiona Hill and Pamela Jewett, *Back in the USSR: Russia's Intervention in the Internal Affairs of the Former Soviet Republics and the Implications for United States Policy toward Russia* (Cambridge, Mass.: Strengthening Democratic Institutions Project, John F. Kennedy School of Government, Harvard University, 1994).

24. The term "frozen conflicts" has from the beginning been criticized as something of a misnomer; but for want of a better general term for the conflicts in Transdniestria, South Ossetia, Abkahzia, and Nagorno-Karabakh, it has continued in broad usage; see P. Terence Hopmann, *Building Security in Post–Cold War Eurasia: The OSCE and U.S. Foreign Policy,* Peaceworks 31 (Washington, D.C.: U.S. Institute of Peace Press, 1999). And on OSCE efforts at conflict resolution, see Victor-Yves Ghebali, *L'OSCE dans l'Europe post-communiste, 1990–1996: Vers une identité paneuropéenne de sécurité* (Brussels: Emils Bruylant, 1996), 258–301.

25. For basic information about the history and current OSCE involvement in Georgia, Moldova, and Nagorno-Karabakh, see the section "Field Operations" in the OSCE Web site, www.osce.org.

26. See the annual OSCE ministerial and summit declarations at www.osce.org/ documents.

27. See the adapted CFE Treaty, "The Final Act of the Conference of the States Parties to the Treaty on Conventional Armed Forces in Europe," signed in Istanbul on November 19, 1999, www.osce.org/documents/doclib/1999/11/13761_en.pdf. Also see OSCE, "Charter for European Security," Istanbul, November 1999, www.osce .org/documents/mcs/1999/11/17497_en.pdf.

28. OSCE, "Operational Document—the Platform for Co-operative Security," 2 (*Istanbul Document 1999*, 44), www.osce.org/documents/mcs/1999/11/4050_en.pdf.

29. OSCE, "Charter for European Security," 2.

30. Russian Federation deputy foreign minister Evgeniy Gusarov to the author, July 1999; former prime minister Primakov to the author, August 2000.

31. For a good detailed account of the deterioration in relations, see James M. Goldgeier and Michael McFaul, *Power and Purpose: U.S. Policy toward Russia after the Cold War* (Washington, D.C.: Brookings Institution Press, 2003), 211–86.

32. Ibid.

33. On the OSCE Assistance Group on Chechnya, see www.osce.org/item/15721 .html.

34. On the Georgian Border Monitoring Operation, see www.osce.org/georgia.

35. Ibid.; also De Waal, *Caucasus,* 190.

36. E.g., in the autumn of 1999 the Finnish EU Presidency visited Moldova at the senior working level, but was wholly unsuccessful in prompting interest in follow-up EU action in Moldova at the 1999 EU Helsinki Summit. This was in stark contrast with extensive senior-level EU interest in the region, such as possible EU peace-keeping, by 2003.

37. A number of senior Russian diplomats and Ministry of Foreign Affairs officials made this complaint to me, especially after 2004–5.

38. The decisions of the 2002 OSCE Porto Ministerial Council Meeting are discussed in greater detail in chapter 4.

39. For the Porto Ministerial Declaration and other documents adopted at the meting, see www.osce.org/documents/mcs/2002/12/4174_en.pdf.

40. OSCE, "Russian Federation: Elections to the State Duma, 7 December 2003: OSCE/ODIHR Election Observation Mission Report" Warsaw, January 27, 2004, www.osce.org/documents/odihr/2004/01/1947_en.pdf. Also see OSCE, "Russian Federation: Presidential Election, 14 March 2004: OSCE/ODIHR Election Monitoring Mission Report," Warsaw, June 2, 2004, www.osce.org/documents/odihr/2004/ 04/3033_en.pdf.

41. Putin's September 4, 2004, speech on Beslan is still available in English, http:// archive.kremlin.ru/eng/speeches/2004/09/04/1958_type82912_76332.shtml. For one account of Putin's bitterness toward the West, see Jonathan Steele, "Angry Putin Rejects Public Beslan Inquiry," *The Guardian,* September 7, 2004.

42. On Kolerov's mission, e.g., see "Putin Appoints Velvet Counterrevolution-ary," *Kommersant,* March 23, 2005, www.kommersant.com/page.asp?id=556859.

43. Russian Federation State Duma Deputies Kokoshin, Kosachev to the author, May 2005.

44. For the SCO, see www.sectsco.org. For the CSTO, see www.dkb.gov.ru.

45. For the Eurasian Economic Community, see www.evrazes.com.

46. Ukrainian and Moldovan senior officials and diplomats to the author, 2003–4.

47. Putin notoriously has blown hot and cold on prospective Russian membership in the World Trade Organization. E.g., after pursuing membership for years, in 2009 he abruptly announced (to the apparent consternation of other Russian officials, including President Medvedev) that Russia was abandoning its unilateral application for membership in favor of a joint application with the other two members of the prospective Russia-Belarus-Kazakhstan customs union. More recently, Putin has combined support for Russia's membership application with a litany of complaints about Western discrimination and unfair practices. E.g., see "Putin Tells Clinton to Help Russia with WTO Bid: Putin Greets Clinton with Litany of Trade Complaints," Reuters, March 19, 2010, available at www.reuters.com.

48. E.g., I had a conversation in January 2000 with a senior Russian diplomat who saw nothing untoward in pressing both the Moldovans and Transdniestrians to adopt a more cooperative approach to the settlement negotiations by cutting off deliveries of natural gas to both sides.

49. E.g., Gazprom cut off all natural gas deliveries to Moldova on February 28, 2000, while I was there, apparently to induce a more forthcoming attitude in ongoing negotiations for a base bilateral treaty.

50. There is an enormous literature on Russia's use of energy as a political instrument. E.g., see Fiona Hill, *Energy Empire: Oil, Gas and Russia's Revival* (London: Foreign Policy Center, 2004) www.brookings.edu/views/articles/FHill/20040930 .pdf. See also Keith C. Smith, "Russia and European Energy Security: Divide and Dominate," October 2008, http://csis.org/files/media/css/pubs/081024_smith_russiaeuroenergy_web.pdf. And see Marshall I. Goldman, *Petrostate: Putin, Power, and the New Russia* (Oxford: Oxford University Press, 2008); on the BTC pipeline, see 160–62.

51. Smith, "Russia," 7ff. For basic information on the charter, see its Web site www.encharter.org.

52. I have made this argument elsewhere; see William Hill, "Reflections on Negotiation and Mediation: The Frozen Conflicts and European Security," *Demokratizatsiya*, 18, no. 3 (summer 2010), 219–27.

Chapter 4

1. For attitudes of right- and left-bank elites in Moldova, see Stuart J. Kaufman, *Modern Hatreds: The Symbolic Politics of Ethnic War* (Ithaca, N.Y.: Cornell University Press, 2001), 129–63; and Charles King, *The Moldovans: Romania, Russia, and the Politics of Culture* (Stanford, Calif.: Hoover Institution Press, 2000), 145–208.

2. The best account of this period in English is given by King, *Moldovans.* See also Vasile Stati, *Istoriia Moldovy* (Chisinau: Biblioteka Pro Moldova, 2003). For an eclectic source of historical and contemporary information of all kinds on Moldova, see Andrei Brezianu and Vlad Spanu, *Historical Dictionary of Moldova,* 2nd ed. (Lanham, Md.: Scarecrow Press, 2007).

3. For the best description of this process, see King, *Moldovans,* 120–42.

4. Ibid., 187–89; also see Kaufman, *Modern Hatreds,* 145–49. The Transdniestrian regime has gone to great lengths to record and make available its version of events. The Web site of Olvia Press, the official press agency, contains a substantial history of the conflict from the left-bank point of view; see www.olvia.idknet/oglavl.htm. For those with considerable time and interest, a multiauthor, two-volume history sponsored by Tiraspol State University and the Transdniestrian Ministry of Education is available: *Istoriia Pridnestrovskoi Moldavskoi Respubliki* (Tiraspol, RIO PGU, 2000).

5. See especially the discussion of this tactic by Kaufman, *Modern Hatreds,* 148–49.

6. Jack F. Matlock Jr., *Autopsy of an Empire: The American Ambassador's Account of the Collapse of the Soviet Union* (New York: Random House, 1995), 504. A member of the Soiuz group is cited extensively on its involvement in the Transdniestrian crisis and conflict in Moldova by the International Crisis Group, *Moldova: Regional Tensions over Transdniestria,* ICG Report 157 (Brussels: International Crisis Group, 2004), 2–4.

7. King, *Moldovans,* 150–51; Matlock, *Autopsy,* 607, 610.

8. On the redistribution of the assets of the Soviet armed forces, see Richard A. Falkenrath, *Shaping Europe's Military Order: The Origins and Consequences of the CFE Treaty* (Cambridge, Mass.: MIT Press, 1995), esp. 169–76. There are many detailed accounts of the armed conflict, written by participants on both sides. For relatively short, readable accounts of the war, see King, *Moldovans,* 184–98; Kaufman, *Modern Hatreds,* 151–58; Edward Ozhiganov, "The Republic of Moldova: Transdniester and the 14th Army," in *Managing Conflict in the Former Soviet Union,* edited by Alexei Arbatov, Abram Chayes, Antonia Handler Chayes, and Lara Olson (Cambridge, Mass.: MIT Press, 1997), 164–83; and Mikhail Bergman, *Vozhd v chuzhoi stae* (Moscow: Bioinformresurs, 2004), esp. 49–102. As General Lebed's chief of staff, Colonel Bergman had a particularly good vantage point from which to follow the war; his account is particularly valuable for the insight it affords on the relationship between the Russian and Transdniestrian forces.

9. See Bergman, *Vozhd,* 34–38.

10. Bergman, *Vozhd,* provides a good breakdown on the composition of the Fourteenth Army and the Transdniestrian Army. For a good account in English of the demographics of the Fourteenth Army and the Russian dilemma on what to do with it, see Ozhiganov, "Republic of Moldova," 179–82.

11. Bergman, *Vozhd,* 50ff.; Ozhiganov, "Republic of Moldova," 147–48. My account is also based on numerous conversations over the course of my years stationed in Moldova with leading figures involved in these events, such as former President Snegur, Transdniestrian leader Smirnov, Nicolae Chirtoaca (one of the founders of the Moldovan Army), and Transdniestria's chief negotiator, Valeriy Litskai. The opinions and conclusions expressed in this narrative are my own.

12. Bergman, *Vozhd,* 89–102.

13. The is from communications from Moldovan participants to the author; also see King, *Moldovans,* 196. Bergman, *Vozhd,* 101, mistakenly states that Smirnov signed the cease-fire agreement with Snegur. The actual agreement is "Soglashenie o printsipakh mirnogo uregulirovaniia vooruzhennogo konflikta v pridnestrovskom regione Respubliki Moldova, g. Moskva," July 21, 1992, OSCE Mission to Moldova archive.

14. There is a great, continuing controversy over the number of casualties suffered by each side during the 1992 fighting in Moldova. Although there are no convincing official or unofficial figures for the dead and wounded, most credible estimates claim several hundred dead. As of this writing, the tripartite Joint Control Commission, the Moldovan-Transdniestrian-Russian body established by the 1992 cease-fire agreement, is still engaged in identifying the fate of a small number of human remains and missing persons whose fate remains unknown.

15. For the early involvement of the international community and initial negotiating positions, see especially OSCE Mission to Moldova, "Report Number 13 by the CSCE Mission to Moldova," November 13, 1993, www.osce.org/documents/mm/1993/11/454_en.pdf. The mission documents on this Web site also include a good short recapitulation from mid-1994 of the causes and course of the conflict and initial efforts at reaching a settlement.

16. OSCE Mission to Moldova, "Report Number 13."

17. The text of the February 1996 Protocol is given by H. N. Perepelitsa, *Konflikt v Pridnestrov'e. Prichiny, Problemy,i Prognoz Razvitiia* (Kiev, 2001), 84–86.

18. Communication from senior officers of the Operative Group of Russian Forces to the author, October 1999.

19. "Soglashenie mezhdu Respublikoi Moldova i Rossiiskoi Federatsiei o pravovom statuse, poriadke i rokakh vyvoda voinskikh formirovanii Rossiiskoi Federatsii, vremenno nakhodiashchikhsia na territorii Respubliki Moldova" Moscow, October 21, 1994.

20. The OSCE Ministerial and Summit statements are available at www.osce .org/mc/documents.html. Both the Moldovan Foreign Policy Association and the OSCE Mission to Moldova in the late 2000s put together collections of all high-level OSCE statements on Moldova and the Transdniestrian conflict. The Moldovan collection is available as "Press Digest on Transdniestrian Conflict, December 8, 2005, Special Issue 5," at www.ape.md. The 1994 Budapest OSCE Summit welcomed signing of the Moldova-Russia Treaty on withdrawal of Russian forces, and called for a "timely, orderly, and complete withdrawal." By the 1996 Lisbon Summit, this had become a call for an "early, orderly, and complete withdrawal."

21. "Memorandum on the Bases for Normalization of Relations between the Republic of Moldova and Transdniestria" signed in Moscow, May 8, 1997; in English, www.osce.org/documents/mm/1997/05/456_en.pdf.

22. In fact, during the Lucinschi administration there was so much working level contact between Moldovans and Transdniestrians and a relatively nonhostile relationship between the leadership that Transdniestrian security officials later told OSCE Moldova Mission members that they were relieved by the hostility to Tiraspol and Smirnov displayed by the Voronin administration. This made it easier, they explained, to control and restrict working level contacts between the two populations that they felt had been eroding Transdniestria's claim to be distinct from and threatened by the regime on the right bank.

23. Communications from the Operative Group of Russian Forces senior officers to the author, August–September 1999.

24. Ibid. Also Transdniestrian commanders to the author, conversations in 1999–2000. Although Ozhiganov, "Republic of Moldova," 179, has some data from 1992, precise statistics are not available to document what portion of the Transdniestrian armed forces came from local youths who were originally in the

Soviet Fourteenth Army, but none of my interlocutors—Transdniestrians, Russians, or Moldovans—disputed that this was the case.

25. OGRF senior officers and former prime minister Primakov to the author, August 1999–July 2000.

26. "Agreement on Confidence Measures [*sic*] and Contacts between Republic of Moldova and Transdniestria," Odessa, March 20, 1998, www.osce.org/documents/ /m/1998/03/457_en.pdf. Protocol 4, on the division of proceeds from the sale of Russian military equipment, has never been released publicly, although neither Transdniestrian nor Russian officials deny its existence or content.

27. OSCE Mission to Moldova, "Spot Report No. 5/99," October 28, 1999; William H. Hill (WHH) personal report to the OSCE Chair, November 22, 1999. In late October and mid-November, I was present on the OGRV base in Tiraspol for destruction by explosion of a good bit of this ammunition and heavy weaponry.

28. On the establishment of the Voluntary Fund, see OSCE Permanent Council, "26lst Plenary Meeting, PC Journal No. 261, Agenda item 8, Decision No. 329"; figures for arms and ammunition withdrawal and destruction are contained in the OSCE Mission to Moldova Monthly Activity Reports for 2000 and 2001, as well as separate reports provided periodically by the Mission to Moldova to VF donor states. On the hanging in effigy, see OSCE Mission to Moldova Report, July 2001. On the amounts withdrawn, see also "Report to the OSCE Permanent Council," Ambassador William H. Hill, Vienna, October 25, 2001.

29. For the ammunition project, see "The Elimination of Russian Ammunition in Moldova/Transdniestria: An OSCE Voluntary Fund Project," October 2, 2001; also see "OSCE Submits Plan to Dispose of 40,000 Tons of Russian Munitions in Moldova," OSCE Press Release, Vienna, October 4, 2001.

30. Moldovan news Web sites are full of reports and comment on these political developments; e.g., see http://old.azi.md for 2000, passim. I also discussed these issues and events during the year with President Lucinschi, Prime Minister Sturza, Speaker Diacov, and PCRM leader Voronin. The judgments and conclusions are my own.

31. President Voronin expressed his desire to make settlement of the Transdniestrian conflict the first priority of his administration in his first meeting with me, in early March 2001, after his election but before he took office. He was subsequently inaugurated on April 7, 2001, and held his first meeting with Transdniestrian leader Smirnov in Chisinau on April 9, graphic evidence of his desire to proceed swiftly.

32. Senior Moldovan officials to the author, June–August 2001.

33. WHH personal reports to the OSCE Chair, June 20 and July 14, 2001; OSCE Mission to Moldova Monthly Activity Reports, June–October 2001.

34. The Russian-language text of the Kiev Document was quickly published in the then–state newspaper *Nezavisimaia Moldova:* "Soglashenie. Proiekt: Respublika Moldova i Pridnestrov'e," July 9, 2002, www.nm.md/daily/article/2002/07/09/0102/ html. Commentary came almost immediately from longtime commentator Vladimir Socor, "Federalization Experiment in Moldova," *Russia and Eurasia Review* (Jamestown Foundation) 1, issue 4 (July 16, 2002). Moldovan commentary on the proposal was quick and almost uniformly negative; see, e.g., "PSDM a chemat populatia sa se consolideze impotriva 'politicii de transnistrizare si federalizare a Moldovei," Info-tag, July 10, 2002, http://old.azi.md/19826/Ro. A more technical contemporary Western constitutional and legal analysis of the Kiev Document is given by Bruno Cop-

piters and Michael Emerson, *Conflict Resolution for Moldova and Transdniestria through Federalisation?* Policy Brief 25 (Brussels: Centre for European Policy Studies, 2002), available at www.ceps.be.

35. Members of both the Moldovan and Transdniestrian negotiating teams separately and independently provided me this narrative and these explanations in meetings on the margins of negotiating sessions in January 2003.

36. U.S. Mission to the OSCE delegation members to the author, December 12, 2002.

37. See the joint United States–Moldova declaration adopted during Voronin's December 16–20, 2002, visit to Washington, available at www.state.gov. Voronin expressed great satisfaction after his meeting with President George W. Bush; see, e.g., "Vstrecha s Prezindentom Bushem 'prevzoshla vse ozhidaniia,'" Infotag, December 18, 2002, http://old.azi.md/news?ID=22079.

Chapter 5

1. William H. Hill (WHH) personal report to the OSCE Chair, February 1, 2003.

2. Ibid.

3. Moldovan ambassador to Moscow Vladimir Ţurcan to the author, February 2003; Moldovan negotiator Vasile Şova to the author, February 2003.

4. WHH personal report to the OSCE Chair, February 1, 2003; Zaiavlenie Prezidenta Respubliki Moldova Vladimira Voronina, February 9, 2003; Zaiavlenia Prezidenta Pridnestrovskoi Moldavskoi Respubliki I. N. Smirnova, February 14, 2003; "Pridniestrov'e zaiavilo o gotovnosti prodolzhat' peregovornyi protsess i nachat' rabotu had novoi Konstitutiei Moldovey," Infotag, February 14, 2003, http://old.azi .md; Moldovan Ministry of Foreign Affairs, "Regarding the Initiative of the President of the Republic of Moldova on the Settlement of the Transnistrian Conflict," OSCE document SEC.DEL/30/03, February 20, 2003.

5. According to established custom, the results of the negotiating round were recorded in an agreed signed document: "Protokol rabochego zasedaniia 'Postoiannogo soveshaniia po politicheskim voprosam v ramkakh peregovornogo protsessa po pridnestrovskomu uregulirovaniiu," Tiraspol-Chisinau, February 27–28, 2003. The agreed-on language on the joint constitution was in "Protokol o sozdanii mekhanizma razrabotki i utverzhdeniia Konstitutsii Federativnogo Gosudarstva," Chisinau, February 28, 2003. OSCE Mission to Moldova files.

6. WHH personal report to OSCE Chair, March 4, 2003.

7. Ibid.

8. See "Council Common Position 2003/139/CFSP of 27 February 2003," in *Official Journal of the European Union,* L 53/60, February 28, 2003. For background and description of the motives and arguments leading to the measure, see, inter alia, International Crisis Group, *Moldova: No Quick Fix,* ICG Europe Report 147 (Brussels: International Crisis Group, 2003), 10–11. See also John Loewenhardt, "The OSCE, Moldova, and Russian Diplomacy in 2003," *Journal of Communist Studies and Transition Politics* 20, no. 4 (December, 2004): 105–6.

9. Telephone conversation with Dutch OSCE/EU official, February 12, 2003.

10. "Tiraspol vyskazyvaet 'nedoumenie' po povodu nedavno vvedenykh Soed-

inennymi Shtatami Ameriki i Evropeiskim Soiuzom sanktsii," Info-Prim, March 3, 2003, http://old.azi.md/news?ID=23083. I transmitted the positive Moldovan reaction in WHH personal report to the OSCE Chair, March 4, 2003.

11. The Transdniestrian action, which will be discussed further below, was announced in a "Foreign Ministry" note published by the official press service Olvia Press: "Chetyrnadtsad' predstavitelei rukovodstva Moldovy ob'iavleny v Pridnestrov'e personami non-grata," Olvia Press, March 21, 2003, accessed at www.olvia .idknet.com/ol74-03-03.htm.

12. The Porto OSCE Ministerial Council Statement placed most of the blame for failing to meet the Istanbul Summit deadline on the lack of cooperation from Transdniestrian authorities; see "Statements by the Ministerial Council," www.osce.org/ documents/mcs/2002/12/4174_en.pdf. On fulfillment of the 2001 deadline, see William Hill, "Making Istanbul a Reality: Moldova, Russia, and Withdrawal from Transdniestria," *Helsinki Monitor* 13, no. 2 (February 2002): 129–45.

13. Conversation between Primakov and the author, August 2000.

14. See OSCE, "Agreement on Confidence Measures and Development of Contacts between Republic of Moldova and Transdniestria," March 20, 1998, www.osce .org/documents/mm/1998/03/457_en.pdf.

15. E.g., see "Piketirovaniia OGRV seichas vedetsia postoianno," Olvia Press, August 24, 2001, www.olvia.idknet.com/ol69-08-01.htm. The Transdniestrian demonstrations against destruction of Russian armor on the OGRF base, which continued through much of July and August 2001, stopped abruptly as soon as a high-level Russian Ministry of Defense delegation arrived in the region at the end of August and met with Smirnov.

16. "Verkhovnyi Sovet PMR rekomendoval prezidentu obespechit' vyvoz s territorii Pridnestrovia i utilizatsiiu voennogo imushestva OGRV," Olvia Press, March 5, 2003, www.olvia.idknet.com/ol21-03-03.htm.

17. WHH personal report to OSCE Chair, March 8, 2003.

18. The process of withdrawal and destruction of Russian arms and ammunition from Moldova's Transdniestrian region was regularly chronicled in the Monthly Activity Reports of the OSCE Mission to Moldova to the OSCE Chair and Secretariat in Vienna. In addition, the mission made regular, detailed written and oral reports to OSCE participating states that had made contributions to the OSCE Voluntary Fund established for the purpose of supporting the Russian withdrawal from Moldova.

19. WHH personal report to OSCE Chair, March 14, 2003.

20. Ibid.

21. "Protokol zasedaniia 'Postoiannogo soveshaniia po politicheskim voprosam v ramkakh peregovornogo protsessa po pridniestrovskomu uregulirovaniiu (Kishinev, 18 Marta 2003 goda)," OSCE Mission to Moldova files; see also "Eksperty Kishineva i Tiraspola zavizirovali protocol o poriadke razrabotki novoi konstitutsii Moldovy," Infotag, March 19, 2003, www.old.azi.md.news?ID=23327.

22. "Protokol vstrechi posrednikov v pridniestrovskom uregulirovaii ot OBSE, Rossiiskoi Federatsii i Ukrainy (Missiia OBSE, Kishinev, 18 Marta 2003 g.)," OSCE Mission to Moldova files.

23. "Chetyrnadtsat' predstavitelei rukovodstva Moldovy ob'iavleny v Pridnestrov'e personami non-grata."

24. The following narrative on the Moldova-Netherlands football match is based

on extensive conversations in late March and early April 2003 with—among others —Moldova Football Federation officials, Dutch OSCE Chairmanship representatives, President Voronin, and Smirnov.

25. WHH personal report to OSCE Chair, March 31, 2003.

26. Ibid. See also "Moldovskoe rukovodstvo obviniaet tiraspol'skuiu administratsiiu v opasnom obostrenii otnoshenii s Kishinevom," Basa Press, March 28, 2003, http://old.azi.md/news??ID=23462.

27. WHH personal report to OSCE Chair, March 31, 2003.

28. Ibid.

29. WHH personal report to OSCE Chair, April 4, 2003. De Hoop Scheffer's visit was widely covered by local broadcast and print media; representative coverage can be accessed at http://old.azi.md/news for April 2 and 3, 2003, for right-bank Romanian- and Russian-language coverage, and the Transdniestrian agency Olvia Press at www.olvia.idknet.com.

30. WHH personal report to OSCE Chair, April 4, 2003.

31. Parlamentul Republicii Moldova, "Hotarire privind unele aspect ale mecanismului de elaborare a proiectului noii Constituţii a Republicii Moldova," Chisinau, April 4, 2003, in OSCE Mission to Moldova files. See also "Parlamentul a aprobat mecanismul de elaborare a noii Constituţii," Basa Press, April 4, 2003, http://old.azi.md/news?ID=23556; "Priniatie resheniia o mekhanizme razrabotki proekta novoi Konstitutii vyzvalo skandal v parlamente," Info-Prim, April 4, 2003, at http://old.azi.md/news?ID=23562. Also see OSCE Mission to Moldova, *Spot Report No. 4/2003,* April 4, 2003.

32. Verkhovnyi Sovet Pridnestrovskoi Moldavskoi Respubliki, "Postanovlenie o nekotorykh printsipakh mekhanizma razrabotki i utverzhdeniia proekta Konstitutsii federativnogo gosudarstva, obrazuemogo Pridnestrovskoi Moldavskoi Respublikoi i Respublikoi Moldova na dogovornoi osnove," April 9, 2003, in OSCE Mission to Moldova files.

33. Protokol dvustoronnei vstrechi prestavitelei po politicheskim voprosam ot Respubliki Moldova i Pridnestrov'ia, Tiraspol', April 15, 2003, in OSCE Mission to Moldova files.

34. "Moldavskii Parlament naznachil trekh iuristov, prizvannykh razrabotat' vmeste s predstaviteliami Tiraspolia konstitutsiiu budushchego federativnogo gosudarstva," Basa Press, April 17, 2003, http://old.azi.md/news?ID=23744; "Verkhovnyi sovet PMR utverdil sostav kommissii po razrabotke konstitutsii budushchego federativnogo gosudarstva," Olvia Press, April 23, 2003, at www.olvia.idknet.com/ ol121-04-03.htm; Verkhovnyi Sovet Pridnestrovskoi Moldavskoi Respubliki, "Postanovlenie ob utverzhdenii polnomochnykh predstavitelei Pridnestrovskoi Moldavskoi Respubliki v sostave sovmestnoi Kommissii po razrabotke proekta Konstitutsii Federativnogo Gosudarstva, obrazuemogo Pridnestrovskoi Moldovaskoi Respublikoi i Respublikoi Moldova na dogovornoi osnove," April 23, 2003, in OSCE Mission to Moldova files. Conversation of Transdniestrian negotiators with the author, April 22, 2003.

35. "Protokol vestrechi posrednikov v pridnestrovskom uregulirovanii ot OBSE, Rossiiskoi Federatsii i Ukrainy," Kishinev, April 24, 2003; "Protokol zasedaniia 'Postoiannogo soveshaniia po politicheskim voprosam v ramkakh peregovornogo protsessa po pridnestrovskomu uregulirovaiiu' Tiraspol'-Kishinev, 22–24 aprelia 2003," in OSCE Mission to Moldova files. See also, e.g., "Glava missii OBSE v

Moldove dal otsenku sovremennoi situatsii v Moldo-pridnestrovskom uregulirova-nii," Olvia Press, April 24, 2003, www.olvia.idknet.com/oll28-04-03.htm.

Chapter 6

1. William H. Hill (WHH) personal report to OSCE Chair, May 23, 2003.
2. Conversation with the author, May 13, 2003; also WHH personal report to OSCE Chair, May 23, 2003.
3. WHH personal report to OSCE Chair, May 23, 2003.
4. Ibid.
5. For a more detailed depiction of the political atmosphere in Moldova during the local and municipal election campaign, see OSCE, *OSCE/ODIHR Election Observation Mission Report: Republic of Moldova Local and Municipal Elections 25 May and 8 June 2003* (Warsaw: OSCE, 2003), www.osce.org/documents/odihr/2003/08/560_en.pdf.
6. See OSCE, "Report No. 13 by the CSCE Mission to Moldova," November 13, 1993, www.osce.org/douments/mm/1993/11/454_en.pdf. Though the details of OSCE analyses and proposals have changed over time to reflect changes in the situation on the ground and approaches of various Moldovan governments, the basic conclusions of this report—the desirability of a special status for the Transdniestrian region and the probable nonviability of a unitary state—have remained the basic OSCE approach since 1993.
7. An English-language text of the May 8, 1997, Moscow Memorandum—"Memorandum on the Bases for Normalization of Relations between the Republic of Moldova and Transdniestria"—is at www.osce.org/documents/mm/1997/05/456_en.pdf.
8. Descriptions of the proceedings of the seminar can be found in the early reports of the CSCE Mission to Moldova to the CSCE Conflict Prevention Center, and seminar papers and reports in the OSCE Mission to Moldova files.
9. See, inter alia, OSCE Mission to Moldova Mission Report No. 3/2000, February 27–March 25, 2000; and Report to the OSCE Permanent Council of Ambassador William Hill, Head of the OSCE Mission to Moldova, June 1; 2000.
10. Conversations of the author with President Voronin and Moldovan negotiator Vasile Sturza, late August–early September 2001.
11. For some of the criticisms of the Kiev Document and federalization proposal, see the sources cited in note 34, chapter 4, above. The fiercest opponents of a federal solution came from Chisinau-based Romanophone intellectuals and nationalists. However, a large number and wide variety of Romanian speaking intellectuals and professionals in the capital opposed the idea. The chief print outlets criticizing the Kiev proposal were *Flux,* the organ of the Christian Democrat Popular Party (Partidul Popular Creştin Democrat—heir to the Popular Front of the late 1980s and early 1990s), and *Timpul,* edited by one of Chisinau's leading Romanian speaking publicists. Opponents also included a former Moldovan government negotiator for the Transdniestrian issue, a leading former deputy from former president Mircea Snegur's party, and a number of center and center-right sitting parliamentarians. See, e.g., an immediate, harsh criticism from a former negotiator: "Liberali se arata

ingrijorati de proiectul privind federalizarea Republicii Moldova," Basa Press, July 7, 2002, http://old.azi.md/news?ID=19807.

12. For an example of early coverage after my return, see "Şeful misiunii OSCE e de un 'optimism moderat' in ceea cepriveste soluţionarea conflictului transnistrean," Infotag, January 31, 2003, http://old.azi.md/news?ID=22637.

13. For overview of the criticism of and debate over a proposed federal solution in Moldova for the Transdniestrian question, see International Crisis Group, *Moldova: No Quick Fix,* ICG Europe Report 147 (Brussels: International Crisis Group, 2003), esp. 18–24; and Steven D. Roper, "Federalization and Constitution-Making as an Instrument of Conflict Resolution" *Demokratizatsiya* 12, no. 4 (Fall 2004): 527–39.

14. For examples of surveys of Moldovan public opinion, see the Institute for Public Policy's Barometers of Public Opinion, www.ipp.md/barometru.php?l=en. Surveys during the period covered by this essay were taken in November 2002, May 2003, and November 2003.

15. Conversation with Mark Tkachuk, March 2003.

16. Conversations of the author with Iurie Roşca, Vladimir Cubreacov, Stefan Secareanu, Vasile Nedelciuc, Vitalie Cosarciuc, and Vladimir Socor, April–June 2003.

17. See International Crisis Group, *Moldova,* 19.

18. Vladimir Socor, "How to Discredit Democracy and Federalism," *Wall Street Journal Europe,* June 6, 2003; Vladimir Socor, "The EU Can Secure Its Own Neighborhood," *Wall Street Journal Europe,* July 25, 2003; and Stephan M. Minikes, Rudolf V. Perina, and Pamela Hyde Smith, "It Takes an International Effort to Unify Moldova," *Wall Street Journal Europe,* August 5, 2003—all available at http://online.wsj.com.

Chapter 7

1. Conversations of the author with Isakov, Russian Foreign Ministry officials, and Russian Embassy officials, April 2003.

2. "Protokol zasedaniia 'Postoiannogo soveshaniia po politicheskim voprosam v ramkakh peregovornogo protsessa po pridnestrovskomu uregulirovaniiu' Tiraspol'-Kishinev, 22–24 aprelia 2003," in the OSCE Mission to Moldova files. In particular, in point 4 all five participants agreed to pay particular attention to questions of guarantees for a comprehensive political settlement.

3. Meetings and conversations with Dutch OSCE officials and officials of the U.S. Department of State, U.S. Department of Defense, and National Security Council, Washington, April 29–May 1, 2003.

4. Conversations with NSC and Department of State officials, April 30–May 1, 2003. This was a case in which being in the field, rather than in Washington, was a real disadvantage. A committed advocate working inside the bureaucracy might have been able to keep the Transdniestria issue high enough on the list of urgent agenda items that crowd the plate for any summit. For a traditionally less important issue like Moldova in Washington, constant presence and pressure are essential to gain and keep the attention of cabinet level principals.

5. Conversation with EU and European Commission officials, May 6, 2003.

6. Conversation with senior EU Council official, May 6, 2003.

7. Conversation of the author with senior Russian Federation official, May 7, 2003; also William H. Hill (WHH) personal report to OSCE Chair, May 12, 2003.

8. Conversation with President Voronin, May 9, 2003; also WHH personal report to OSCE Chair, May 9, 2003.

9. WHH personal report to OSCE Chair, May 9, 2003.

10. Conversations with senior Moldovan officials, May 2003, related in WHH personal report to OSCE Chair, May 23, 2003.

11. WHH personal report to OSCE Chair, May 23, 2003; conversations with Dutch OSCE representatives, May 2003; conversations with Deputy Foreign Minister Stavila and Reintegration Minister Şova, May 26, 2003.

12. WHH personal report to OSCE Chair, May 23, 2003; WHH personal report to OSCE Chair, May 27, 2003.

13. WHH personal report to OSCE Chair, June 10, 2003.

14. Ibid.

15. President Snegur and three successive Moldovan negotiators for the Transdniestrian issue—Ion Leşanu, Vasile Sturza, and Vasile Şova—at various times from 1999 to 2003 (and beyond) provided me the Moldovan perspective on the segment of the border with Ukraine controlled by authorities in Tiraspol. The situation in 2003 is encapsulated fairly successfully in the reports from the International Crisis Group (ICG): ICG, *Moldova: No Quick Fix,* ICG Europe Report 147 (Brussels: ICG, 2003), 24–27; and ICG, *Moldova: Regional Tensions over Transdniestria,* ICG Europe Report 157 (Brussels: ICG, 2004), 12–15. The text of the February 1996 Protocol is given by H. N. Perepelitsa, *Konflikt v Pridnestrov'e: Prichiny, Problemy,i Prognoz Razvitiia* (Kiev, 2001), 84–86. The Moldovan and Ukrainian viewpoints are well represented in a collection of essays by regional experts published under the aegis of the Central European Initiative and Chisinau-based Institute for Public Policy: *New Borders in South Eastern Europe: The Republic of Moldova, Ukraine, Romania,* edited by Arcadie Barbarosie and Valeriu Gheorghiu (Chisinau: Ştiinţa, 2002). In this collection, the following essays are of particular interest for background to the events described here: Natalia Belitser, "Conflicting Security Concerns across the Ukraine-Moldova Border," 233–57; Vitaly Kulik, "Settlement of the Transnistrian Conflict as a Way to the Creation of the Regional Stability Zone in Eastern Europe," 258–71; and Hryhory Perepelytsa, "The Influence of Regional Factors on Possible Scenarios of Development of Moldovan-Transnistrian-Ukrainian Relations," 272–87.

16. The Transdniestrian authorities regularly published economic statistics on the region's economic activity, some of which are available on the official Web site www.olvia.idknet.com. However, as was the case with Soviet statistics, one often needed to read skillfully between the lines to make the figures given correspond to other aspects of empirically measured reality in the region's economy. During my time in Moldova, I benefited greatly from the expertise and analyses of the leading Moldovan economist, the late Anatol Gudym of the Center for Strategic Studies and Reforms, whose personal connections, deep knowledge, and keen understanding of the region's economy were unmatched. Gudym's most comprehensive analysis of the Transdniestrian economy was released in 2005: *Transnistrian Market and Its Impact on Policy and Economy,* available at www.cisr-med.org. A good short discussion of

the role of the border and legal and illegal trade in the Transdniestrian economy is given by ICG, *Moldova: Regional Tensions over Transdniestria,* 14–15.

17. Since 1992, the Moldovan press has been filled with such accusations, and one does not have to search hard to find representative examples. E.g., see President Voronin's denunciation of Transdniestrian authorities in his speech on Moldova's independence day, August 27, 2001, as reported in "Moldova otmetila 10-uiu godovshchinu svoei nezavisimosti," Infotag, August 28, 2001, http://old.azi.md/news? ID=13478.

18. Conversations with President Voronin and Moldovan negotiator Vasile Sturza, August–September, 2001. See also ICG, *Moldova: No Quick Fix;* and "Preşedintele Moldovei, Vladimir Voronin, a plecat pe calea aerului la Moscova intr-o visita privata," Infotag, September 3, 2001, http://old.azi.md/news?ID=13545.

19. E.g., see "Moldova ob'iavila Pridnestrov'iu ekonomicheskuiu i diplomaticheskuiu blokadu," Olvia Press, August 31, 2001, www.olvia.idknet.com/ol02-08-01 .htm.

20. Director of the Moldova Metallurgical Factory (MMZ) to the author, January 2000.

21. Report of Assessment Team to OSCE Chair, December 2002.

22. Report to the OSCE Permanent Council, Ambassador William Hill, February 18, 2003. See also WHH personal report to the OSCE Chair, March 7, 2003.

23. WHH personal report to the OSCE Chair, March 7, 2003.

24. WHH personal report to the OSCE Chair, March 21, 2003.

25. As quoted by OSCE Mission to Moldova, "Border Monitoring along the Moldovan-Ukrainian Border: A Food for Thought Paper," May 2, 2003.

26. Ibid.

27. Discussions with director, OSCE Conflict Prevention Center, and OSCE secretary-general, May 7, 2003.

28. WHH personal report to OSCE Chair, May 23, 2003.

29. Ibid.

30. Ibid.

31. WHH personal report to OSCE Chair, June 29, 2003: see also "Novye pravila dlia Pridnestrovtsev," *Nezavisimaia Moldova,* June 13, 2003, www.nm.md/daily/ article/2003/06/13/0302.html.

32. WHH personal report to OSCE Char, June 29, 2003.

33. WHH personal report to OSCE Chair, July 7, 2003.

34. WHH personal reports to OSCE Chair, June 29 and July 7, 2003.

35. Report to the OSCE Permanent Council, Ambassador William Hill, September 16, 2003.

36. OSCE Mission to Moldova Reports to OSCE Voluntary Fund Donor States, April–June 2003; also WHH personal report to OSCE Chair, June 10, 2003, and Report to the OSCE Permanent Council, Ambassador William Hill, September 16, 2003.

37. Conversations with OSCE Military Mission Members and Head of OSCE Mission to Moldova Project Management Cell, June 16, 2003; also WHH personal report to OSCE Chair, June 29, 2003.

38. WHH personal report to OSCE Chair, June 29, 2003.

39. Ibid.; also conversations with Moldovan negotiator Vasile Şova, June–July 2003.

40. Netherlands Ministry of Foreign Affairs, "Food for Thought Paper: Peace Consolidation Mission Moldova," June 2003.

41. Based on conversations with Netherlands Ministry of Foreign Affairs OSCE Task Force and Netherlands Delegation to the OSCE, June–July, 2003.

42. Conversations with Ambassadors Aleksandr Novozhilov, Adriaan Jacobovits, and Petr Chaliy, at meetings of the Mediators from the OSCE, Russian Federation, and Ukraine, July 3–4, 2003; also WHH personal report to OSCE Chair, July 7, 2003.

43. WHH personal report to OSCE Chair, July 7, 2003; conversation with Smirnov, July 18, 2003.

44. Meetings and conversations with Russian Federation deputy minister of foreign affairs Viacheslav Trubnikov and Netherlands Ministry of Foreign Affairs OSCE Task Force members, September 11, 2003.

45. Conversations with the head of the Netherlands Ministry of Foreign Affairs OSCE Task Force and Ambassador Adriaan Jacobovits, September 2003.

Chapter 8

1. William H. Hill (WHH) personal report to OSCE Chair, May 23, 2003.

2. Memorandum from OSCE Mission to Moldova Members to WHH, June 16, 2003; also "Protkol'naia zapis' zasedaniia Sovmestnoi Konstitutsionnoi Kommissii, Missiia OBSE, Kishinev," June 16, 2003, in OSCE Mission to Moldova files.

3. WHH personal report to OSCE Chair, June 25, 2003.

4. Ibid.; also "Predlozheniia polnomochnykh predstavitelei Respubliki Moldova v Sovmestnoi Konstitutsionnoi Kommissii (SKK) po proekty Reglamenta," June 16, 2003, in OSCE Mission to Moldova files.

5. WHH personal report to OSCE Chair, June 29, 2003.

6. Ibid.

7. WHH personal report to OSCE Chair, July 7, 2003.

8. "Reglament Sovmestnoi Konstitutsionnoi Kommissii," April 10, 2003, in OSCE Mission to Moldova files; also WHH personal report to OSCE Chair, July 13, 2003.

9. "Comiţia Constituţional Miata s-a introit la Bender (Tighina)," Basa Press, July 21, 2003, http://old.azi.md/news?ID=24971. I personally heard Smirnov use the phrase "na dogovornoi osnove" literally dozens of times, and on the other hand, President Voronin stress that the Commission was writing a new constitution of the present Republic of Moldova, not creating some new state.

10. Meeting of Netherlands Foreign Ministry OSCE Task Force, Netherlands Delegation to the OSCE, and OSCE Mission to Moldova representatives, Vienna, July 28, 2003.

11. "Vladimir Voronin s-a intelnit cu şeful administrative preşedintului Federaţiei Ruse," Moldpres, July 8, 2003, http://old.azi.md/news?ID=24797.

12. "Prezident Rossii Vladimir Putin vysoko otsenil rost promyshlennogo proizvodstva v Moldove," Infotag, July 24, 2003, www.infotag.md/news/432529/.

13. E.g., see Infotag reports for July 31 that cited extensive talks between Kozak and Smirnov, cited by Radio Free Europe / Radio Liberty, *Newsline,* August 1, 2003, www.rferl.org/content/article/1142971.html. Senior Moldovan negotiators subsequently confirmed to me Kozak's July visit during meetings in August 2003.

14. "V Moldove i Pridnestrov'e zavershili rabotu predstaviteli Venetsianskoi Kommissii," Olvia Press, July 25, 2003, www.olvia.idknet.com/oll16-07-03.htm. On

July 25, President Voronin met in Chisinau with the visiting chief of political affairs of the Council of Europe secretary and the council's new resident representative. In the course of the meeting, they discussed the contribution of the Council of Europe to the work of the Joint Constitutional Commission; see www.president.md/press .php?lang=rom.

15. Conversations with Russian delegation members during the July 30–31, 2003, negotiating round.

16. Conversation with Minister for Reintegration Vasile Şova, Chisinau, August 28, 2003. The document (written in Russian) is titled "Memorandum: Ob osnovnykh printsipakh gosudarstvennogo ustroistva dlia tselei razrabotki novoi Konstitutii Respubliki Moldova" and was labeled "konfidential'no—proekt, 21.08.03" (hereafter, "Memorandum: August 21 Draft"). From OSCE Mission to Moldova files.

17. "Memorandum: August 21 Draft."

18. Ibid.

19. Ibid.

20. WHH personal report to OSCE Chair, July 7, 2003. The list Adriaan Jacobovits and I presented was "Perechen' podpisannykh i prorabotannykh formulirovok na zasedaniiakh Postoiannogo soveshchaniia po politicheskim voprosam v ramkakh peregovornogo protsessa po pridnestovskomu uregulirovaniiu," in "Protokol zasedaniia 'Postoiannogo soveshchaniia po politicheskim voprosam v ramkakh peregovornogo protsessa po pridnestrovskomu uregulirovaniiu' (Tiraspol'-Kishinev, 3–4 Iiulia 2003 goda)."

21. Meeting of Netherlands Ministry of Foreign Affairs OSCE Task Force, Netherlands Delegation to the OSCE, and OSCE Mission to Moldova representatives, Vienna, July 28, 2003; conversation with Ambassador Adriaan Jacobovits upon conclusion of negotiating round, Chisinau, July 31, 2003.

22. WHH communications with Ambassador Adriaan Jacobovits, August 20–21, 2003.

23. Meeting with Ambassador Adriaan Jacobovits, Ambassador Aleksandr Novozhilov, and Ambassador Petr Chaliy, Chisinau, September 4, 2003.

24. Ibid.

25. "Protokol zasedaniia 'Postoiannogo soveshchaniia po politicheskim voprosam v ramkakh peregovornogo protsessa po pridnestrovskomu uregulirovaniiu' (Tiraspol'-Kishinev, 4–5 Sentiabria 2003 goda)." The Moldovan proposals were titled "Deklaratsiia ob osnovnykh printsipakh razgranicheniia polnomochii pri razrabotke novoi Konstitutsii Respubliki Moldova." The Transdniestrians submitted a paper: "Polozheniia dlia vkliucheniia v Itogovyi politicheskii dokument." All in OSCE Mission to Moldova files.

26. Distributed by the Bulgarian OSCE Chair as "Predlozheniia i Rekomendatsii posrednikov ot OBSE, Rossiiskoi Federatsii, Ukrainy po uregulirovaniiu pridnestrovskoi problemy," February 13, 2004, CIO/GAL/11/04; English-language version, www.osce.org/documents/mm/2004/02/2079_en.pdf.

Chapter 9

1. Meeting with Smirnov, Tiraspol, September 22, 2003; the first document, which Smirnov so disliked, was titled "Memorandum ob osnovnykh printsipakh gosudarstvennogo ustroistva dlia tselei razrabotki novoi Konstitutsii Respubliki

Moldova," and dated September 11, 2003 (hereafter, "Memorandum: September 11 Draft") (for the text of this document, see appendix B). The second, Transdniestrian document was captioned "Soglashenie o bazovykh printsipakh konstitutsionnogo i gosudarstvennogo ustroistva Federativnogo Gosudarstva, obrazuemogo Respublikoi Moldova i Pridnestrovskoi Moldavskoi Respublikoi," and dated September 22, 2003 (hereafter, "Transdniestrian September 22 Draft"). Litskai also gave me a ten-page, single-spaced, article-by-article critique of the Kozak draft by the Transdniestrian experts. The Transdniestrian draft was clearly a throwaway, designed only to obstruct the process, and is eminently forgettable. The biggest substantive differences between Chisinau and Tiraspol are clearly reflected in the titles of the documents, without any need to refer to the text.

2. Conversations with senior Moldovan and Transdniestrian negotiators, Chisinau and Tiraspol, September 2003.

3. "Memorandum: September 11 Draft."

4. Ibid.

5. Ibid.

6. "Transdniestrian September 22 Draft."

7. "Report No. 13 by the CSCE Mission to Moldova, 13 November 1993," www.osce.org/documents/mm/1993/11/454_en.pdf.

8. "Zamechaniia/predlozheniia Pridnestrovia k proektu politicheskogo dokumenta ob osnovnykh printsipakh gosudarstvennogo ustroistva dlia tselei razrabotki Konstitutsii Federativnogo gosudarstva" and "Predvaritel'nye predlozheniia i zamechaniia predstavitelei Pridnestrovskoi Moldavskoi Respubliki v Sovmestnoi Konstitutsionnoi Komissii po povodu 'Proekta ot 11.09.2003 goda'," received from Transdniestrian negotiator Litskai, Tiraspol, September 22, 2003.

9. The paper that I circulated was untitled, and was cast in the format of a formal agreement between Chisinau and Tiraspol authorities. It had been through at least four revisions inside OSCE by the time the other mediators saw it. Henceforth, I refer to the version we began working with on September 24 as the "Zagreb Draft." Also see William H. Hill (WHH) personal report to OSCE Chair, October 3, 2003.

10. WHH personal report to OSCE Chair, October 3, 2003.

11. Ibid.

12. Ibid.

13. The agreed-on text was the same as that released by the Bulgarian OSCE Chairmanship in February 2004: "Predlozheniia i Rekomendatsii."

14. The following account of this October 11, 2003, meeting between President Voronin and Foreign Minister De Hoop Scheffer is based on my notes and a memorandum of conversation that I composed for the OSCE Chair.

15. This assertion in itself was odd, inasmuch as withdrawals of ammunition from Colbasna were still blocked by the Transdniestrian authorities, as they had been since mid-June. Ammunition trains in fact did not resume rolling again until October 26; see OSCE Mission to Moldova, Activity Report 10/2003 (October 2003), SEC/FR/561/03.

16. Meeting with Mark Tkachuk, Chisinau, October 23, 2003.

17. Meeting with Dmitri Kozak, Chisinau, October 23, 2003.

18. "Sovmestnyi memorandum Parlamenta Respubliki Moldova i Verkhovnogo Soveta Pridnestrov'ia: Ob osnovnykh printsipakh gosudarstvennogo ustroistva ob'edinennogo gosudarstva," October 22, 2003, marked "Confidential (until agreement is achieved)," in OSCE Mission to Moldova files.

19. "Protokol zasedaniia 'Postoiannogo soveshchaniia po politicheskim vopro-sam v ramkakh peregovornogo protsessa po pridnestrovskomu uregulirovaniiu' (Tiraspol'-Kishinev, 29–30 oktiabria 2003 goda)," in OSCE Mission to Moldova files. See also "Reprezentatul OSCE a communicat ca mediatorii in solutionarea diferendului transnistrean vor face noi propuneri in timpul apropriat," Infotag, October 30, 2003, http://old.azi.md/news?ID=26441.

20. The Joint Constitutional Commission provided the negotiators and mediators with a spreadsheet, dated October 28, 2003, of the Moldovan and Transdniestrian versions of this section of the new Constitution. There were significant substantive differences between the two versions on every article; sometimes the two variants were barely recognizable as being intended for the same document on the same subject.

21. My working notes from this session are a depressing list of unresolved problems and disputes, punctuated by references to bitter accusations and denunciations from each side toward the other.

22. The "telephone war" was chronicled in great detail in both the Moldovan and Transdniestrian press; readers interested in the details of the accusation, denials, and explanations should peruse the Moldovan news Web site, http://old.azi.md, and the site for Olvia Press, the official Transdniestrian agency, www.olvia.idknet.com, for September–November 2003.

23. See "Protokol zasedaniia 'Postoiannogo soveshchaniia . . . ,'" October 29–30, 2003, paragraph 5.

24. The account here of this meeting is based on my own working notes.

25. The account here of this meeting is based largely upon my working notes. See also "OSCE Chairman-in-Office, Civil Society Representative (sic) Discuss in Transnistrian Issue," Basa Press, November 6, 2003, http://old.azi.md/news?ID=26541.

26. My efforts to corral the Ukrainian and Russian ambassadors and obtain their signatures on a common letter of transmittal for the Mediators' Document and the reactions and instructions of the Dutch OSCE Chair were recorded in a series of email messages from late October to mid-November 2003. I received my instructions to either get agreement or present the document myself from The Hague on the morning of November 14, 2003.

Chapter 10

1. This was the "Memorandum ob osnovnykh printsipakh gosudarstvennogo ustroistva ob'edinennogo gosudarstva," containing fifteen numbered articles (with subarticles) (hereafter, "Memorandum: November 14 Redaction").

2. I reported my November 14 meeting with Kozak and provided written analysis and recommendations in William H. Hill (WHH) personal report to OSCE Chair, November 16, 2003. There are a number of published accounts of events leading up to and of the appearance of the Kozak Memorandum, and events in Chisinau that followed. The two that best accord with my own notes and recollections are International Crisis Group, *Moldova: Regional Tensions over Transdniestria,* ICG Europe Report 157 (Brussels: International Crisis Group, 2004), 22–27; and John Loewen-

hardt, "The OSCE, Moldova, and Russian Diplomacy in 2003," *Journal of Communist Studies and Transition Politics* 20, no. 4 (December 2004): 103–12, esp. 108ff. Loewenhardt clearly based his narrative on input from my Dutch colleagues. For another report, also based on interviews with Chisinau participants in the process, including me and my Moldovan colleagues, see Steven D. Roper, "Federalization and Constitution-Making as an Instrument of Conflict Resolution," *Demokratizatsiya* 12, no. 4 (Fall 2004): 527–39.

3. Unless otherwise indicated, the analysis and discussion immediately following is based on the "Memorandum: November 14 Redaction."

4. OSCE Mission staff collected their comments and analysis of the "Memorandum: November 14 Redaction" in an eleven-page, single-spaced document: "Comments on the 'Memorandum of the Basic Principles of the State Structure of a United State,'" November 15, 2003 (revised November 16).

5. WHH personal report to OSCE Chair, November 16, 2003.

6. Ibid.

7. Ibid.

8. Ibid.

9. The following account of this meeting is based on my own personal working notes.

10. For the announcement, see, e.g., "Rossiiskaia Federatsiia predlozhila dlia ob'edineniia Moldovy plan asimmetrichnoi federatsii," Infotag, November 17, 2003, http://old.azi.md/news?ID=26680. For the text, see *Nezavisimaia Moldova,* November 18, 2003, www.nm.md/daily/issue/2003/11/18.html.

11. "Prezident Voronin vstretilsia s liderami parlamentskikh grupp," Basa Press, November 18, 2003, http://old.azi.md/news?ID=26699.

12. "Moldavskii president proinformiroval akkreditovanykh v Kishineve diplomatov o svoei ofitsial'noi pozitsii po memorandum, razrabotannomu rossiiskimi ekspertami," Basa Press, November 21, 2003, http://old.azi.md/news?ID=26753. This account of the meeting is based on my personal working notes.

13. Kozak *Memorandum,* November 23 Redaction.

Chapter 11

1. See, e.g., "Vo vtornik v Kishinev priezhaet president Rossii Vladimir Putin," Infotag, November 24, 2003, http://old.azi.md/news?ID=26782.

2. "Opoziţia a infiintat un comitet ce va coordona acţiunile impotriva planului rusesc de reglementare transnistreana," Basa Press, November 24, 2003, http://old .azi.md/news?ID=26775; "Apelul Comitetului pentru Apararea Independenţiei si Constituţiei Republicii Moldova," Basa Press, November 25, 2003, http://old.azi .md/news?ID=26794. A brief but good account of the November 24–25 events in Chisinau is given by International Crisis Group, *Moldova: Regional Tensions over Transdniestria,* ICG Europe Report 157 (Brussels: International Crisis Group, 2004), 25–26.

3. Like most of my Moldovan colleagues, I watched Moldovan and Russian television coverage of Georgia's "Rose Revolution" on Chisinau cable the evening of November 23. For a good contemporaneous review of the chronological sequence of

events in Tbilisi in November 2003, see International Crisis Group, *Georgia: What Now?* ICG Europe Report 151 (Brussels: International Crisis Group, 2003).

4. "Apelul Comitetului. . . ."

5. "Grupuri organizate de student s-au alaturat protestatarilor din central capitalei," Basa Press, November 25, 2003, http://old.azi.md/news?ID=26797.

6. "Președintele Voronin a discutat cu ambasadorul American despre planul rusesc de reglemntare a crizei transnistrene," Basa Press, November 24, 2003, http://old.azi.md/news?ID=26776. Based on the Presidential press release, Chisinau press accounts of the meeting did not really reflect the substance of the discussion, which was relayed to me by both American and Moldovan participants.

7. OSCE, "OSCE Does Not Endorse Russian Plan on Moldova," press release (PR-CiO-Voronin-FINAL), November 24, 2003.

8. "OBSE otkloniaet rossiiskii proekt federalizatsii Respubliki Moldova," Info-Prim, November 25, 2003, http://old/azi.md/news?ID=26806.

9. Conversations with staff members, Office of the Special Representative of the Chairman of the Council of Europe and Office of the High Representative of the European Council, November 25–26, 2003.

10. "Leonid Kuchma: Dlia Ukrainiy glavnym iavliaetsia skoreishee uregulirovanie pridnestrovskogo konflikta," *Nezavisimaia Moldova,* November 25, 2003, at www.nm.md/daily/news/2003/11/25.html. The descriptions of the circumstances of Kozak's visit to Kuchma in Kiev are based on conversations with Ukrainian delegation members at the OSCE Ministerial Council meeting in Maastricht, December 2003, and at the January 2004 Mediators' Meeting in Sofia.

11. "Vizit rossiiskogo prezidenta v Kishinev otmenen," Basa Press, November 25, 2003, http://old.azi.md/news?ID=26804.

12. "Zaiavlenie prezidenta Vladimira Voronina po povodu memorandum ob osnovnykh printsipakh gosudartstvennogo ustroistva Respubliki Moldova," Moldpres, November 25, 2003, http://old.azi.md/news?ID=26805.

13. Again, I watched Kozak's airport press conference in its entirety on Russian television on the Chisinau cable channel. The gist of Kozak's remarks was reported, inter alia, in "Predstavitel' prezidenta Rossii schitaet, chto plan pridnestrovskogo uregulirovaniia ne podpisan po vine rukovodstva Moldovy," Infotag, November 25, 2003, http://old.azi.md/news?ID=26807.

14. I was present at the Maastricht Ministerial Meeting when Ivanov spoke, and I recall his voice being filled with deep emotion—real anger, indignation, and frustration. For one account, from the Russian Federation perspective, of the first day of the Maastricht Meeting, see Natalia Babsian, "Igor' Ivanov pred'iavil pretenzii Evrope," *Izvestiia,* December 1, 2003, www.izvestiia.ru/russia/article41706/index.html.

15. Conversations with U.S. OSCE Delegation members, Maastricht, December 1–2, 2003.

16. "Dmitri Kozak: On prosil proshchenia i nazyval sebia obmanshchikom," *Kommersant,* November 25, 2005, www.kommersant.ru/doc.html?path=/daily/2005/222/29256616.htm. The Kozak interview was also carried on the Russian news agency Lenta.ru, http://lenta.ru/articles/2005/11/25/kozak/.

17. "Ruka Moskvy ne poluchila ot Rossii nikakoi pomoshchi: Sovetnik prezidenta Moldavii otvetil Dmitriiu Kozaku," *Kommersant,* December 2, 2005, www.kommersant.ru.doc.html?docld=631793.

18. Report to the OSCE Permanent Council, Ambassador William Hill, head of the OSCE Mission to Moldova, February 5, 2004, PC.FR/2/04.

Chapter 12

1. William H. Hill (WHH) personal reports to OSCE Chair, March and May 2004.

2. WHH personal reports to OSCE Chair, April and May 2004.

3. WHH personal report to OSCE Chair, October 30, 2004; conversation with President Voronin, February 2, 2004.

4. E.g., for Lavrov's less-than-enthusiastic public endorsement at a meeting with Moldovan foreign minister Stratan, see "Moldovan Foreign Minister Favours Agreement over Stability and Security Pact for Moldova," Basa Press, July 15, 2004, http://old.azi.md/newsID?=30001.

5. OSCE Mission to Moldova reports to Voluntary Fund donors, April 2004.

6. WHH personal report to OSCE Chair, March 23, 2004.

7. The proposed CSBM package of has never been released to the public. The delivery of the CSBM package to the Moldovan and Transdniestrian representatives was widely reported; e.g., see "Preşedintele in exercitiu al OSCE a ţinut la Chisinau o conferinţa de presa imediat dupa ce a visitat Tiraspolul," June 22, 2004, http://old .azi.md/news?ID=29646.

8. Report to the OSCE Permanent Council, Ambassador William H. Hill, June 29, 2004, PC.FR/20/04.

9. I summarized the history of the development, presentation, and attempts to implement the CSBM package; see William H. Hill, "The Transdniestrian Settlement Process: Steps Forward, Steps Back—The OSCE Mission to Moldova in 2005/2006," in *OSCE Yearbook 2006,* edited by Institute for Peace Research and Security Policy at the University of Hamburg (Baden-Baden: Nomos, 2007), 153–72; see esp. 162–63.

10. "Autoritatile transnistrene au sechestrat bunurile şcolii nr 20 din Tiraspol si a şcolii internat din Tighina," Moldpres, July 15, 2004, http://old.azi/news?ID=29990; "Reintegration Minister Says Transdniestrian Security Forces 'Stormed' the Only Romanian-Language School in Tiraspol," Basa Press, July 16, 2004, http://old.azi .md/newsID?=30021. Early in the morning of July 15, police in Tiraspol occupied and closed the Moldovan school there. At the same time, police in Bendery moved against both a Moldovan Romanian-language school and a Moldovan state-run orphanage located in the city. Parents, teachers, and students in the two Moldovan institutions in Bendery refused to leave the premises, and they managed to keep out the Transdniestrian police, who then encircled and blockaded the grounds of both schools. In the northern city of Ribniţa, parents and teachers held the beleaguered Moldovan school building for two weeks, until on July 29 local police wielding chain saws and bolt cutters broke into the building and evicted the parents. See also WHH personal reports to OSCE Chair, July 26, July 29, and August 4, 2004.

11. "Reintegration Minister Says Transdniestrian Security Forces 'Stormed' the Only Romanian-Language School."

12. "Moldova işi suspenda participarea la procesul de negocieri," Moldpres, July 21, 2004, http://old.azi.md/newsID?=30076; also see "Preşedintele a calificat situatia din stinga Nistrului drept capitularea tutoror mecanismulor de reglementarea a conflictului trasnistrean in faţa acţiiunilor unilateral ale administraţiei tiraspolene" Moldpres, July 21, 2004, http://old.azi.md/newsID?=30072.

13. WHH personal report to OSCE Chair, September 19, 2004.

14. WHH personal report to OSCE Chair, August 4, 2004; also see "OSCE Mission to Moldova Summary of Recent Events: Fact Sheet," August 5, 2004.

15. WHH personal report to OSCE Chair, August 4, 2004; "OSCE Mission to Moldova Summary of Recent Events"; WHH sitrep to OSCE Chair, September 1, 2004; WHH personal report to OSCE Chair, September 6, 2004.

16. "The Three-D Strategy & Action Plan for the Settlement of the Transnistrian Conflict," in English, www.ad-astra.ro/library/papers/moldova_3d_strategy.pdf. A good, brief description of the plan can be found at the Open Society Policy Center's Web site, www.opensocietypolicycenter.org/resources/publication.php?docId=87. In addition to its domestic proponents, the proposal enjoyed tremendous support from elements in the Moldovan diaspora in Europe and North America.

17. See Oazu Nantoi, "Strategia '3D': De la 'extremism' la consens?" www.-e-democracy.md/comments/political/20041031, November 3, 2004.

18. See EU, *EU/Moldova Action Plan,* http://ec.europa.eu/world/enp/pdf/action_plans/moldova_enp_ap_final_en.pdf.

19. See "OSCE/ODIHR Election Monitoring Mission Report, Republic of Moldova: Parliamentary Elections: 6 March 2005," Warsaw, June 3, 2005, www.osce .org/documents/odihr/2005/06/14919_en.pdf. Also see the Moldovan NGO site www .elections2005.md.

20. On the Romanian election results, see "OSCE/ODIHR Assessment Mission Report, Romania: Parliamentary and Presidential Elections: 28 November and 12 December 2004," www.osce.org/documents/odihr/2005/02/4281_en.pdf. On the Moldovan government reaction and increasingly active contacts with the new Romanian administration, I spoke at length with senior Ministry of Foreign Affairs and Presidential Administration officials in the period January–April 2005. An unmistakable sign of change came with President Băsescu's active presence at the April 22, 2005, GUAM Summit in Chisinau.

21. On the effects of the Orange Revolution on various Moldovan politicians, see, e.g. Jeremy Page, "Moldova Has Pro-Western Revolution Even before Poll Is Held: The Communist President Responds to the Public Mood with Anti-Russian Rhetoric," *The Times* (London), March 5, 2005, www.timesonline.co.uk/tol/news/world/article419357.ece. The far-reaching effects of the recent political upheaval in neighboring Ukraine were obvious to anyone living in Moldova during the 2005 parliamentary election campaign.

22. OSCE, "Statement Delivered by H.E. Mr. Andrei Stratan, the Minister of Foreign Affairs of the Republic of Moldova at the 12th OSCE Ministerial Council Meeting (Sofia, 6–7 December 2004)," MC.DEL/21/04, December 6, 2004, www .osce.org/documents/mcs/2004/12/3873_en.pdf.

23. WHH personal report to the OSCE Chair, March 11, 2005. The incident is reflected, without the operational details, in "OSCE/ODIHR Election Observation Mission Statement of Preliminary Findings and Results, Chisinau, 7 March 2005," in the discussion of Moldova's failure to accredit some international observers, p. 10.

24. WHH personal report to the OSCE Chair, March 11, 2005. Former minister of defense Valeriu Pasat attended one of these rallies, along with former Premier Braghiş and alleged organized crime figure "Bolgar" Karamalak in early March, which allegedly contributed to Moldovan authorities' decision to arrest Pasat when he returned to the country after the election.

25. "Parliament Defines Principles of Holding Elections in Transnistria and Approves of Yushchenko Plan," Infotag, June 10, 2005, http://old.azi.md/news?ID= 34592. The Voronin administration drafted texts of the parliamentary resolution in Romanian (Moldovan) and Russian, because the negotiators were working in Russian. The text is available in the *Monitorul Oficial al Republicii Moldova,* nos. 83–85 (1682–84), June 17, 2005, pos. 385; the text is also available in Russian in a collection of key documents on the Transdniestrian question published by the Moldovan government in 2006: *Sbornik Dokumentov otnosiashchikhsia k Sovmestnomu zaiavleniiu Prem'er-ministrov Moldovy i Ukrainy* (Kishinev, 2006), 52–59.

26. "Yushchenko Presents Ukraine's Plan of Transnistrian Conflict Settlement," Infotag, April 22, 2005, http://old.azi.md/news?D=33949. The seven points of the plan in this article accurately reflect the points distributed by the Ukrainian delegation at the GUAM Summit, but contain key differences and retreats from points included by Yushchenko's advisers in the draft they presented him before the meeting. Ukrainian officials who described the rationale for the initiative to me in mid-March were a bit more cynical, expressing the opinion that Smirnov would win any election on the left bank no matter what the conditions, and the Moldovans would then be forced finally to negotiate seriously with him. See WHH personal report to OSCE Chair, March 28, 2005.

27. This process of bilateral Moldova-Ukraine negotiations is reflected in my own reports: WHH personal reports to OSCE Chair, May 4, May 7, and May 18, 2005. The final text of the Yushchenko Plan is contained in the Moldovan *Sbornik Dokumentov,* 44–52. The OSCE Mission did an informal English translation of the plan as agreed to at the Vinnitsa meeting in May 2005.

28. *Monitorul Oficial al Republicii Moldova,* nos. 101–3 (1700–1702), July 29, 2005, pos. 478. The text is available in Russian in *Sbornik Dokumentov,* 60–64. For a good discussion of adoption of the law, see Claus Neukirch, "Managing the Crises: Restarting the Process—The OSCE Mission to Moldova in 2004/2005," in *OSCE Yearbook 2005* (Baden-Baden: Nomos, 2006), 139–53 (esp. 149–51); see also Oleh Protsyk, "Democratization as a Means of Conflict Resolution in Moldova," in *European Yearbook of Minority Issues, Volume 4 (2004/2005),* edited by European Centre for Minority Issues and European Academy Bozen/Bolzano (Leiden: Brill, 2006).

29. U.S. and EU diplomats to the author, July 2005.

30. The Yushchenko Plan, which Smirnov accepted in principle in early July 2005, called for inclusion of the United States and the EU as participants in the negotiation process. On July 22, 2005, Litskai and I worked out a twelve-point draft list of rights and responsibilities of the United States and the EU as observers, which was all Smirnov and Moscow were willing to accept. As it turned out, the draft was accepted with objection by all seven parties to the process and was formally approved at a meeting in Odessa in late September 2005. See also "Report to the Permanent Council," Ambassador William H. Hill, November 10, 2005.

31. WHH personal report to the OSCE Chair, October 31, 2005.

32. WHH personal reports to the OSCE Chair, June 28 and October 31, 2005; "Report to the OSCE Permanent Council," Ambassador William H. Hill, November 10, 2005; "OSCE Mission to Moldova Monthly Activity Report," October and November 2005.

33. For basic background information, see the EU Border Assistance Mission's Web site, www.eubam.org. My comments are based largely on my personal and

working contacts with all of the parties involved in agreeing upon and setting up the Border Assistance Mission.

34. The basic documents and statements regarding the Transdniestrian-Ukrainian border crisis of late winter and early spring 2006 are in the Moldova government's *Sbornik dokumentov.* We had considerable warning that trouble was coming on the border; a WHH private report to the OSCE Chair, January 23, 2006, warned of Moldovan expectations that the Ukrainians could be convinced in the near future to close the Transdniestrian segment of the border.

35. Extensive local press coverage of the economic crisis occasioned by the new regime on the border, beginning on March 3, 2006, can be found at http://old.azi.md. The OSCE Mission sent daily patrols to the Transdniestrian region during the crisis, and reported extensively to the Secretariat and the Chair. E.g., I sent personal reports and sitreps on March 4 and March 9; a summary of the humanitarian situation on the left bank on March 24; and personal reports summarizing Russian, Ukrainian, Moldovan, and Transdniestrian actions and responses to the crisis, all of which form a basis for this account. See also my account of these events: Hill, "Transdniestrian Settlement Process," 166–69. Western accounts of this period in Moldovan-Ukrainian-Transdniestrian affairs are gradually appearing. E.g., see Robert Weiner, "Whither Moldova? East or West?" in *The Boundaries of Enlargement,* edited by Joan DeBardeleben (New York: Palgrave Macmillan, 2008); and Ryan Kennedy, "Trains, Trade, and Transnistria: Russian Influence in Moldova," unpublished paper for presentation at the 2007 World Conference of the Association for the Study of Nationalities, New York (available from the author).

36. The Russian ban on importing wine from Moldova and Georgia in the spring of 2006 was widely reported and interpreted as aimed at exerting political pressure and retaliation against the governments of the two states for their anti-Russian policies. E.g., see C. J. Chivers, "A Russian 'Wine Blockade' against Georgia and Moldova," *New York Times,* April 6, 2006, www.nytimes.com/2006/04/06/world/europe/06russia.html. For a longer-term perspective on the motivation and effects of the ban, see Ryan Kennedy, "Moldova: Counting Losses as Wine Ban Lingers," Radio Free Europe / Radio Liberty, April 4, 2007, www.rferl.org/content/article/1075697.html. Conversations at the time with senior Russian representatives clearly showed the political nature of the ban; WHH personal report to the OSCE Chair, April 16, 2006.

37. On the Dorotskaia issue, see "OSCE Mission to Moldova Monthly Activity Reports," April and May, 2006. On the Transdniestrian referendum on September 17, 2006, see "Reactions on Referendum in Transnistria," Infotag, September 18, 2006, at http://old.azi.md/news?ID=41023; "Pridnestrov'e progolosovalo za prisoedinenie k Rossii: Za eto vyskazalis' bole 97% grazhdan respubliki, uchastvovavshikh v referendum," Olvia Press, September 18, 2006, www.olvia.idknet.com/oll60-09-06.htm; Vladimir Soloviev and Mikhail Zygar, "The Old Guard Wins in Transdniestria," *Kommersant,* September 19, 2006, www.kommersant.com/p705753/r_1/The_Old_Guard_Wins_in_Transdniestria/; and OSCE, "OSCE Does Not Recognize Transdniestrian Independence Referendum, Recalling July Statement," OSCE Chairmanship Press Release, September 18, 2006, www.osce.org/cio/item_1_20620.html.

38. OSCE, "OSCE Mission to Moldova, Special Report: Visit to Colbasna (13 November 2006)," Vienna, November 28, 2006, SEEC.FR/553/06. There have been

no official visits by OSCE representatives to the Russian facility at Colbasna since that time.

39. The Transdniestrians were quite happy with the statement; for the text and comment, see "V khode trekhstoronnei vstrechi v Moskve podpisanno sovmestnoe zaiavlenie," Olvia Press, March 18, 2009, www.olvia.idknet.com/ol171-03-09.htm. Many Moldovans and other observers were not so sure about the results of the meeting. E.g., see Eugen Tomiuc, "Moscow Moves to Draw Moldova, Transdniester Leaders Back into Fold," Radio Free Europe / Radio Liberty, March 18, 2009, www .rferl.org/content/Moscow_Moves/to_Draw_Moldova_Transdniester_Leaders_Back _Into_Fold/1512603.html.

40. This narrative, on the Moldovan "package," derives from conversations with OSCE heads of mission Louis O'Neill and Philip Remler, Moldvan negotiators Vasile Şova and Mark Tkachuk, and former Transdniestrian negotiator Valeriy Litskai, from late 2006 to early 2009. Any errors or conclusions are mine.

41. On the State Duma Resolutions and Tiraspol's disappointment at the failure to include Transdniestria in the call for independence and recognition, see, e.g., "Russia: Duma to Weigh In on Abkhaz, South Ossetian, Transdniestrian Status," Radio Free Europe / Radio Liberty, March 13, 2008, www.rferl.org/content/article/ 1079631.html. Smirnov and his colleagues were deeply frustrated by their failure to convince Moscow to include them in the Duma initiative. My Moldovan and Russian colleagues generally portrayed the move as a message to Voronin that he would be rewarded if he took a "constructive" approach toward relations with Russia. For the text of the resolution, see "Postanovlenie GD FS RF ot 21.03.2008 N 245-5 GD 'O zaiavlenii gosudarstvennoi dumy federal'nogo sobraniia rossiiskogoi federatsii o politike rossiiskoi federatsii v otnoshenii abkhazii, iuzhnoi osetii i prodnestrov'ia,'" accessed at http://duma.consultant.ru/page.aspx?953940.

42. Medvedev made the statement about Russia's "privileged interests" in some countries in the region during the course of an interview on Russian television, August 31, 2008, in which he laid out five basic principles of Russian foreign policy. A transcript of the interview is available at www.kremlin.ru.

43. One good recent example of the genre is Viktor Litovkin, "DOVSE pretknoveniia: Razgovory o vozvrashchenii k Dogovoru ob obychnykh vooruzhennykh silakh v Evrope mogut prevratit'sia v obeshchanie otmenit' popravku Dzheksona-Venika," *Nezavisimaia Gazeta,* September 17, 2010, www.ng.ru/245291. For one Russian's comment on the continuing inner contradictions of many of his compatriots' views of NATO and the West, see Yevgeny Bazhanov, "Why Russia Needs a Strong NATO," *Moscow Times,* September 22, 2010.

44. Svetlana Gamova, "Moskva ustupaet Moldaviiu Bukharestu," *Nezavisimaia gazeta,* August 25, 2011, www.ng.ru/258584.

Bibliography

A Note on Sources

A considerable portion of the descriptions of events and analyses is based at least in part upon my personal experience and recollections, supported by working notes, diaries, calendars, and other personal papers from the period of my two terms serving as head of the Organization for Security and Cooperation in Europe (OSCE) Mission to Moldova. Where appropriate, I have also cited conversations and interviews with a number of colleagues, officials, journalists, and academics from the OSCE Mission to Moldova, the OSCE Secretariat, various national delegations to the OSCE, the European Union, and NATO, and from Moldova, Transdniestria, Ukraine, Russia, Romania, the United States, and the OSCE Chairs under which I served—Norway, Austria, Romania, Portugal, the Netherlands, Bulgaria, Slovenia, and Belgium. The negotiation records cited in this work are all collected in the files of the OSCE Mission to Moldova; many of them are also duplicated in the files of the OSCE Conflict Prevention Center in Vienna. OSCE documents and records, such as Permanent Council decisions, are available either online or through the OSCE Secretariat in Vienna.

Many documents and contemporary news accounts and analyses of the material covered by this study are now available online. Almost anything relating to the OSCE can be found through the organization's Web site, www.osce.org. For news accounts of Moldova during the period covered, two major news sites are the most comprehensive: www.azi.md, a collection of news service reports from Moldova (pre-2008 items now can be retrieved from http://old.azi.md; and www.nm.md, the site of the official newspaper *Nezavisimaia Moldova.* For Transdniestria for the period covered in this book, the best source is the Web site of the official agency Olvia Press, www.olvia.idknet.com. There are additional Transdniestrian and Russian Web sites (e.g., www.nr2.ru) that are as good or better for post-2006 events. The Moldovan government Web site—www.moldova.md—is also useful, but now problematic for retrieving some documents from a decade or more ago. The same might be said for the official Russian Web sites—www.kremlin.ru and www.mid.ru. Though useful for more contemporary events, it is at times difficult to retrieve older documents. I have attempted in the notes to consistently indicate the URL at which

I accessed a particular document; given the vagaries of the Internet, one hopes these links will remain active for some time.

The bibliography for this work is essentially in the notes. However, some works stand out in each of the major areas covered in this narrative. These are cited, with occasional comments, as a guide to the interested reader for further investigation.

Sources

Moldova

Brezianu, Andrei, and Vlad Spanu. *Historical Dictionary of Moldova,* 2nd ed. Lanham, Md.: Scarecrow Press, 2007.

Chinn, Jeff, and Steven Roper. "Ethnic Mobilization and Reactive Nationalism: The Case of Moldova." *Nationalities Papers* 23, no. 2 (June 1995): 291–325. This periodical is filled with useful articles by these and other authors on Moldova, Transdniestria, and other conflicts in the post-Soviet periphery.

Crowther, William. "The Politics of Ethnic Confrontation in Moldova." National Council for Soviet and East European Research, Washington, D.C., September 23, 1993. Especially useful for its data and discussion of the Moldovan public's attitudes on reunification with Romania.

Haynes, Rebecca. "Historical Introduction." In *Occasional Papers in Romanian Studies, No. 3: Moldova, Bessarabia, Transnistria,* edited by Rebecca Haynes. London: School of Slavonic and East European Studies, University College London, 2003. One of the best works available on Moldovan history in its regional context.

King, Charles. *The Moldovans.* Stanford, Calif.: Hoover Institution Press, 2000. Still by far the best general work on Moldova—a classic, and the place to start.

Ronnås, Per, and Nina Orlova. *Moldova's Transition to Destitution.* SIDA Studies 1. Gothenburg: Novum Grafiska AB, 2000. A stunning analysis of the reasons for Moldova's poverty and poor economic performance in the decade after the Soviet collapse.

Stati, Vasile. *Istoriia Moldovy.* Chisinau: Pro Moldova, 2002. A recent Moldovan survey; also available in Romanian.

van Meurs, Wim P. *The Bessarabian Question in Communist Historiography: Nationalist and Communist Politics and History-Writing.* East European Monographs 337. New York: Columbia University Press, 1994. Interesting, useful background to contemporary disputes over whether Moldova should be independent or part of Romania.

Way, Lucan. "Pluralism by Default in Moldova." *Journal of Democracy* 13, no. 4 (October 2002): 127–41. One of this author's many useful analyses of contemporary Moldovan politics.

The Transdniestrian Conflict

Barbarosie, Arcadie, and Oazu Nantoi, eds. *Aspects of the Transnistrian Conflict.* Chisinau: Ştiinţa and Institute for Public Policy, 2004. A collection of Moldovan Romanophone views of the conflict from Moldova's leading think tank.

Bergman, Mikhail. *Vozhd v chuzhoi stae.* Moscow: Bioinformresurs, 2004. The memoirs of General Lebed's aide; indispensable.

Burla, Mikhail, V. Gushan, and I. Kazmali. *Ekonomika Pridnestrov'ia na perekhodnom etape* Tiraspol: IPTs 'Sherif', 2000. Along with the work of Anatol Gudym (see below) one of the best explanations of how the Transdniestrian economy works.

Coppieters, Bruno, Michael Emerson, and Marcus Vahl, eds. *Europeanization and Conflict Resolution: Case Studies from the European Periphery.* Gent: Academia Press, 2004.

Flikke, Geir, and Jakub M. Godzimirski. *Words and Deeds: Russian Foreign Policy and Post-Soviet Secessionist Conflicts.* Oslo: Norwegian Institute of International Affairs, 2006. Includes a good discussion of the Kozak history, as well as other post-Soviet conflicts.

Gribincea, Mihai. *Trupele Ruse in Republic Moldova: Factor stabilizator sau sursa de pericol.* Chisinau, 1998. The classic Moldovan nationalist view of the Russian troop presence.

Gudym, Anatol. *Transnistrian Market and Its Impact on Policy and Economy.* Chisinau: Center for Strategic Studies and Reforms, 2005. Available at www.cisr-med .org.

Hanne, Gottfried. "Der Transnistrien Konflikt: Ursachen, Entwicklungsbedingungen und Perspektiven einer Regelung." *Berichte des Biost,* no. 42.1 (1998). An excellent analysis of the early stages of the conflict based on extensive onsite interviews.

Hill, Ronald. *Soviet Political Elites: The Case of Tiraspol.* New York: St. Martin's Press, 1977. A classic study of a Soviet provincial elite that retains its usefulness by helping to explain the origins of separatist sentiment in Transdniestria.

Istoriia Pridnestrovskoi Moldavskoi Respubliki. Tiraspol: RIO PGU, 2000. A collection of pieces by Transdniestrian academics; the authoritative left-bank history.

Kaufman, Stuart J. *Modern Hatreds: The Symbolic Politics of Ethnic War.* Ithaca, N.Y.: Cornell University Press, 2001. A classic chapter on the Transdniestrian conflict; also includes chapters on Georgia and Nagorno-Karabakh.

Loewenhardt, John. "The OSCE, Moldova, and Russian Diplomacy in 2003." *Journal of Communist Studies and Transition Politics,* 20, no. 4 (December, 2004). An account of the Kozak dénouement, based on interviews with Dutch officials.

Lynch, Dov. *Engaging Eurasia's Separatist States: Unresolved Conflicts and De Facto States.* Washington, D.C.: U.S. Institute of Peace Press, 2004. Sections on Moldova-Transdniestria, Abkhazia, South Ossetia, and Nagorno-Karabakh.

Nantoi, Oazu. "Strategia '3D'—de la 'extremism' la consens?" November 3, 2004. www.-e-democracy.md/comments/political/200411031.

New York Bar Association. "Thawing a Frozen Conflict: Legal Aspects of the Separatist Crisis in Moldova." *Record of the Association of the Bar of the City of New York* 61, no. 2 (2006): 196–304. The results of a 2005 visit to the region; the best discussion available on the juridical bases for the Transdniestrian separation.

Ozhiganov, Edward. "The Republic of Moldova: Transdniester and the 14th Army." In *Managing Conflict in the Former Soviet Union: Russian and American Perspectives,* edited by Alexei Arbatov, Abram Chayes, Antonia Handler Chayes, and Lara Olson. Cambridge, Mass.: MIT Press, 1997. Very good on the role of the Fourteenth Army.

Perepelitsa, H. N. *Konflikt v Pridnestrov'e: Prichiny, Problemy, i Prognoz Razvitiia.* Kiev, 2001. A study of the first decade of the conflict by one of the leading Ukrainian experts.

Protsyk, Oleh. "Moldova's Dilemmas in Democratizing and Reintegrating Transnistria." *Problems of Post-Communism* 53, no. 4 (July–August 2006): 29–41. One of many pieces on the Transdniestrian conflict by this leading expert.

Roper, Steven D. "Federalization and Constitution-Making as an Instrument of Conflict Resolution." *Demokratizatsiya* 12, no. 4 (Fall 2004): 527–39. One of many articles by this U.S. expert on the Transdniestrian conflict and Moldovan politics.

Sbornik Dokumentov otnosiashchikhsia k Sovmestnomu zaiavleniiu Prem'er-ministrov Moldovy i Ukrainy. Kishinev, 2006. Contains the 2005 Moldovan law and the Yushchenko Plan.

Troebst, Stefan. "The Transdniestrian Moldovan Republic: From Conflict-Driven State-Building to State-Driven Nation-Building." In *European Yearbook of Minority Issues, Volume 2 (2002/2003),* edited by European Centre for Minority Issues and European Academy Bozen/Bolzano. Leiden: Brill, 2004. An interesting discussion of the development of a Transdniestrian "national identity."

Other *"Frozen Conflicts"*

Arbatov, Alexei, Abram Chayes, Antonia Handler Chayes, and Lara Olson, eds. *Managing Conflict in the Former Soviet Union: Russian and American Perspectives.* Cambridge, Mass.: MIT Press, 1997. An excellent collection, with particularly good introduction and conclusion by Arbatov.

De Waal, Thomas. *Black Garden: Armenia and Azerbaijan through Peace and War.* New York: New York University Press, 2003. The best available study of this conflict. Together with the following work, indispensable reading on recent history in the Caucasus.

———. *The Caucasus: An Introduction.* Oxford: Oxford University Press, 2010.

Hill, Fiona, and Pamela Jewett. *Back in the USSR: Russia's Intervention in the Internal Affairs of the Former Soviet Republics and the Implications for United States Policy toward Russia.* Cambridge, Mass.: Strengthening Democratic Institutions Project, John F. Kennedy School of Government, Harvard University, 1994.

Hill, William. "Reflections on Negotiation and Mediation: The Frozen Conflicts and European Security." *Demokratizatsiya* 18, no. 3 (Summer 2010): 219–27.

King, Charles. "The Benefits of Ethnic War: Understanding Europe's Unrecognized States." *World Politics* 53, no. 4 (July 2001): 524–52. A fascinating discussion of the transformation over time of the post-Soviet separatist movements.

Kremenyuk, Viktor A. *Conflicts in and around Russia: Nation-Building in Difficult Times.* Westport, Conn.: Greenwood Press, 1994. A Russian view of the post-Soviet conflicts.

O'Prey, Kevin P. "Keeping the Peace in the Borderlands of Russia." In *UN Peacekeeping, American Politics, and the Uncivil Wars of the 1990s,* edited by William J. Durch. New York: St. Martin's Press, 1996.

Zuercher, Christoph. *The Post-Soviet Wars: Rebellion, Ethnic Conflict, and Nationhood in the Caucasus.* New York: New York University Press, 2007.

Moldova's Neighbors: Ukraine and Romania

Barbarosie, Arcadie, and Valeriu Gheorghiu, eds. *New Borders in South Eastern Europe: The Republic of Moldova, Ukraine, Romania.* Chisinau: Ştiinţa, 2002. A collection of essays by regional experts published under the aegis of the Central European Initiative and the Chisinau-based Institute for Public Policy.

Belitser, Natalia. "Conflicting Security Concerns across the Ukraine-Moldova Border." In *New Borders in South Eastern Europe: The Republic of Moldova, Ukraine, Romania,* edited by Arcadie Barbarosie and Valeriu Gheorghiu. Chisinau: Ştiinţa, 2002.

Perepelytsa, Hryhory. "The Influence of Regional Factors on Possible Scenarios of Development of Moldovan-Transnistrian-Ukrainian Relations." In *New Borders in South Eastern Europe: The Republic of Moldova, Ukraine, Romania,* edited by Arcadie Barbarosie and Valeriu Gheorghiu. Chisinau: Ştiinţa, 2002.

Russia and European Security

Gaidar, Yegor. *Collapse of an Empire: Lessons for Modern Russia.* Washington, D.C.: Brookings Institution Press, 2007.

Goldman, Marshall I. *Petrostate: Putin, Power, and the New Russia.* Oxford: Oxford University Press, 2008. One of the best discussions of Russia as an energy superpower.

Jackson, Nicole J. *Russian Foreign Policy and the CIS: Theories, Debates, and Actions.* London: Routledge, 2003.

Legvold, Robert, ed. *Russian Foreign Policy in the Twenty First Century and the Shadow of the Past.* New York: Columbia University Press, 2007. An excellent collection, including a particularly good article by the editor.

Matlock, Jack F., Jr. *Autopsy of an Empire: The American Ambassador's Account of the Collapse of the Soviet Union.* New York: Random House, 1995. By far the best general work on the Soviet collapse and its consequences.

Nygren, Bertil. *The Rebuilding of Greater Russia: Putin's Foreign Policy towards the CIS Countries.* London: Routledge, 2008.

Shevtsova, Lilia. *Putin's Russia,* revised and expanded edition. Washington, D.C.: Carnegie Endowment for International Peace, 2005. The classic liberal domestic criticism of Putin's regime and policies.

European Security and Security Institutions

Asmus, Ronald D. *Opening NATO's Door: How the Alliance Re-made Itself for a New Era.* New York: Columbia University Press, 2002. Along with Goldgeier's work, the best study on NATO expansion.

Baker, James A., III. *The Politics of Diplomacy: Revolution, War, and Peace 1989–1992.* New York: G. P. Putnam's Sons, 1995.

Burg, Steven L., and Paul S. Shoup. *The War in Bosnia-Herzegovina: Ethnic Conflict and International Intervention.* Armonk, N.Y.: M. E. Sharpe, 1999. One of the best-informed, most intelligent studies of the war in Bosnia-Herzegovina.

Bush, George H. W., and Brent Scowcroft. *A World Transformed.* New York: Alfred A. Knopf, 1998.

CSCE Helsinki Document 1992: The Challenges of Change. www.osce.org/documents/mcs/1992/07/4048_en.pdf. Along with the Charter of Paris and the Copenhagen Document, essential reading for anyone desiring to understand the origins of the present-day OSCE.

Charter of Paris for a New Europe. November 19, 1990. www.osce.org/mc/39516.

Dinan, Desmond. *Ever Closer Union: An Introduction to European Integration,* 3rd ed. Boulder, Colo.: Lynne Rienner, 2005. The place to start to understand the European Union.

Document of the Copenhagen Meeting of the Conference on the Human Dimension of the CSCE. June 29, 1990. www.osce.org/odihr/elections/14304.

Falkenrath, Richard A. *Shaping Europe's Military Order: The Origins and Consequences of the CFE Treaty.* Cambridge, Mass.: MIT Press, 1995.

Ghebali, Victor-Yves. "Growing Pains at the OSCE: The Rise and Fall of Russia's Pan-European Expectations." *Cambridge Review of International Affairs* 18, no. 3 (October 2005): 375–88. In addition to the next work below, Ghebali's classic survey, this article is essential for understanding Russian disillusionment with the OSCE.

———. *L'OSCE dans l'Europe post-communiste, 1990–1996: Vers une identité paneuropéenne de sécurité.* Brussels: Emils Bruylant, 1996.

Glenny, Misha. *The Fall of Yugoslavia.* New York: Penguin Books, 1992. My favorite to obtain an understanding of the origins and beginnings of the Balkan wars.

Goldgeier, James. *Not Whether but When: The U.S. Decision to Enlarge NATO.* Washington, D.C.: Brookings Institution Press, 1999.

Hopmann, P. Terence *Building Security in Post-Cold War Eurasia: The OSCE and U.S. Foreign Policy.* Peaceworks 31. Washington, D.C.: U.S. Institute of Peace Press, 1999.

Hutchings, Robert L. *American Diplomacy and the End of the Cold War: An Insider's Account of U.S. Policy in Europe, 1989–1992.* Washington, D.C., and Baltimore: Woodrow Wilson Center Press and Johns Hopkins University Press, 1997. The best insider's view of the George H. W. Bush administration's foreign policy in Europe.

Kemp, Walter, ed. *Quiet Diplomacy in Action: The OSCE High Commissioner on National Minorities.* The Hague, 2001.

Pond, Elizabeth. *The Rebirth of Europe.* Washington, D.C.: Brookings Institution Press, 1999. A sympathetic but cogent study of EU development and expansion.

Yost, David S. *NATO Transformed: The Alliance's New Roles in International Security.* Washington, D.C.: U.S. Institute of Peace Press, 1998.

Zimmermann, Warren. *Origins of a Catastrophe: Yugoslavia and Its Destroyers—America's Last Ambassador Tells What Happened and Why.* New York: Random House, 1996. The ultimate insider's account on the origins of the Balkan wars.

Russia–United States Relations

Goldgeier, James M., and Michael McFaul. *Power and Purpose: U.S. Policy toward Russia after the Cold War.* Washington, D.C.: Brookings Institution Press, 2003.

Goodby, James E. *Europe Undivided: The New Logic of Peace in U.S.-Russian Relations.* Washington, D.C.: U.S. Institute of Peace Press, 1998.

Matlock, Jack F., Jr. *Superpower Illusions: How Myths and False Ideologies Led America Astray—and How to Return to Reality.* New Haven, Conn.: Yale University Press, 2010.

Perry, William J., and Ashton B. Carter. *Preventive Defense: A New Security Strategy for America.* Washington, D.C.: Brookings Institution Press, 1999.

Talbott, Strobe. *The Russia Hand: A Memoir of Presidential Diplomacy.* New York: Random House, 2002.

Index